SUBURBAN DOMESTIC ARCHITECTURE SERIES

NORTH SHORE CHICAGO

HOUSES OF THE LAKEFRONT SUBURBS, 1890–1940

SUBURBAN DOMESTIC ARCHITECTURE SERIES

NORTH SHORE CHICAGO

HOUSES OF THE LAKEFRONT SUBURBS
1890–1940

STUART COHEN AND SUSAN BENJAMIN

FOREWORD BY

FRANZ SCHULZE

ACANTHUS PRESS
NEW YORK : 2004

Published by Acanthus Press LLC
Barry Cenower, Publisher
48 West 22nd Street
New York, New York 10010
www.acanthuspress.com
800.827.7614

Copyright © 2004, Stuart Cohen and Susan Benjamin

Every reasonable attempt has been made to identify the owners of copyright.
Errors of omission will be corrected in subsequent printings of this work.

All rights reserved. This book may not be reproduced in whole or in any part
(except by reviewers for the public press) without written permission from the publisher.

Library of Congress Cataloging-in-Publication Data
on file at the Library of Congress
isbn: 0-926494-26-0

Frontis: Map of Chicago Suburbs on the North Western Line, 1909

Book design by Maggie Hinders

Printed in China

URBAN AND SUBURBAN DOMESTIC ARCHITECTURE SERIES

For three hundred years, Americans have sought to fulfill the promise of a better life that a rich wilderness held out to the first settlers as they stepped onto the shores of the North Atlantic. The American engagement with a vast continent has been defined by the necessary development and expansion of cities and the simultaneous preservation and enjoyment of a bucolic countryside.

The Acanthus Press series on Urban and Suburban Domestic Architecture present landmark domestic buildings of the last two centuries that display the innovative housing solutions of Americans and their architects as they addressed their desires for the ideal domestic life.

Contents

Acknowledgments • [9]
Foreword • [11]
North Along the Lakeshore • [15]
In the Cause Conservative • [35]
A Community of Architects • [38]
Authors' Note • [44]

1890–1899

WAVERLY, *Kenilworth* • [48]
CHARLES GATES DAWES HOUSE, *Evanston* • [52]
ROOT–BADGER HOUSE, *Kenilworth* • [58]
EASTBANK, *Evanston* • [63]
RAGDALE, *Lake Forest* • [67]

1900–1909

WARD W. WILLITS HOUSE, *Highland Park* • [74]
JAMES PATTEN HOUSE, *Evanston* • [80]
WESTMORELAND, *Lake Forest* • [86]
HARRY RUBENS ESTATE, *Glencoe* • [91]
INDIANOLA, *Glencoe* • [97]

AUGUSTUS MAGNUS ESTATE, *Winnetka* • [102]
CHARLES FERNALD HOUSE, *Lake Forest* • [106]
MELLODY FARM, *Lake Forest* • [110]
HOUSE OF THE FOUR WINDS, *Lake Forest* • [117]
VILLA TURICUM, *Lake Forest* • [123]
FINLEY BARRELL HOUSE, *Lake Forest* • [131]
RAVINE BLUFFS DEVELOPMENT, *Glencoe* • [137]

1910–1919

HAVENWOOD, *Lake Forest* • [142]
NATHAN WILBUR WILLIAMS HOUSE, *Evanston* • [148]
C. PERCY SKILLIN HOUSE, *Wilmette* • [153]
ROSEMOR LODGE, *Glencoe* • [156]
STONEBRIDGE, *Lake Bluff* • [158]
WYLDWOOD, *Lake Forest* • [165]
HOUSE IN THE WOODS, *Lake Forest* • [171]
MRS. CAROLYN MORSE ELY ESTATE, *Lake Bluff* • [176]
DAVID ADLER ESTATE, *Libertyville* • [184]

1920–1929

BENJAMIN MARSHALL HOUSE AND STUDIO, *Wilmette* • [192]
FAIRLAWN, *Lake Forest* • [199]
BICHL AND SCHAGER HOUSES, *Wilmette* • [203]
FELIX LOWY HOUSE, *Winnetka* • [208]
NOBLE B. JUDAH ESTATE, *Lake Forest* • [214]
CRAB TREE FARM, *Lake Bluff* • [223]
ROBERT MANDEL HOUSE, *Highland Park* • [233]

HARLEY LYMAN CLARKE HOUSE, *Evanston* • [238]
MILL ROAD FARM, *Lake Forest* • [244]
SHADOW POND, *Lake Forest* • [252]
WALTER T. FISHER HOUSE, *Winnetka* • [258]

1930–1940

EDGECLIFF, *Winnetka* • [264]
TANGLEY OAKS, *Lake Bluff* • [271]
MRS. KERSEY COATES REED HOUSE, *Lake Forest* • [276]
HERBERT BRUNING HOUSE, *Wilmette* • [284]
BERTRAM J. CAHN HOUSE, *Lake Forest* • [290]

Appendices

Portfolio of Houses 1880–1940 • [296]
Architects' Biographies • [305]
Bibliography • [323]
Index • [328]
Photography Credits • [336]

Acknowledgments

In our search for photographs, history, and engaging stories we are indebted to a great many people. We would like to thank all of them for their invaluable contributions to this volume:

Arthur Miller, Archivist and Librarian for Special Collections, Lake Forest College, who generously provided us with information, photographs, encouragement, and his invaluable expertise, and whose book, *Classic Country Estates of Lake Forest*, has been a valuable resource. He was a diligent reader of our text • Franz Schulze, the Betty Jane Schultz Hollender Professor of Art, Emeritus, Lake Forest College, the consummate professional Architectural Historian, who not only contributed the preface, but endorsed our efforts and served as a reader, making numerous helpful corrections and suggestions • Richard Solomon, F.A.I.A., Director, and Board of Trustees, Graham Foundation for Advanced Studies in the Fine Arts, for a grant that enabled us to purchase many of the fine illustrations in this book • Pauline Saliga, Executive Director, Society of Architectural Historians; Wim De Wit, Director, Special Collections, The Getty Research Institute, who wholeheartedly endorsed our efforts • Julie McKeon, who diligently researched the images in the Portfolio and was a constant source of support • Gwen Sommers Yant, who read the text, providing numerous helpful suggestions • Mary Woolever and Amy Babinec, Burnham Library, Art Institute of Chicago, who generously provided us with recently accessioned photographs • Lesley A. Martin, Robert Medina, and Aimee L. Marshall, who shared with us with images from the invaluable photographic archive at the Chicago Historical Society • Eden Pearlman, Evanston Historical Society • Lori A. Walker, Harrison Conference Center, formerly the Lake Forest estate known as Stonebridge • Alan Leder, Evanston Art Center, formerly the Harley Lyman Clarke House • Kathleen Roy Cummings, whose history of Northwestern University architecture and wealth of knowledge on architect George Maher has been invaluable • Eben Gilette, Tangley Oaks, now owned by Paterno Imports • John Notz, whose historical papers provided us with invaluable background information on Jens Jensen and the properties he landscaped • Mary and Jim McWilliams, whose information on Crab Tree Farm, the Frances Willard House, and the introduction history was enormously helpful • John Bryan, whose time and expertise solidified our understanding of Crab Tree Farm • Kathy Hussey-Arntson and Patrick Leary, Wilmette Historical Museum • Melinda Kwedar, Kenilworth Historical Society • Joan Evanich, Winnetka Historical Society • Ellen Paseltiner, who served as a reader and provided us with considerable help. Glencoe Historical Society • Julia Johnas, Highland Park Public Library • Mike Mills, Highland Park Historical

Acknowledgments

Society • Janice Hack and Elizabeth Hedsen, Lake Forest–Lake Bluff Historical Society • Janet Nelson, President, Vliet Center for Lake Bluff History, Lake Bluff • Dianna Monie, David Adler Cultural Center • Virginia Beaty, Frances Willard House and Museum • Stephen Salny, who constantly and generously offered us the benefit of his experience and expertise and whose book, *David Adler, Architect: Elements of Style*, is an invaluable resource • Pauline Mohr, Lake Forest Preservation Foundation • Gail Hodges, Lake Forest Preservation Foundation, who loaned us photos and gave us many helpful suggestions • Betty Blum, Chicago Architects Oral History Project, Department of Architecture, the Art Institute of Chicago • Martha Thorne, Architecture Department, Art Institute of Chicago • Luigi Mumford, Architecture Department, Art Institute of Chicago • Homeowners and former homeowners, many of whom provided photographs: Martin and Maribeth Rahe, Terry McKay, Lyn Redfield, Sue Bush, Joel Falk, Tom and Jane O'Neil, Herb Stride, Laureen Grieve • Jennifer Kenny, who frequently helped with historical information and computer glitches • Adam Blumenthal, who loaned us a beautiful photograph of the McGann House • Paul Lane of Photo Source, Evanston, who scanned and repaired many of the historic images in our book • Thomas Rajkovich who recommended us to Acanthus Press for this project • Julie Hacker, Stuart's partner, and Victoria Granacki, Susan's former partner, who never complained when we spent worktime away from our firms • Paul Bergmann, Curator of Stanley D. Anderson Archives, for his suggestions and generosity • Suzanne Nyren, Lake Forest College • Nan Greenough, who read the introduction and whose excellent advice contributed to a better manuscript • Dr. Karen Pierce, Phyllis Higgins and numerous other friends, who constantly encouraged Susan's writing • Ann Swallow and Tracey Sculle, former and present National Register Coordinators, State of Illinois • Bill McNaught, Oysterponds Historical Society • David Phillips, Chicago Architectural Photographing Company • Christine Cordazo, ESTO Photographics, Inc. • Scholars whose research and writing enabled us to think through and work out our ideas for the book, including: Leonard Eaton, Richard Guy Wilson, and H. Allen Brooks • Our mentors, William Jordy (Susan) and Colin Rowe (Stuart), who cultivated the intellectual skills that made this book possible.

We want to thank Barry Cenower, our editor and publisher, for his enthusiasm for this project and for his help in narrowing down the selection of wonderful houses, which he tackled impartially.

We especially want to thank our respective spouses, Wayne Benjamin and Julie Hacker, and our children, Michael and David Benjamin and Gabriel Cohen, who never complained, offered continuous support and were never upset when we disappeared to tour the North Shore or sequester ourselves to write.

Foreword

During the last decade, the history of Chicago architecture has undergone a noteworthy shift of scholarly emphasis. The customary approach has been to concentrate on the achievements of the great innovators of form and plan—Louis Sullivan, Daniel H. Burnham, Frank Lloyd Wright, and Ludwig Mies van der Rohe. More recently, however, closer attention has been paid architects of more traditional stylistic orientation. David Adler, a designer almost totally dependent on manners associated with the historical past, has been the subject of two books as well as one major museum exhibition. Moreover, the estates of the wealthy suburb that boasts many of Adler's buildings, Lake Forest, have been treated to a substantial study documenting that town's aesthetically conservative tastes.

This book in turn provides the latest evidence of a change in the direction of Chicago architectural historiography as well as a provocative interpretation of several aspects of it. Susan Benjamin and Stuart Cohen have confined themselves here to a single genre, the private residence, built over a brief, 50-year period, in a geographically limited space, the nine communities that border Lake Michigan north of the Chicago city limits. Most of these works are traditional in character, but a number are closer to the relatively more progressive Prairie School, and the authors evaluate the ideological relationship between architects of both groups. The breadth of coverage offered by Benjamin and Cohen leaves us with a vision of a far richer townscape along the North Shore than we might have known earlier. For many of the houses illustrated have been demolished, and our only way of remembering them is through the photographs unearthed by the authors and described in their text entries.

How many readers are familiar with Indianola, the Hermann Paepcke estate, completed in 1903 in Glencoe after the designs of the Chicago firm of Frommann & Jebsen? It was a frankly historicist work in the Queen Anne mode that mixed lavishly gabled half-timbered passages with shingled turrets and even a Palladian window tucked beneath an eave on the top story. Indianola projected authority with unmistakable assurance from its twenty-acre site atop the great Glencoe bluff overlooking Lake Michigan. The quality of the landscape design by Jens Jensen was at least equal to that of the house. We read, moreover, that the commission was of consequence to the advancement of Jensen's career, since it brought him into mutually profitable contact with a wealthy suburban residential clientele.

And if Paepcke did Jensen a favor, he was also the figure behind a man of comparable consequence for the arts. Hermann was a lumber baron whose paper mills and packing box company inspired his son Walter to found the Container Corporation of America, a firm famous for a highly original post-World

War II campaign that singularly advanced the cause of modern art in advertising. Walter and his wife Elizabeth were also responsible for turning the sleepy village of Aspen, Colorado, into a world-renowned community serving ski lovers as well as more sedentary types who preferred the Aspen Institute of Humanistic Studies. The personal stories, interwoven with the authors' analysis of Indianola as a building, provide the reader of this book with a measure of cultural as well as architectural history.

The same can be said of another house rich in both social and architectural lore. When in 1895 Edith Rockefeller of New York married Harold Fowler McCormick of Chicago, two of the wealthiest American families and the two largest American cities took on new connections. Having decided to build a house in Lake Forest, the couple awarded the commission to Charles Platt of New York, but only after rejecting the proposed plans of a pair of architects with equally famous names: Frank Lloyd Wright and James Gamble Rogers. The house Platt designed, Villa Turicum, was a sumptuous country estate indebted to the manner of the Italian Renaissance. The grounds, also designed by Platt, demonstrated that his knowledge of landscape architecture in the Beaux-Arts tradition was as sound as his understanding of Classicist form. Villa Turicum was one of the most grandiose residences erected in America during the early twentieth century, and the photographs in this book are enough to remind us that its demolition, like that of Indianola, constituted a major architectural loss.

While both houses and more have disappeared, numerous others discussed here still stand. However, they may have changed over the decades, sometimes significantly, and the illustrations are in some instances uniquely informative. One of the rules the authors followed was to publish exclusively archival photographs that show the houses in their original state. Mellody Farm, the spectacular Lake Forest estate designed by Arthur Heun for J. Ogden and Lolita Sheridan Armour, completed in 1908, has been part of a private secondary school, the Lake Forest Academy, since 1947. Hence its furnishings have changed accordingly, and the photographs published in this volume show the interiors as they were when the Armours lived there. While the Academy has preserved the richness of Heun's design, the image of the building when it was still a private house conveys more sheer luxury than would that of the public institution. A similar lesson can be learned from the entry on the Nathan Williams House in Evanston, designed by Robert Spencer and completed in 1912. It is still standing on Sheridan Road, but no longer in the form the architect intended. The open entry porch has been enclosed, and much of the original space around the house, including vegetable gardens and a tennis court, was removed after the property was sub-divided and a newer house built to the east.

Of the twenty-nine architects whose work appears in this book, twenty-four practiced in Chicago, and Spencer was one of them. He was also a close friend of Frank Lloyd Wright, and the two men enjoyed a relationship that was as professional as it was social. Nor were they in this regard unique in Chicago, where lively communication among designers in the late nineteenth and early twentieth centuries was evidence of, in the authors' words, "a stimulating collegial architectural culture." In the essay "A Community of Architects," that culture is discussed in detail. The location of offices in a single building and even the occasional sharing of a single office space brought the architects into close contact and led to endless conversations about their respective practices and the theoretical ideas of

FOREWORD

the day. Dwight Perkins, who had worked for H. H. Richardson before joining Daniel H. Burnham's staff, was the designer of Steinway Hall, which at various times after its completion in 1895 accommodated Perkins himself, Wright, Spencer, Walter Burley Griffin, Marion Mahony, Irving and Allen Pond, and Arthur Heun—all names well known to students of Chicago architectural history. Clients played a role as well. The owner and developer of Steinway Hall was William H. Winslow of River Forest, for whom Wright designed a house that still occupies a special place in his catalogue.

Among this group, membership in the Chicago Architectural Club was customary, and meetings featured papers on a variety of topics. As Benjamin and Cohen recall, "[Louis] Sullivan spoke, John Root read his translations from the German of essays by Gottfried Semper, and George Maher presented a paper on his 'Motif Rhythm Theory'." The exchange of ideas among the members at the Arts and Crafts Society was just as vigorous and involved many of the same architects. Like the Chicago Architectural Club, the Society sponsored a yearly exhibition at the Art Institute of Chicago. It is worth pointing out that these people were not the only artists of accomplishment in Chicago, nor were they the only designers who left houses of special merit on the North Shore. No one was more committed to the Arts and Crafts aesthetic than Howard Van Doren Shaw, as his own house, "Ragdale," demonstrates. And no Chicago firm contributed more to Chicago architecture at the turn of the twentieth century than Holabird & Roche, an office responsible, moreover, for one of the finest urbanistic achievements on the North Shore, the sober common brick buildings comprising Fort Sheridan. In another essay in this book, "In the Cause Conservative," Cohen and Benjamin pay homage to gifted architects including Henry Ives Cobb, and Harrie Lindeberg, and well-informed clients like Edward L. Ryerson, Noble Judah—all of more antiquarian than advanced taste. Nonetheless, it was no less a modernist than Frank Lloyd Wright who used the term "a cause conservative" in referring to the Ward W. Willits house, one of his most distinguished efforts. The longest of the essays, "North Along the Lakeshore," traces the historical development of the nine North Shore towns. Textual material concludes with biographical sketches of the featured designers.

In sum, the authors have added depth and perspective to the subject of Chicago's suburban residential architecture built before the end of World War II. In addition to the remarkable quantity of work presented on these pages, they leave the reader to ponder one of their central arguments: that intentions of the progressive and historicist designers of this period had more than a little in common.

FRANZ SCHULZE

INTRODUCTION

NORTH ALONG THE LAKESHORE

IN HIS BOOK WELCOMING VISITORS to the 1933 Century of Progress Exposition, architect Alfred Granger wrote, "This whole North Shore district is the chosen pleasure ground of Chicago's richest people and has been developed with an eye to harmony not found in other places."

Although not as sociologically or architecturally homogeneous as Granger would have us believe, the North Shore of Chicago conjures up images of elegant houses lining the shore of Lake Michigan, of tree-shaded streets, of forested ravines, and of a gracious lifestyle. Historically, the North Shore has always had cachet. Chicago's finest residential architects as well as prominent East Coast practitioners designed homes for the city's movers and shakers. Whether bankers, meatpackers, grain traders,

Lake Michigan bluffs, Highland Park, c. 1895

Glencoe railway station, built 1891

or retailing entrepreneurs, North Shore clients tended to demand excellence from their architects, and typically, they got it. If this is suburbia, it represents the best American suburbs have to offer.

To understand the North Shore, some facts are in order. It stretches along the lakefront due north of Chicago, and is made up of nine suburbs located between 13 and 35 miles from the Loop, the city's business district. The largest community is the city of Evanston (population 75,000) and the smallest is the village of Kenilworth (population 2,500). Most of the cities and villages were incorporated in the 1860s and 1870s. The last was Kenilworth, incorporated in 1896. In 2000, the population of the North Shore towns numbered 190,000. Despite neighborhood and community differences, the demographics have always reflected the wealth, education, and social status of residents.

Natural forested beauty characterizes the North Shore and influenced its designed landscapes, but the most defining topographical feature of the North Shore is Lake Michigan itself. From Calumet Harbor on the south side of Chicago to just south of Waukegan, almost at the Wisconsin border, there is no industry along its pristine shoreline. Commerce is confined to freighters seen far offshore. The lake is important insofar as it regulates the climate, which is somewhat more moderate than in the western reaches of Chicago and provides the North Shore's water supply. But the persistent draw lies in its compelling beauty, its changing moods, and alluring vistas. Although many of the most elegant

Introduction

North Shore mansions face Lake Michigan, this was not always the case. Prior to 1900, sewage poured into the lake; the spread of disease was a significant problem, and homeowners feared the polluted "vapors." In the 19th century, houses tended to be built closer to town centers or along the ridges and deep-cut ravines formed by receding glaciers that carved out the Great Lakes. By 1900, when flow of the Chicago River had been reversed, sewage flowed toward the Mississippi River system instead. With this change, building houses along the lake became a more attractive choice.

Before the construction of the Chicago and Milwaukee Railroad in 1854 and 1855, small settlements grew up along the ridges that previously had served as Indian trails between Chicago and Green Bay, Wisconsin. Erastus Patterson built a tavern in the area today known as Winnetka, which was then a day's journey out of Chicago. A sawmill, a chapel, and a log schoolhouse grew up around it. Just to the north, Anson Taylor laid out a small village known as Taylorsport, with a post office, a small store, and an inn along the Green Bay Trail. Still farther north, where Fort Sheridan is located, the town of St. Johns was founded. With no transportation system—no road or rail—none of these small villages established in the 1830s and 1840s became the thriving communities their founders envisioned.

All nine towns making up the North Shore owe their existence to the rail line that became, in 1866, the Chicago and North Western Railway. Two-term Chicago mayor Walter S. Gurnee was president of the railway. As ambitious a man as any of the residents who were to populate the North Shore, his real focus was land speculation. In the early 1850s, while the railroad was being constructed, Gurnee purchased real estate near where the stations of Winnetka, Glencoe, Highland Park, and Lake Bluff were to be built. His unwillingness to build passenger stops at the existing settlements, including Taylorsport, erased them from the map. As the towns developed and ridership increased, hourly service, skip-stop trains, and private subscription cars carried commuters to their destinations in a comfortable and efficient manner—it is still possible to set one's watch by the train. Thanks to the railroad, North Shore residents were able to "have it all." They could live in the country and commute to the city for work, as well as ride in for shopping and entertainment.

Unlike major East Coast cities, Chicago developed almost entirely during the period of the railroad. Regarded as the rail center of America and the gateway to the West, Chicago in the second half of the 19th century was the fastest growing city in the world. In 1860, the city had a population of 200,000; by 1870, it had grown to 300,000. But by 1890, three years before the World's Columbian Exposition, it had reached a million, and by 1920, 2.7 million. Growing congestion forced an exodus from Chicago as the city's expanding business district was encroaching on the historic enclaves of the rich. Factories moved south toward Prairie Avenue—called by Lake Forest resident Arthur Meeker, who once lived there, "the sunny street that held the sifted few"—and west toward the elegant town houses lining Washington and Warren boulevards. Businesses moved north toward the area of Rush Street, which was know as McCormickville because several members of the McCormick family, who manufactured farming equipment, had ostentatious mansions there. The destination for many who could afford it was the North Shore.

In addition to congestion, other prime factors driving migration to the North Shore were a lingering fear of another great fire like that of 1871 and, among Chicago's business leaders, a fear of persistent labor unrest. Carl Smith describes the powerful impact of the fire and Chicago's labor problems in his book *Urban Disorder and the Shape of Belief*. Statistics relating to the 1871 Chicago Fire are sufficient to inspire apprehension: 18,000 buildings destroyed, 90,000 residents left homeless, 2.7 square miles of the city, including a growing business district, obliterated. The perceived danger remained in people's memories. Tension between labor and management was also a powerful force. Factory owners no longer wanted to live anywhere near their factories. Railroad strikes in the 1870s, and turmoil that climaxed in uprisings at the McCormick Reaper Works and in the infamous Haymarket Riots of May 1886, led prominent businessmen and politicians—including George Pullman, Marshall Field, and Senator Charles B. Farwell—to push for the construction of an army presence to protect their commercial interests in Chicago and to ensure the safety of those who had homes on the North Shore. Fort Sheridan was built between Lake Forest and Highland Park between 1889 and 1891, and troops stationed there aided in keeping peace during the violent 1894 Pullman Strike, thus preventing an anticipated confrontation at the Union Stock Yards.

For rich and poor residents, Chicago took on the problems of a 19th-century commercial-industrial center. Erik Larson's 2003 popular history *The Devil in the White City*, set during the 1893 World's Columbian Exposition, paints as grim a picture of Chicago in the 1890s as any academic history, portraying the city as corrupt, filthy, and crime-infested. A high percentage of families who could afford to leave the city did, building homes in the northern suburbs bordering the lake.

Traditionally, Chicago has always been a city whose residents preferred living in detached, single-family homes. Unlike Parisians or New Yorkers, most Chicago families would not choose apartment life. Even when elegant apartment buildings by the same talented architects who designed North Shore country houses became available, agents had to convince renters that it was actually desirable to live in what was referred to by one realty company as "apartments of the better class." Multi-family living was for those who could not afford better. In 1874, William Everett Chamberlin wrote in *Chicago and its Suburbs* that a detached house is "the right of every Chicago family that had pulled itself out of poverty to a cottage and a garden plot in a sylvan suburb, away from the squalor and stink of the city." For the affluent, however, the desire was frequently not just for a house and a small yard but for a home resting on extensive acreage, sometimes facing the lake or a ravine, sometimes part of an immense, park-like estate, but typically on the North Shore. And, when the rich left Chicago, the upwardly mobile followed them.

The very names of many North Shore towns were designed to conjure up images of a sylvan landscape as an idyllic destination. "Winnetka" is thought to be an Algonquin word meaning "place of beauty." Because of its ravines resembling valleys, the name of the village of Glencoe was a reversal of Coe's Glen, named by Gurnee, after his father-in-law, Matthew Coe. Highland Park, Highwood, Lake Forest, and Lake Bluff refer directly to the North Shore's beautiful forested setting on Lake Michigan.

Although the name North Shore has long been used to refer to Chicago's northern suburbs, this was not always the case. The name was part of a public relations campaign mounted in an attempt to encourage the diverse suburban communities to consider joint public improvements. The name was not generally used until 1889, when the North Shore Improvement Association was established. Its

INTRODUCTION

Fort Sheridan barracks and water tower, c. 1900

immediate purpose was to construct Sheridan Road as an extension of Chicago's Lake Shore Drive. Although it was envisioned as a beautiful roadway linking the towns, there was also another, not-so-hidden agenda. Discussions were underway with the United States Department of War to designate it a military highway as early as 1887, at the same time that plans were taking shape for building the permanent army installation that became Fort Sheridan. In 1900, the federal government agreed to pay for the section of road that passed through Fort Sheridan but refused to dedicate the road as military highway, saying there was no need for it. In fact, some North Shore residents were adamantly against the plan, claiming a widened road would destroy hundreds of trees and harm the shoreline. Ultimately, Sheridan Road was constructed as a scenic drive, and to this day commercial traffic is restricted.

When the War Department agreed to construct a fort to protect the interests of Chicago leaders, it did so under the auspices of establishing "an artillery school and military station in the area." The elite Commercial Club of Chicago purchased a 632-acre tract of land and donated it to the federal government. In 1888, the fort was named for Civil War hero Philip Sheridan, who had kept order during the 1871 Chicago Fire and was himself a member of the Commercial Club. Soon, contracts for the fort's construction were let by Brigadier General Samuel B. Holabird, quartermaster general of the army. No doubt prompted by a desire to promote his son's newly formed architectural firm, the commission to design buildings for the fort was awarded to Holabird and Roche. Though they would later receive worldwide recognition for pioneering the skeleton-frame skyscrapers that characterize the Chicago

School of architecture, Holabird and Roche designed monumental Richardsonian Romanesque structures set in a Prairie-style landscape laid out by Ossian C. Simonds. The effect of General Holabird's nepotism was long lasting. In 1896, after the Fort Sheridan commission, legislation was passed that expressly prohibited the employment of a private architectural firm to design military installations except by special act of Congress.

Fort Sheridan was closed in 1993 and today is the site of an upscale residential community that falls under the jurisdiction of Highland Park and Highwood. The historic buildings have been thoughtfully renovated, and the stables as well as barracks and officers' homes have become private residences. The fort's most prominent feature, a tower modeled on the campanile of Piazza San Marco in Venice, functions as an ornamental central archway that Sheridan Road once passed through.

A drive up Sheridan Road, as it wends its way north from Chicago through Evanston to Lake Bluff, is a favorite Sunday leisurely pastime. On the north side of Chicago, Lake Shore Drive turns into Sheridan Road even before it reaches Evanston's boundary, passing through the community areas of Edgewater and Rogers Park, which were suburbs themselves before being annexed to the city in 1889 and 1893 respectively. Where stately homes like those at the south end of Evanston once lined Sheridan Road, few are left. High- and low-rise apartment buildings, commercial strips, and a variety of buildings designed for Loyola University have replaced them. Only a small number of elegant houses suggest what lies ahead in Evanston.

After rounding the bend where Sheridan Road passes between Lake Michigan and Calvary Cemetery, commercial buildings are left behind and the North Shore's suburbs begin. Driving north, at first glance, one is impressed by the apparent seamlessness of the elegant residential neighborhoods, but this is an illusion. Each of the nine communities that make up Chicago's North Shore from Evanston to Lake Bluff has its own character and its own story to tell. There is a progression from somewhat urban streetscapes, lined with houses of similar size built on similar lots, to a more rural setting where homes are set in park-like landscapes.

Initially, the transition to the North Shore from Chicago is subtle. The roads of Evanston continue Chicago's street grid, even its strict numbering system. In addition, many buildings in the southeast section of Evanston are three-and-a-half-story red brick apartment buildings dating from the early 1890s to 1930. They are not, however, typical railroad flats, but rather gracious courtyard buildings with handsome colonial or Tudor embellishments, broad lawns, and interiors resembling those of well-designed houses, complete with fireplaces, paneled walls, art glass, and spacious floor plans. Apart from this apartment zone, established by the creation of restricted residence districts in 1916, and its business district, commercial pockets, and school and university buildings, Evanston is entirely residential. The houses tend to be large and built quite close to one another on relatively uniform lots.

Named for John Evans, a founder of Northwestern University, Evanston is a large city composed of many diverse neighborhoods. Its downtown skyline is now distinguished from those of other North Shore communities by tall office and residential towers. The only other contemporary high-rise buildings are to be found in Wilmette's "No Man's Land," a strip along the lake between Wilmette and Kenilworth that remained unincorporated for many years. The area to the west of Northwestern

INTRODUCTION

Frances E. Willard house, Evanston, built 1865

University and Evanston's business district is generally modest, with small homes surrounding Evanston High School. Sections of northwest Evanston are upper-middle class, with residences barely distinguishable from those in areas of Wilmette or Winnetka. Yet its shoreline is lined with mansions that rest on city-size lots and would fit comfortably in Lake Forest.

Historically, Evanston has been considered a university town. Chartered in 1851 by Methodists with a clear religious mission, the site of Northwestern University was selected for its distance from the lurid temptations of Chicago. It was to be a school dedicated to "sanctified learning," and by extension, the town was presented to potential students as "strictly moral and religious." Its motivating spirit was the temperance movement led by resident Frances E. Willard, who in 1873 became Northwestern's first dean of women. Under Willard's influence, Evanston also embraced education and women's rights. However, so strong was the influence of temperance that a "four-mile limit" was written into an amendment to the university charter shortly after the school opened. The 1855 proclamation read: "No spirituous, vinous, or fermented liquors shall be sold under license, or otherwise, within four miles of the location of the said University, except for medicinal, mechanical, or

[21]

Sheridan Road, Winnetka, looking southwest toward Wayside, house of Henry Demarest Lloyd, 1894

sacramental purposes." The zeal of temperance set the moral tone for Evanston and the example for most of the North Shore. Only Gross Point (today part of Wilmette) and Highwood, the "watering hole" for Fort Sheridan, were not dry during the Prohibition era. Elsewhere, people drank at home or at their clubs, and oddly, it is only in recent times that North Shore diners have been able to order a drink with dinner.

Buildings on Northwestern's beautiful lakeside campus date from 1869, when Chicago architect Gordon Randall designed University Hall, a medieval-looking structure of Joliet limestone, to house classrooms, a library, offices, dormitory rooms, and a chapel. The growing university's diverse architectural character was established when several buildings were designed by world-class architects whose names ring familiar to many North Shore residents. Evanstonian Daniel H. Burnham designed Fisk Hall, completed in 1899. Harris Hall was built in 1915 by the Boston firm of Shepley, Rutan, and Coolidge, H. H. Richardson's successors, who also built the Chicago Public Library and the Art Institute of Chicago. In 1922, former Chicagoan James Gamble Rogers was appointed campus architect. He designed the quintessential place of study, Northwestern's Collegiate Gothic–style Deering Library, completed in 1932.

Located immediately north of Evanston, the town of Wilmette was not platted until the late 1860s. However, Gross Point, now part of Wilmette, was settled 20 years earlier at the west end of New Trier

INTRODUCTION

Miralago Ballroom and shops, Wilmette, c. 1929

Township along Ridge Road. It was populated by hardworking farmers from Trier who emigrated to escape German oppression. The township, which lay outside the "four-mile-limit," was known for its saloons, and its residents were described in 1873 as "Teutonic revelers." In 1919, after passage of the Prohibition amendment, the little village no longer had a viable economic base and was immediately absorbed by Wilmette. Today, the Gross Point Village Hall serves as home to the Wilmette Historical Society, and the surrounding area along Ridge and Lake avenues continues to look like a small-town crossroads. Its vernacular cottages differ greatly from Wilmette's large, east-side homes and are a far cry from architect Benjamin Marshall's own opulent villa that once overlooked Wilmette Harbor.

Wilmette was incorporated in 1872, shortly after the Chicago Fire, and it had hoped to attract fire-weary Chicagoans. It was founded by real estate developers expressly for the purpose of building a train stop to create a suburban community. The original 1869 plat shows 525 acres that were a subdivision of the "Ouilmette Reservation." The streets east of the tracks are an extension of Evanston's rectangular grid. Like in Evanston, large homes were built close to each other with uniform setbacks. One 1890s real estate promotion touted Wilmette as "The Elm Forest of the North," advertising "beautiful grove lots" for $250 to $500 cash and $5 per month, "elegant homes on easy monthly payments." Wilmette's location was described as "immediately adjoining the aristocratic suburb of Evanston."

[23]

Just before Sheridan Road enters Kenilworth, there is the place commonly known to the local population as "No Man's Land." Today it consists of a lakeside strip of tall apartment buildings across the road from the picturesque Plaza del Lago. This complex actually lay outside the corporate boundaries of both Wilmette and Kenilworth until 1942, the year it was annexed to Wilmette. When the first highrises were built in the early 1960s, the beach area was the site of closed and abandoned ruins of the Vista del Lago nightclub and the Breakers Beach Club, along with gas stations, hot dog stands, and Peacock's Dairy Bar, a popular North Shore hangout. Designed as the Spanish Court in 1928 by Edwin Hill Clark, the shops at Plaza del Lago are the last remnant of a whole entertainment complex that included the Clark-designed Teatro del Lago and the art deco-style Miralago Ballroom designed by George Fred Keck. When it caught fire in 1932, only three years after it was built, the ballroom building burned to the ground—it lay outside the boundaries of the adjacent villages and no fire department would respond. Edwin Clark lived in Winnetka and designed North Shore houses as well as the Georgian-style Winnetka City Hall and Indian Hill Country Club. While Clark's residences were conservative and recalled America's colonial past, Plaza del Lago, with its white stucco Spanish buildings sporting red tile roofs and a bell tower, was pure Hollywood (or perhaps pure Addison Mizner).

The transition from glamorous shopping complex to conservative residences occurs at a pair of stone gate posts designed by architect George Maher, signaling that Sheridan Road is passing into Kenilworth. The smallest and newest North Shore town with the highest median home value ($972,000 in 2000), Kenilworth was a planned community laid out by Joseph Sears in 1889. After spending summers away from his Prairie Avenue home with Glencoe resident Dr. John Nutt, a member of the firm that developed Glencoe in the late 1860s, Sears decided to move to the North Shore. But instead of buying a house, he created a village, establishing the Kenilworth Company, and for the princely sum of $150,300 purchased 223.6 acres of farmland between Lake Michigan and the Chicago and North Western railroad tracks. Inspired by an 1883 family visit to England's Warwickshire countryside and a boyhood romance with the region evoked by Sir Walter Scott's novel *Kenilworth*, Sears named his venture Kenilworth after Scott's novel, eventually drawing from the book Scottish and English names for streets (including Abbotsford, Essex, and Warwick). The streets were laid out on a northeast-southwest axis to allow sunlight into the houses during part of each day. The east-west spine of the village continues to allow commuters a clear vista to the lake. According to an 1890 sales brochure, the village of Kenilworth was to be "The Model Suburban Community." It was envisioned as a family-centered community, in proximity to the amenities of the city, yet providing the wholesome life that country living afforded. It was intended to be beautiful and to retain the quality planned from the day the village was incorporated. Deed restrictions required large 100-by-175-foot lots, no alleys, and high standards of construction. In keeping with the social mores of the day, the restrictions also specified sales to Caucasians only, a requirement long abandoned.

Much of Kenilworth's earliest architecture has roots in late-19th-century romanticism, with picturesque styles favored. Resident Franklin Burnham, the Kenilworth Company's original architect, built the train station in the style of H. H. Richardson's suburban Boston train stations, and built houses in the Shingle and Queen Anne styles. Kenilworth also has a handful of Classical

Introduction

Revival and several Prairie-style houses. In the early 20th century, architect George Maher, an early resident actively involved in the development and planning of the community until shortly before his death in 1926, created simplified geometric designs, establishing a second look to the town's residential character.

As Sheridan Road extends into Winnetka, estate-size homes, many with coach houses at the street, are set far back from the road against steep bluffs facing Lake Michigan. Although many riparian lots have been subdivided, with 1950s ranch style and Colonial Revival houses built between the road and the lake, there are still a number of grand homes visible from Sheridan Road. The lakefront topography gradually changes, with the flat landscape so apparent in Evanston becoming slightly rolling (for Chicago) as bluffs rise and ravines cut in from the lake.

Winnetka was, like Wilmette and Kenilworth, developed as a speculative business venture. In 1854, Charles F. Peck formed a partnership with railroad president Walter Gurnee, built his family home in Winnetka, and encouraged others to purchase property from him. Mercifully, his wife insisted the settlement not be called Pecktown, suggesting instead the more lyrical Indian name "Winnetka," meaning "beautiful land." The Pecks' most lasting contribution was the donation of land for the Village Green, stipulating that nothing would be built on the property. Preservation of the wooded landscape was important to Peck and those who incorporated Winnetka. The 1869 village charter included a provision "to enforce the setting of shade-trees upon the streets, and to punish by fines the cutting or injury of any shade trees." Winnetka's main streets—Elm, Oak, Maple, and Chestnut—bear the names of trees, as do many streets in other North Shore towns and villages.

Social justice and progressive education are values often associated with Winnetka. The focus on local political activism was largely the result of Henry Demarest Lloyd's residence there from 1878 until his death in 1903. At Wayside, his home on Sheridan Road, Lloyd hosted social reformer Jane Addams, socialist and labor activist Eugene Debs, African American educator and civil rights leader Booker T. Washington, and men and women just needing respite from their sometimes dreary daily lives. Winnetka served as a laboratory for Lloyd's ideas on direct democracy, and his legacy includes founding the Winnetka Town Meeting in 1890 and promoting construction of the municipally owned water works and electric plant in 1900. The revolutionary Winnetka system of elementary education was introduced when Carleton Washburne was named school superintendent in 1919. His innovations included goal- instead of grade-oriented report cards, learning through doing, and studying less by rote and more via independent research. His innovative approach to education was applied early on at the Skokie School, and embodied architecturally in the award-winning Crow Island School designed in 1940 by Perkins, Wheeler, and Will with Eliel and Eero Saarinen. This modern, flat-roofed brick building featured private courtyards and work areas adjacent to each classroom, child-size furniture, and plentiful light and storage, setting a new, nationally recognized standard for elementary school design.

Glencoe is approached northward from Winnetka through a wooded ravine. Sheridan Road dips and turns and takes on a different character as it enters the village. It winds through neighborhoods, with the lake accessible only by roads extending east. This rolling topography was taken into account when the village was first platted in 1868, with large lots on the more desirable ravine-cut land east of

Lake Shore Country Club, Glencoe, c. 1911

the tracks. But even the roads west of the tracks, where there were no ravines, were given highly descriptive topographical names such as Greenwood, Grove, Bluff, and Valley. Glencoe was described on a promotional map as the "Queen of Suburbs."

In 1866 and 1867, the Glencoe Company was formed by Dr. Alexander Hammond, a retired physician who envisioned a utopian village. Glencoe already had a railroad station built by Walter Gurnee, whose own house in Glencoe became known as the Castle. Dr. Hammond approached Charles E. Browne, a successful Evanston realtor, and together they assembled a team of nine Chicago and Evanston businessmen including Luther Greenleaf and Charles Hosmer Morse, two highly successful partners in the Fairbanks Morse Scale Company. Each of the nine participants was to build a home for himself and one to sell to create further development. They also agreed to invest $5000 and provide an additional $500 for a church and school, pastor, teacher, roads, and shrubbery. Land was set aside on the lakefront for a public park. Reserving 25 acres for himself, Hammond moved into Gurnee's Castle.

As Glencoe grew, it attracted a nucleus of German Jewish businessmen who built country houses in the vicinity of their summer lodestar, Lake Shore Country Club. The elite membership of the club included grain broker and Chicago Board of Trade chairman Edward Glaser, department store magnate Robert Mandel, art collector Max Epstein, and architect Samuel Marx. Designed by Howard Van Doren Shaw, Lake Shore Country Club was built between 1908 and 1910. At the time, Shaw was not only Chicago's foremost country house architect of his generation, but also the residential architect of

INTRODUCTION

Ravinia Park, entrance from railway, Highland Park, c. 1904

choice for many prominent Jewish families, including investment banker A. G. Becker in Highland Park, and members of the Foreman banking family in Glencoe. Straddling the boundaries of Glencoe and Highland Park, Lake Shore Country Club is immediately adjacent to Minoru Yamasaki's North Shore Congregation Israel, which occupies the lakefront site of David Adler's first commission. It was a Louis XIII chateau designed in 1911 for his uncle Charles A. Stonehill while Adler was still working in Howard Van Doren Shaw's office.

Sheridan Road briefly runs east-west, coinciding with Lake Cook Road (the dividing line between Cook and Lake counties), before it continues north. At this juncture, the Braeside train stop was built to accommodate Lake Shore golfers coming up from the city. The community area of Braeside was not annexed to Highland Park as part of Ravinia until 1899, many years after Highland Park was incorporated.

Highland Park, like Glencoe, Winnetka, Kenilworth, and Wilmette, was a suburban development competing for residents. Walter Gurnee had purchased land on speculation surrounding the train stop that he established in 1854, in what is today central Highland Park. Even though a small town with a dry goods store and hotel grew up around the station, substantial growth did not take place until 1867, when a group of Chicago businessmen formed the Highland Park Building Company and bought the 1,200 acres that Gurnee had assembled when he was president of the railroad. Before house construction even began, Frank Hawkins, the resident manager for the company, hired the firm of Cleveland and French to plat the company's land. Boston landscape architect Horace W. S. Cleveland

[27]

had connections with railroad magnates, so he was drawn to the Chicago area for work. His partner, civil engineer William M. R. French, would make his mark in the city by becoming founding director of the Chicago Art Institute. Cleveland and French's goal in Highland Park was to maximize the aesthetic impact of the existing natural landscape of woods, ravines, and the lakefront. This was accomplished by laying out streets in curvilinear patterns reflecting the picturesque aesthetic of Andrew Jackson Downing, Cleveland's mentor, and his close friend Frederick Law Olmsted, whom Cleveland had worked for on Brooklyn's Prospect Park. The early homes built by the Highland Park Building Company were typical Italianate and Carpenter Gothic rural cottages popularized by Downing in his pattern books and constructed by local carpenters.

The passion for landscape in Highland Park was so persistent that the Ravinia neighborhood, which began as a Baptist settlement in the 19th century, was named for its most characteristic topographical feature. It is also the spot where landscape architect Jens Jensen—considered a dean of American landscape architecture—chose to build his studio. Jensen, who landscaped estates for Chicago's business elite, enjoyed a North Shore clientele that included Mrs. Cyrus McCormick, steel barons Edward L. Ryerson and William V. Kelley, beer-brewing magnate Harry Rubens, Ravine Bluffs developer and attorney to Frank Lloyd Wright, Sherman Booth, and utility company owner Harley F. Clarke. Jensen subscribed to the strong midwestern regionalism associated with Frank Lloyd Wright and his followers, using design elements that were metaphors for the prairie, the region's most characteristic landscape feature, and the flat horizon. Jensen translated the horizontality of the prairie into broad meadows reinforced through the use of native plants and laterally branching trees like Hawthorns and Redbuds, and rocks with stratified layers like limestone. Noting that there are no straight lines in nature, Jensen created lawns with undulating edges approached by curving roads. Jensen's imprint is found throughout the North Shore, but especially in Highland Park. His most important and easily accessible landscape is Rosewood Park, formerly the estate of Julius Rosenwald, philanthropist and president of Sears, Roebuck and Company. The house was demolished in the 1930s, but its landscape has been largely restored.

Although many distinguished Highland Park residences are designed in popular historical revival styles, Highland Park has a particularly high number of 20th-century houses designed by prominent Prairie School and early modernist architects. Of note are Frank Lloyd Wright's Ward W. Willits House of 1902, Henry Dubin's own 1929 International Style house, and several postwar solar houses by George Fred Keck and his brother, William Keck.

Highland Park's best-known attraction is Ravinia Park. As with Tanglewood, in the Berkshire Mountains of Massachusetts, and Aspen, Colorado, Ravinia Park hosts one of America's great summer music festivals and is the summer home of the Chicago Symphony Orchestra. Located on 36 acres at the south end of Highland Park, Ravinia was opened in 1904 by the Chicago, North Shore and Milwaukee electric railroad line for the purpose of attracting ridership. It was designed in the Arts and Crafts tradition by Peter Weber as a high-class amusement park that included a merry-go-round, Ferris wheel, toboggan slide, and a pavilion featuring classical music and later opera. Since streetcars ran from Evanston to Waukegan, it was the hope of A. C. Frost, president of the line, that Ravinia Park

INTRODUCTION

patrons riding the rail between the towns would become so enamored with the beautiful North Shore streetscapes lining the route that they would purchase property and become regular riders. In 1931, the Depression forced the park's closure. Stipulations in the will of Mrs. Louis Eckstein, who along with her husband bailed out the park during the lean years, stated that if music performances ceased for four consecutive years, the property would have to be turned over to the United Jewish Charities of Chicago. Ravinia Park has historically featured the world's greatest conductors and soloists, including Igor Stravinsky, Artur Rubenstein, Jascha Heifetz, Gregor Piatagorsky, Leonard Bernstein, and Sir Georg Solti. This classical tradition continues today, although programming has expanded to include ballet, jazz, and popular music.

North of Highland Park is the tiny city of Highwood, located across from Fort Sheridan. Highwood is seldom recognized for the superlative garden heritage within its boundaries. Fountains, topiary, and stone walls grace the landscape.

Just west of Green Bay Road, Highwood's restaurant-lined commercial thoroughfare, there is a compact residential area of relatively modest houses that flank winding streets 33 feet wide. With meticulously trimmed formal landscapes, the neighborhood resembles a small Italian village. Like other North Shore towns, Highwood was laid out during the speculative real estate frenzy of the late 1860s. When the national economy crashed in 1873, 300 people, including architect William W. Boyington, who later resided in Highland Park, lived within the 20-acre community. Established by the investment partnership of E. Ashley Mears and Reverend William W. Everts, Highwood's demographics changed in the early 1900s. Italians from Modena and its surrounding villages immigrated to the area and found jobs on construction crews at Fort Sheridan. Their talent as stonemasons and landscape gardeners also afforded them positions working on the huge formal estates built in Lake Forest between the late 1800s and the mid 1930s. After landscaping the multi-acre Italian- or French-inspired properties owned by the Armours, Ryersons, and McCormicks, Highwood artisans came home and re-created such large formal landscapes in microcosm.

If charming describes the village-like atmosphere of residential Highwood, magnificent applies to the park-like setting of Lake Forest. Words such as "elegant," "elite," "exclusive," and "aristocratic" come to mind. Building lots are spacious; homes are large. When the community was platted in 1857, most lots were three to five acres; estate properties, especially to the west, were considerably larger. The early cottages, styled after Andrew Jackson Downing's Italianate villas, were comparable in scale to those of Newport, Rhode Island.

Like the city of Evanston, Lake Forest's foundations were religious. Following Evanston's lead, when, in 1850, Methodists purchased farmland and built Northwestern University, a group of affluent Chicago Presbyterians met in 1856 to establish a community of residents who shared religious, educational, and social values. They too began by building a school. Initially called Lind University after the most substantial donor, it was renamed Lake Forest University, which, beginning in 1888, evolved into Lake Forest College. Like Northwestern, the college is graced by several stunning buildings designed by well-known architects, including Henry Ives Cobb, Charles Frost, Alfred Granger, Pond and Pond, and Howard Van Doren Shaw. The Lily Reid Holt Chapel features windows made by New York's Tiffany Studios.

While the university was being planned, the Lake Forest Association, which had purchased 2,000 acres on both sides of the railroad tracks, was founded to sell lots to investors, with the proceeds from alternate parcels used to fund the university. To accomplish this, Almerin Hotchkiss, experienced as a designer of rural cemeteries, was hired in 1857 to plat 1,200 of the acres, between the railroad and the lake. With curvilinear roads branching out from the train station, Hotchkiss created a picturesque romantic suburb, based on English precedents 11 years before Olmsted and Calvert Vaux laid out the western Chicago suburb of Riverside. The plan by Hotchkiss was as philosophically distinct from the urban grid of Evanston as it was geographically. A note on his original plat read: "nature has lavished a world of beauty here. Persons who have traveled the world over are charmed with Lake Forest."

Lake Forest's stunningly beautiful site was sufficient to attract Chicago's most affluent businessmen. Some built large, elegant homes by Chicago's foremost country house architects—Henry Ives Cobb, Howard Van Doren Shaw, and David Adler—as well as by many less well-known Chicago-area architects, including Arthur Heun, Stanley Anderson, and Edwin Hill Clark. Others chose prominent East Coast architects such as Delano and Aldrich, Harrie T. Lindeberg, and Philip Goodwin. The clients were Chicago's aristocracy. They were railroad men, retail merchants, financiers, or attorneys. Many bore names closely identified with Chicago's early economic growth, such as Armour and Swift (meatpacking) or McCormick (farm equipment).

Lake Foresters built residences to create an image to accompany their economic and social status. The Anglophile tradition of naming houses was particularly popular. Examples of English names include: Rathmore (Ambrose Cramer, manufacturers' agent), Ardleigh (John V. Farwell, Jr., dry goods merchant), and Argyllshire (Cyrus McCormick III, farming equipment manufacturer). The town's bucolic setting inspired other choices: Forest Lawn (David J. Lake, realtor and secretary of the Lake Forest Association), Pinewold (Bernard Eckhart, flour merchant), Fairlawn (Senator Charles B. Farwell, and later, Grace and Robert McGann), Linden Lodge (Henry Calvin Durand, wholesale grocer), Havenwood (Edward L. Ryerson), and House in the Woods (Mrs. Cyrus H. McCormick, Sr.). Some of these places, such as House in the Woods and Havenwood, were very large estate properties with outbuildings as handsome as the main house. Coventry, Meyer, and Miller point out in their excellent book, *Classic Country Estates of Lake Forest,* that estate buildings were typically connected by exquisite designed landscapes, some formal—Italian or French—and some Prairie style. America's most talented landscape architects, including Frederick Law Olmsted, Jens Jensen, Warren Manning, Ferruccio Vitale, and Rose Standish Nichols, were selected to lay out the plans.

By the late 19th century, leisure activities had supplanted religion as the main focus of social gatherings. The Onwentsia Country Club, established in 1895, set the pace. Golf was introduced to Lake Forest in 1893 by Rose and Hobart Chatfield-Taylor, who built a short seven-hole course at Fairlawn, the estate of Rose's father, Senator Charles B. Farwell. Taken with the sport, Lake Foresters started their own club and 18-hole course, Onwentsia, a Native American word meaning "country." In 1895, the course was located on architect Henry Ives Cobb's farm, with his sprawling Shingle Style house serving as clubhouse. It remained in use until 1927, when members demanded a new clubhouse with more amenities. Harrie T. Lindeberg, who had built a number of Lake Forest estates, was hired to

INTRODUCTION

Onwentsia Country Club, Lake Forest, 1928

design the new clubhouse. The royal sport of polo was added to the club's roster of activities in 1899, and matches were frequently held between Lake Foresters and officers at Fort Sheridan.

After Onwentsia was completed and huge estate properties began to be built west of the train tracks, commuters lamented the decrepit look of the town's business district located just west of the train station. It was a rag-tag grouping of retail buildings sandwiched between elite residential areas. Architecture critic Peter B. Wight, in a 1917 issue of *Western Architect*, called Lake Forest's downtown "a disgrace to civilization." Howard Van Doren Shaw and real estate developer Arthur T. Aldis, both of whom lived west on Green Bay Road, set out to remedy the problem. In 1912, they and other property owners formed the Lake Forest Improvement Trust, with the idea of raising money for the project by subscription for a new town center. Shaw's masterpiece, Market Square, completed in 1916, was arguably the first shopping center in the United States built to accommodate the automobile. It was also Lake Forest's town green, a civic space significant enough to be included in Hegemann and Peets' seminal book *The American Vitruvius: An Architects' Handbook of Civic Art* (1922). Opposite the station, it is the point of entry to the town by train. Two paired towers, one sporting a curving copper roof

[31]

South Tower, Market Square, Lake Forest, c. 1916

resembling a Bavarian helmet, flank the entrance to the square like giant gateposts facing Western Avenue and the station. The picturesque, gabled shops, built with apartments above that today serve as offices, have arcaded walkways and bow windows. Rich in detail and variety, with Tudor half-timbering, stepped Belgian gables, and English Arts and Crafts brackets, these structures reflect Shaw's eclectic, creative approach. At the end of the square is a freestanding bank building (today, Marshall Field and Company) with two-story Doric columns. The English village flavor of Market Square inspired the character of every North Shore town center, including Lake Bluff's, the North Shore's northernmost community.

Lake Bluff conveys the ambience of an inviting resort town and looks like no other place on the North Shore. Established in 1875 by the Lake Bluff Camp Meeting Association of the Methodist Episcopal Church (with close ties to Evanston), this small-scale village grew out of a plan by Solomon Thatcher, Jr. Thatcher wanted to create a summer resort in the Midwest that would equal such prestigious summer enclaves as Oak Bluffs in Martha's Vineyard or the camp meeting grounds in Thousand Islands, New York. Thatcher envisioned a place with a family atmosphere, without the presence of

INTRODUCTION

Bank building (left) and North Tower, Market Square, Lake Forest, c. 1916

alcohol or gambling. Enthralled by its ravines and wooded bluffs, the founders viewed Lake Bluff as a paradise. Some 160 acres were acquired from the estate of North Shore real estate speculator Walter Gurnee, and land was platted for a hotel and a 100-feet-square tabernacle to seat 3,000 people. The hotel and tabernacle were surrounded by 25-foot-wide lots. Church-like, gable-fronted Victorian Gothic cottages were built resembling those contained in the pattern books of Andrew Jackson Downing. Stockholders in the association included J. V. Deering (farm equipment) and C. B. Farwell (dry goods) of Lake Forest, as well as H. N. Higginbotham (later chairman of Chicago's 1893 world's fair), Orrington Lunt (a charter member of Northwestern University's Board of Trustees), and educator Frances Willard of Evanston.

The turn of the century saw the end of the Lake Bluff Camp Meeting Association and the beginning of Lake Bluff's development as a residential suburb. Tudor, Colonial Revival, and several Prairie School houses—one an American System Ready-Cut structure designed by Frank Lloyd Wright—were built. Located at the northern edge of Lake Forest, Lake Bluff also attracted a wealthy clientele, and large estates such as the Shaw-designed Stonebridge, William V. Kelley's residence landscaped by Jens

[33]

Jensen, and Tangley Oaks, Harrie T. Lindeberg's Tudor Gothic manor house for Philip Armour III, were built along Green Bay Road. As Sheridan Road wound into Lake Bluff from Lake Forest, another estate area was developed, with houses designed by Benjamin Marshall, Daniel H. Burnham, and David Adler. Crab Tree Farm, designed by Solon S. Beman, the William McCormick Blair estate, which today encompasses the original Crab Tree Farm property, and the Lester Armour estate by David Adler were sited north of the village, adjacent to the prestigious Adler-designed Shore Acres Country Club. Beyond lies North Chicago, an industrial satellite of the city of Waukegan. This is no longer the North Shore.

In the estate areas lying outside its town center, Lake Bluff is virtually indistinguishable from Lake Forest. But the general impression of Lake Bluff remains that of a small, quiet resort town with some nice shops but no movie theaters or busy restaurants, a town where the streets are rolled up at night. The scale is small, and there is little sense of being connected to Chicago. Commuters ride the train in, but the Loop feels very far away.

The best residential architecture that Chicago has to offer endures on the North Shore, despite the plague of teardowns and the infiltration of characterless McMansions. Just as development interests—then tempered with religious interests—drove its settlement, they now cloud its future, a future that one can only hope will value the qualities that make the North Shore unique.

In the Cause Conservative

In 1908, Frank Lloyd Wright wrote in the *Architectural Record* that "the work illustrated here is dedicated to a cause conservative in the best sense of the word." By 1908 Wright had designed the Ward W. Willits house (1901), arguably his most important Prairie-style house, built in Highland Park. Viewed from the distance that time provides, this fully realized Prairie house does not seem such a radical departure from the residential architecture that influenced it. Its exterior is a transformation of the half-timbering typical of Tudor houses and it borrows from the open interiors of the American Shingle Style as found in Wright's own 1889 house in Oak Park, Illinois.

The conservatism of the North Shore's architecture can be explained in a number of ways. Most area residents preferred houses done in historical styles that provided an architecture with which they felt comfortable. Many believed that historical styles asserted an image of status and respectability. Few thought of architecture as a vehicle for social reform, yet we must not forget the intimate relationship between "progressive" architecture and social reform in the 20th century. The Prairie School, which grew out of the Arts and Crafts movement with its agenda of elevating the common man through manual labor, never became more than a regional style and lasted only a generation. The more radical International Style, with its geometric, machine-like forms suggesting the mass production of standardized building, had an avowed socialist agenda. Le Corbusier, the celebrated modern Swiss architect, wrote in 1922 that "it is a question of building which is at the root of the social unrest of today: architecture or revolution." America had already had its revolution, in 1776, and architectural styles whose message was that of social change had little or no appeal in Chicago's wealthy suburbs.

The question "in what style should we build" dominated architectural discourse for much of the 19th century. During the early part of the 20th century, the question of style, sometimes referred to as "character," was linked with architecture's meaning. Specific styles were believed to be suited to particular building types, and these attributions were based on associative meanings. Banks were classical, more specifically they were designed in the Doric order, the most "masculine" and visually the strongest of the classical orders, to suggest the solidity of the institution and the soundness of its investments. Schools and university buildings tended to be Gothic, because of the association with European monasteries, the bastions of learning during the Middle Ages. Places of worship took on a variety of styles. Smaller buildings frequently recalled Romanesque pilgrimage churches, while larger structures were built in the classical style of Roman churches such as St. Peter's or Gothic cathedrals. Residential architecture borrowed from a variety of European traditions. Sometimes classical influences and sometimes a more romantic approach to building prevailed.

Travel as well as books and magazines shaped residential taste during the 20th century. For the very rich, the early 1900s were still the era of the Grand Tour. The capstone of education for the privileged, it usually encompassed a year or more spent visiting the great monuments of Europe. Letters of introduction helped travelers gain access to well-known country houses, villas, and gardens. That Americans of wealth would want to live in surroundings comparable to those they saw abroad is understandable in terms of their aspirations to status and refinement. American architects, such as David Adler, trained in Paris at the Ecole des Beaux-Arts and also toured Europe, studying the monuments of Italy, England, and France. Those architects and clients who did not travel could leaf through popular magazines, looking at pictures of historic and contemporary English country houses, French chateaux, and East Coast Georgians. While architects were reading *Architectural Record* and *Architectural Forum*, their clients perused *Country Life in America*, *Town and Country*, and *House Beautiful*. That the growing middle class would strive to live in modest versions of what the very rich could build reflects their aspirations to upward mobility.

Like their East Coast counterparts, North Shore barons of industry wanted to exhibit connections, not only to their family ancestry but also to their place of origin. In the absence of real family history, an imagined one would do. For the most part, this meant looking to 15th- and 16th-century English architecture or Georgian colonial architecture of 18th-century America. Those seeking an image of wealth and leisure were attracted to the life of England's landed aristocracy and looked to Tudor manor houses and even large rustic cottages to provide the desired pedigree. Howard Van Doren Shaw is said to have been happiest when he worked for clients who wanted the American version of an English country house. The imposing classicism of American Georgian architecture, which became popular following the 1876 Centennial Exposition, was equally desirable. Associated with patriotism, it engendered a sense of nostalgia for America's "lost" past. It also appealed to Americans who wanted the appearance of having "come over on the Mayflower." Before 1900, organizations such as the Daughters of the American Revolution and the Society of the Cincinnati were founded for the study and appreciation of family heritage, and these organizations were often located in Colonial Revival buildings. Stately Tudor and Georgian Colonial country houses were built by the wealthy. Tudor cottages and Colonial Revivals with small classical porches were their middle-class suburban counterparts.

North Shore clients with enormous wealth and sophistication, such as advertising magnate Albert Lasker, commissioned French chateaux. J. Ogden Armour, Harold and Edith Rockefeller McCormick, and Edward L. Ryerson had palatial Italian-style villas built. All were located on immense, formally-landscaped parcels of land. The ability of architects to produce works patterned after great European houses was assured because the most prestigious architectural education at the time was to be found in Paris at the Ecole des Beaux-Arts, where many of the architects who designed North Shore estates studied. Richard Morris Hunt, considered the dean of American architects, promoted Beaux-Arts-style

Introduction

studio education here in America. As a prominent practitioner, he built immense French chateaux for his wealthiest clients, including the Vanderbilts. On the North Shore, Philip Goodwin and, in particular, David Adler created equally elegant personalized versions of French chateaux. The number of palatial Italian villas on the North Shore were fewer, but nonetheless magnificent and for the most part designed by Howard Van Doren Shaw and the lesser-known but talented Arthur Heun.

While some clients relied on their architects to provide them with a cultural education in the appropriateness of one style over another, many North Shore clients had their own ideas. Leonard Eaton in his study, *Two Chicago Architects and Their Clients*, suggested that Frank Lloyd Wright's clients were progressive-thinking, self-made men, and that Howard Van Doren Shaw's clients were conservatives, vested in maintaining the status quo. The fact of the matter is that the North Shore's taste in houses has been consistently conservative, even when clients were progressive in business, politics, and social reform. Inherent in the choice of an architectural style was not just a client's social or cultural aspirations, but the long-term investment of capital in a house one could believe would not go out of style or depreciate in its desirability or value. Add to this the inherent conservatism surrounding the act of building, with its enormous investment of time and materials, and it is easy to see why North Shore clients wanted houses designed in a style that conveyed permanence and stability. This was the American capitalist version of building for the ages.

A Community of Architects

Chicago is known for its place in 20th-century architecture, in particular the development of balloon-frame construction involving continuous wood studs running from the ground to the roof, which revolutionized 19th- and early-20th-century residential building. More importantly, Chicago was the birthplace of steel-frame construction that made the skyscraper possible. It was in Chicago that Frank Lloyd Wright and the Prairie School architects developed houses with a heightened continuity between interior spaces and to the adjacent landscape. How, if at all, does the residential architecture of Chicago's North Shore relate to the inventions that established Chicago's prominence in the history of architecture? In order to answer, we need to look at the architects who built on the North Shore. Architects who, like their clients, lived or summered on the North Shore, participated in its social and intellectual life, and like their clients, commuted to offices they maintained in Chicago's central business district, the Loop.

During the period covered by this book, Chicago supported a stimulating, collegial architectural culture in which architects worked to promote ideas about a commonly shared agenda—the development of an American architecture. In the 1880s, the civic and residential architecture of H. H. Richardson was lauded as uniquely original and American. For his religious and institutional buildings, Richardson adopted the Romanesque style. With its romantic massing and flexibility of asymmetrical planning, the Romanesque was able to accommodate increasingly complex and modern requirements of building use. Richardson's residential style was based in large part on the work of the English architect Richard Norman Shaw, transformed through the use of wooden wall shingles. In Chicago, Louis Sullivan's philosophical writings on architecture and his highly personal reinterpretation of Richardson's Romanesque style—particularly in terms of ornament—made him a guru for a younger generation of architects who would build significant houses on the North Shore. Their work was to have an important impact on the architecture of the first half of the 20th century.

Dwight Heald Perkins worked in the office of H. H. Richardson in Brookline, Massachusetts, after graduating from MIT, and then returned to Chicago to work for Daniel H. Burnham. Perkins ran Burnham's office while Burnham was busy overseeing work on the 1893 World's Columbian Exposition. At the fair's end, Burnham generously helped Perkins establish his own architectural practice by referring work to him. Among Perkins' first commissions was Steinway Hall in Chicago, an

INTRODUCTION

Entrance to Steinway Hall, Chicago, c. 1896

office building with showrooms on the ground floor for the Steinway Piano Company. Lyon, Potter and Company were agents for Steinway pianos and occupied the first as well as the sixth floors. The rest of the building was comprised of musicians' studios, a recital hall, and office space. The owner and developer of Steinway Hall was William H. Winslow, for whom Frank Lloyd Wright was designing a house in River Forest, Illinois. With the completion of Steinway Hall in 1895, Perkins moved his office to a space on the 11th floor. It had a connecting stairway to the loft space in the building's attic that was used as a drafting room. The space was much more than Perkins needed and he soon invited Myron Hunt, Frank Lloyd Wright, and Wright's good friend Robert Spencer to share the space, expenses, and a secretary. Marian Mahony, who was Perkins' cousin and had graduated from the architecture program at MIT in 1894, worked for him part-time in Steinway Hall along with Walter Burley Griffin, whom Marian later married. Both went to work for Wright when he moved his office to Oak Park. Other tenants of Steinway Hall included Arthur Heun and Irving and Allen Pond. Wright and Perkins collaborated on the Abraham Lincoln Center (also called the All Souls Center), commissioned by Wright's uncle, Jenkin Lloyd Jones. Both Wright and Perkins were members of Jones' All Souls

[39]

Unitarian Church. Wright is also believed to have collaborated with Hunt on the double house in Evanston that he designed for Mrs. Catherine M. White. In his book *The Prairie School*, H. Allen Brooks suggests that the cruciform plan of Wright's Ward W. Willits house of 1901 may well have been based on Robert Spencer's 1901 design for "A Shingled Farmhouse for $2700," published in the *Ladies' Home Journal* in April 1901. The organization of the spaces around a central stair and fireplace core, and the extension of the main rooms out onto covered verandas and terraces, all present in Spencer's plan, were to become leitmotifs of Wright's work.

In his autobiography, Frank Lloyd Wright referred to the group of architects who dined together regularly as the "18," and for Perkins, they were "the committee on the Universe." According to Wright's account, the group was comprised of the architects at Steinway Hall plus colleagues whose work they respected. These were Wright, Robert Spencer, James Gamble Rogers, Hugh Garden, George Dean, Dwight Heald Perkins, Howard Van Doren Shaw, Irving and Allen Pond, Arthur Heun, Myron Hunt, and Alfred Granger. These men worked together and met together to discuss architectural ideas. They were all members of the Chicago Architectural Club and the Chicago Arts and Crafts Society. The Chicago Architectural Club met regularly to listen to papers on everything from architectural engineering to philosophy. Sullivan's partner Dankmar Adler spoke on "raft foundations." John Root read his English translations of Gottfried Semper's essays. George Maher presented a paper on his "Rhythm Motif Theory." The group mounted an annual exhibition of the members' work at the Art Institute of Chicago, sponsored design competitions, and published a yearbook. The Architectural Club also organized social affairs among the membership.

The Arts and Crafts Society was founded in 1897 at Hull House. Irving Pond was the first president of the society, and his brother Allen served as secretary of Hull House. Founded by Jane Addams, one of Chicago's famous social reformers, Hull House provided social services for the poor as well as training in its craft workshops. Hull House sponsored a number of societies, which, like the Arts and Crafts Society, were established for the education and self-improvement of their members. The Arts and Crafts Society was a great success. It met monthly, at which time a paper was presented on a particular craft. Like the Chicago Architectural Club, the Arts and Crafts Society sponsored a yearly exhibition. It would be difficult to overestimate the influence that the Arts and Crafts movement had on Chicago's circle of young architects. *House Beautiful*, launched in Chicago in 1896, illustrated its first issue with works by English designers William Morris, Walter Crane, C. R. Ashbee, and the architect Charles F. A. Voysey, all prominent in the English Arts and Crafts movement. Architect Robert Spencer wrote for the magazine on a regular basis. In 1897, the influential English Arts and Crafts magazine the *Studio* began publication in America. The Arts and Crafts Society, like the Chicago Architectural Club, held their annual exhibition at the Art Institute. Ashbee, who had addressed the society and become friendly with Frank Lloyd Wright, sent silver jewelry to the first exhibition in 1898. Several of Ashbee's pieces were purchased by Mrs. Coonley, the mother of Wright's Riverwood client Avery Coonley, who was the brother of Shaw's Lake Forest client Prentiss Coonley.

Wright's Oak Park house, which he designed for himself, was built in the Shingle Style of his first employer, Joseph Lyman Silsbee. Silsbee, the architect of the Lincoln Park Conservatory, designed

Introduction

many fashionable Shingle Style houses. Early interior photographs of Wright's house show rooms furnished and arranged in the English Arts and Crafts style, similar to Ragdale, the house Howard Van Doren Shaw built for his family in Lake Forest. Shaw's house, showing the influence of Charles Voysey's architecture, was one of the first all-stucco houses to be built on the North Shore and may well have influenced Wright's use of that material in his later designs for stucco and half-timber houses.

Professional clubs and social gatherings provided the architects of the North Shore with a network through which they found their clients. No less important to their future success was their architectural apprenticeship. In *The Favored Circle*, Gary Stevens' sociological study of the profession, a historical database demonstrates that almost every architect of significance worked for or studied under another prominent architect. This relationship provided not only referrals, but also provided an intellectual base of ideas. William Le Baron Jenney, remembered as the father of steel frame construction and clearly an inventive thinker, at various times employed Louis Sullivan, William Holabird, Martin Roche, Irving Pond, Alfred Granger, Howard Van Doren Shaw, and James Gamble Rogers. In addition to Dwight Perkins, North Shore architects Edward Bennett and Thomas Tallmadge worked for Daniel Burnham, who also is said to have offered to pay to send Frank Lloyd Wright to the Ecole des Beaux-Arts. Joseph Lyman Silsbee employed Frank Lloyd Wright, George Maher, and George Grant Elmslie at the same time (1887–88), and Wright, Elmslie, and Elmslie's future partner William Gray Purcell all worked together in Louis Sullivan's office from 1889 to 1893. Perhaps the most influential ideas passed to the younger generation by these mentors related to the interior spatial development of Silsbee's Queen Anne and Shingle Style houses and a divergent understanding of Louis Sullivan's work. Queen Anne– and Shingle Style houses were one of the sources for the development of the interior spatial continuity seen in the work of the Prairie architects. In Sullivan's ornament, George Maher saw the potential to visually unify the elements of a house through the repetition of a single ornamental motif. Wright saw the potential to interrelate all the parts of his houses through repeated compositional ideas that organized the interior spaces, the building's mass, and the building's ornamental details.

The development of shared architectural ideas, particularly in terms of spatial issues, may be seen in a comparison between Wright's Prairie houses and the work of Howard Van Doren Shaw. Shaw's 1908 House of the Four Winds for Hugh J. McBirney is linear in plan, and only one room deep, which, like the arms of Wright's cruciform houses allows for windows, views, and cross ventilation on the sides as well as the ends of the principal rooms. The entry hall in the McBirney house runs from front to back and opens on the side into the living room, which in turn opens onto a sunroom and then a covered porch. The interiors "extend" into the garden, which was designed to function both as a vista and as a lateral extension of the interior spaces of the house, creating the continuity between interior and landscape spaces generally credited to Wright. Coventry, Meyer, and Miller, in their book *Classic Country Estates of Lake Forest*, commented on the English architect Reginald Blomfield's influential 1892 book *The Formal Gardens of England*, noting that "Blomfield urged architects to regain from landscape gardeners the spaces immediately around country houses and develop them as extensions of the interior." Surely this was an important idea understood and shared by many of the architects building on the North Shore.

According to Wilbert Hasbrouck's forthcoming book on the Chicago Architectural Club, George Dean, one of the "18," published an essay in the May 1900 issue of *The Brickbuilder*, entitled "Progress before Precedent." To Dean's dismay, that title had been adopted as a slogan by the Architectural League of America. Fearing a misinterpretation of his title, he wrote that "precedent in architecture has two very distinct and entirely different meanings. If that of slavishly copying the forms of ancient architecture is meant, let us say 'Progress without Precedent.' If, however, the meaning is the following of principles which led the great architects to produce monuments of art which we revere and fondly worship, let the maxim be 'Precedence and Progress.'"

What were these architects, who were calling for a modern American architecture, trying to accomplish? Because of the 20th century's infatuation with abstraction and the avant-garde, we tend to lose sight of their aims. There is no evidence that they sought the invention of a new language of architecture comprised of forms never seen before. For them, invention consisted, as it had in the past, of the use of existing architectural elements and language in ways that were unprecedented and new. A North Shore example of such architectural invention is Wright and Spencer's transformation of the structural half-timbering of Tudor architecture. In Wright's Ward W. Willits house in Highland Park and in Robert Spencer's Prairie-Tudor Nathan house in Evanston, the timbering visually organized and structured the surface of the wall and its openings. Howard Van Doren Shaw's use of pilasters topped by urns as non-structural design elements on the facades of the Donnelley and Fernald houses also functions to visually group openings and subdivide the wall surface in a new and original way. The second-floor window cut through the center of the chimney flue on the rear facade of Shaw's Stonebridge, designed for William V. Kelley, is startling in its originality. Like the blank panel of Palladio's house in Vicenza, it assumes the unexpected power to mark the center of the entire facade. Pond and Pond's C. M. Howe residence in Evanston is a brick Georgian so unassuming as to be nearly invisible. Yet the architects have arranged windows, dormers, an off-center entry, and a window at the stair landing in a way that turn on end our expectations of a normative Georgian house. And what of the highly original Patton house by George Maher, a stone palazzo whose sense of compressed proportions and mass rivals those of the Philadelphia architect Frank Furness, for whom Louis Sullivan had worked? Surely each of these architects believed he was creating an original work rather than slavishly copying the architecture of the past.

For all their theoretical concerns about creating an original American architecture, these architects understood and mirrored the domestic desires of their clients. Wright built his home in Oak Park as an advertisement for his skills. There he subsequently built many houses and the Unity Temple. George Maher built a house for himself in Kenilworth, where he went on to build dozens of residences. In Kenilworth, Maher built the Joseph Sears School, the Kenilworth Club, the clubhouse for the North Shore Golf Club, and an addition to the Kenilworth Union Church. Maher unofficially succeeded Franklin Burnham, who also built his own house in Kenilworth, as town architect. Maher prepared a plan in 1923 for the redesign of the town's civic spaces and originated the idea to install a fountain just east of the train station. Along with his son Philip, Maher purchased and developed houses in Kenilworth on land west of Green Bay Road.

Introduction

Daniel H. Burnham lived in southeast Evanston, which he called "the most beautiful suburb in the world." Burnham designed several buildings in Evanston, including a grammar school near his home. Other architects who made their homes in Evanston and participated in the life of the community included Dwight Perkins, Myron Hunt, and architect-historian Thomas Tallmadge. Benjamin Marshall built a studio and mansion at the lakeshore in Wilmette, where he entertained royalty and rented space to the local Yacht Club. Howard Fisher lived in Winnetka and built his own modern house on family property just a short walk from the house he designed for his brother, Walter. Spencer Solon Beman, the son of Solon Spencer Beman, architect of the town of Pullman, lived in Winnetka and built many houses there. W. W. Boyington, the architect of Chicago's Water Tower, built his own house in Highland Park, where he was elected mayor. Robert Seyfarth, who had worked for George Maher on the Patten house, built his home on Sheridan Road in Highland Park. He designed well over a hundred houses on the North Shore, over 50 of them in Highland Park. John S. Van Bergen lived in the Ravinia section of Highland Park, where he built over a dozen houses and his Prairie masterpiece, the Braeside School. Henry Dubin built his modern flat-roofed "battledeck" house for himself and his family in Highland Park.

Lake Forest residents included Howard Van Doren Shaw, Henry Ives Cobb, James Gamble Rogers, Edward Bennett, Alfred Granger, and his partner Charles Frost, among others. David Adler lived just west of Lake Forest in Libertyville. There he renovated a farmhouse and created a country estate that included a house for his mother. A chauffeur drove Adler to his office in downtown Chicago every day. Alfred Granger observed in his 1933 guidebook to Chicago and the Century of Progress Exposition that there were so many architects who belonged to Lake Forest's Onwentsia Golf Club that the membership felt it had to select an "out-of-town" architect to design their new clubhouse. For many years, the club had occupied a large house that Henry Ives Cobb had built for himself and sold to the club along with the property. The club members selected Harrie T. Lindeberg, a nationally recognized residential architect known for his grand houses on Long Island, as well as a number of handsome country houses in Lake Forest. Henry Ives Cobb, an early Lake Forest resident, designed Lake Forest's First Presbyterian Church and many of the original buildings at Lake Forest College. For the town's most important civic development, Market Square, developer Arthur T. Aldis collaborated with his friend Howard Van Doren Shaw, who along with his wife Frances, a published author, played an important role in the intellectual life of Lake Forest. The Shaws entertained Chicago writers and playwrights and staged noted theatrical evenings at the outdoor theater they built on their property.

The architects who designed the houses of the North Shore formed an integral part of its civic and social history. Drawing their clients from their circle of friends, belonging to the same clubs, holding elected offices, and organizing social, cultural, and intellectual activities, they created total environments—houses and gardens that shaped as well as mirrored the lives of their clients, resulting in what is today the fabled stature of Chicago's North Shore.

Authors' Note

It is our hope that this book will be of broad interest as a social and architectural history of Chicago's North Shore seen through the lens of its houses. It follows the format of the Acanthus Press series on uniquely interesting residential areas of the country. Like other books in the series, it contains historical photographs of both exteriors and interiors. These early photographs allow us to study works of architecture as they were built, which is especially important in the case of houses that have weathered poorly or were subjected to unsympathetic remodeling driven by function or fashion. Historical photographs allow us to consider houses that are no longer extant alongside those that remain standing.

Writing a book reliant on the existence of historic photographs, however, presents some inherent difficulties, not the least of which is the fact that everyone who lives on the North Shore will immediately look to see if we have published a favorite house, a friend's house, or their own house. The inevitable question will be how could they have omitted this or that wonderful house. Unfortunately, many of the houses that we love were never photographed on completion. Others were only photographed from the exterior, leaving interiors undocumented, particularly those built before 1890.

Fortunately, the North Shore's most prominent residential architects, including Howard Van Doren Shaw, Frank Lloyd Wright, George Maher, David Adler, and Mayo and Mayo, all had their work photographed extensively. However, Robert Seyfarth, an architect who built nearly 100 elegant houses in Evanston, Wilmette, Winnetka, Glencoe, Highland Park, and Lake Forest between 1909 and 1948, did not have his work photographed. Only a few examples of his smaller houses appeared in the pages of *Western Architect* in the early 1920s.

In addition to researching interior and exterior photographs, we have also looked for photographs of gardens or grounds, particularly where the interior planning of the house was related to its landscape in a clear and discernable way. Surprisingly, finding landscape photographs for houses designed by Howard Van Doren Shaw has been easier than ferreting out those of his eminent colleague Frank Lloyd Wright. While to the reader, Wright's well-photographed body of work may seem to be a glaring omission from this book, it should be remembered that most of the houses of Wright's early career were built in Chicago and the suburb of Oak Park where he lived. We were fortunate in locating many never- or infrequently-published photographs. However, familiar photographs were too important not to include in our book.

In making our selections, we have defined Chicago's North Shore as the suburbs of Evanston, Wilmette, Kenilworth, Winnetka, Glencoe, Highland Park, Highwood, Lake Forest, and Lake Bluff. Fort

AUTHORS' NOTE

Sheridan, an army installation surrounded by Highland Park, Highwood, Lake Forest, and the shoreline, must also be included, because of the superb quality of its architecture by Holabird and Roche.

Like Philadelphia's Main Line or Long Island's Gold Coast, parts of the North Shore were home to Chicago's wealthiest and most prominent families. They built large estates, country houses, and gentleman's farms. These are largely to be found in Lake Forest and Lake Bluff. While many palatial homes were built in the other suburbs, especially on the east side of Sheridan Road from Evanston north to Lake Bluff, there is considerable variety to North Shore architecture. There are modest vernacular houses and suburban scale homes stylistically derivative of their grander counterparts. Rather than write a book devoted exclusively to estates, it was our intention to portray as best we could the diversity of residential architecture of the North Shore.

Our criteria for selection, in addition to availability of archival photographs, were architectural merit and historical interest. We have also tried to represent, even if only in the portfolio at the back of this book, most of the architects who built significant houses on the North Shore. This has resulted in the inclusion of a number of houses that architects built for themselves. While Libertyville, just west of Lake Forest, doesn't seem to fit our geographic definition of the North Shore, we wanted to include David Adler's house because it is so important and so closely tied to his other residential work on the North Shore. The frustration of decision-making was compensated by the sheer joy of fresh exposure to some of the finest architecture anywhere. We hope that our readers will share the same pleasure.

1890–1899

WAVERLY

JOSEPH SEARS HOUSE

Kenilworth, 1891

It was after a family trip to England in 1883 that Joseph Sears, the developer of the North Shore town of Kenilworth, decided to build a country house for his family. Visiting Kenilworth in Warwickshire to see a business associate, he was taken with the beauty of the English countryside. He also recalled reading Sir Walter Scott's novel *Kenilworth* as a young man. The Sears family lived in a house on Chicago's posh Prairie Avenue designed for them by Joseph's childhood friend, Daniel Burnham. They spent summers in Glencoe with family friends in a rented house. His daughter Dorothy

Lake facade

Waverly

View toward lake

Garden facade

Parlor

Fireplace

Sears recalled: "We loved the country. Father used to ride horseback up and down the North Shore looking for a suitable farm for his family. He liked very much the level area of land on the lakeshore between the villages of Wilmette and Winnetka. Since it was far too large a piece for just a one-family farm he decided to try the experiment of creating a little village."

Sears was taken with the idea of planning a village where he could live in peaceful rural surroundings with his friends. He approached members of the Swedenborgian Church, the Chicago Society of the New Jerusalem, of which his father had been a founder, with his idea. In 1889, he purchased a tract of land between the railroad and Lake Michigan from Charles Simmons, the land commissioner of the Chicago and North Western Railway.

The Kenilworth Company was formed in 1889. Sears asked his friend Daniel H. Burnham to become the company architect and to design a house for his family. Burnham, who was chief architect for Chicago's 1893 World's Columbian Exposition, was in the midst of planning the fair. According to Colleen Kilner's *Joseph Sears and His Kenilworth,* Burnham was too busy to accept the commission and he instead recommended a young man who worked for him. The man Burnham recommended, Franklin Burnham, was not a relative. Franklin Burnham became the official architect for the Kenilworth Company, designing Sears' house, which was completed in 1891. Supposedly based on sketches Daniel Burnham had done for his friend, the house looks more like Franklin Burnham's subsequent work than Daniel Burnham's. Furthermore, there are no records of Franklin Burnham having worked for Daniel Burnham. Prior to becoming chief architect of the Kenilworth Company, Franklin Burnham practiced in partnership with Willoughby Edbrooke between 1887 and 1891. In the year he designed the Sears house, he still would have been in practice with Edbrooke. Franklin Burnham designed three other houses for members of the Kenilworth Company. In addition to these, he also designed the Richardsonian-style train station and Kenilworth Union Church.

The Joseph Sears house, named "Waverly," was built on a bluff overlooking the lake. It was a picturesque, shingled affair with three porches, a curving veranda, a porte cochere, bays, and dormer windows. Designed in the Queen Anne style, it was classically detailed with Palladian windows in both gables, narrow clapboards, and small-scale dentil moldings at the eaves. The house was later extended along its length by the addition of a round bay to the west of the front porch. The extension was balanced by the addition of a dormer window on the new roof to make the existing porch the center of the main facade. Queen Anne and Shingle Style houses would become so fashionable that the young Frank Lloyd Wright built his own 1893 house in Oak Park with symmetrical bays, a gable with a Palladian window, and shingled walls. However, no Chicago architect surpassed Franklin Burnham's skill at handling this picturesque style. Burnham's own stone and shingle house overlooking the lake at the east end of Kenilworth Avenue is a fine example of his residential work.

Joseph Sears lived at Waverly until his death in 1912. The house remained in the family until it was destroyed by fire in 1945. The land was later subdivided and sold.

CHARLES GATES DAWES HOUSE

Evanston, 1895

THE ORIGINAL OWNER AND BUILDER of the 1895 Evanston mansion that would become the home of Charles Gates Dawes, vice president to Calvin Coolidge, was Robert Dickenson Sheppard. Sheppard, a professor of political science and trustee of Northwestern University, was made business manager and treasurer of the university in 1892. He claimed that he had built his mansion as a suitable residence for the president of Northwestern University, a position he desired but never held. After failing to keep his own accounts distinct from those of the university, he was beset by financial problems and forced to sell his house and eventually leave Evanston.

Street facade

Lake facade

It is uncertain how Sheppard came to hire New York architect Henry Edwards-Ficken to build the house. Edwards-Ficken was a prominent architect who had been born in London and married into New York society. He was a gifted artist and renderer, and his work appeared frequently in the architectural periodicals of the day. Edwards-Ficken had been hired to complete the interiors of Grey Towers, a French-chateau-style house, under construction in Milford, Pennsylvania. Grey Towers was designed by Richard Morris Hunt, the architect of Biltmore, George Vanderbilt's estate in Asheville, North Carolina. Hunt, a graduate of the Ecole des Beaux-Arts, popularized the architecture of the French Renaissance for lavish American residences.

There can be little doubt that Hunt's Grey Towers was an important influence on Edwards-Ficken's house for the Sheppards. The round towers of the front facade flanking the entryway, the location of the main hall with the dining room behind it, and the covered terrace at the side of the house overlooking Lake Michigan are all modeled after Hunt's design. Grey Towers also had a porte cochere at the west side that provided covered access to the great hall. The Sheppard house was to have had an art gallery above its porte cochere, but the second-floor gallery was never built. The library, stretching 60 feet along the east side of the house, ends in a glass conservatory. On the third floor was a ballroom. Servants' quarters were located in both the attic and the carriage house. While the exterior was consistently based on French sources, the interior, as evidenced by the English plasterwork on the

Entrance hall

Library

Dining room

Conservatory

Bedroom

dining room ceiling, is a mixture of styles. This approach was not uncommon in the eclectic houses of the time.

Charles Gates Dawes, president of the Central Trust Company of Illinois and an Evanston resident, bought the Sheppard house in 1909. Dawes was born in Ohio and educated at the law school of Cincinnati College. His investment in the Northwestern Gas Light and Coke Company of Evanston first brought him to the North Shore. Dawes was politically active in the 1896 presidential campaign of William McKinley. After his election, McKinley made Dawes comptroller of the currency. Dawes returned to Evanston from Washington after McKinley's death. A veteran of World War I, Dawes rose to the rank of brigadier general and served as the head purchasing agent for the United States Army. After the war, Warren G. Harding asked Dawes to reorganize what would become the Veterans Bureau, and later to serve as comptroller of the currency, the first director of the federal budget. Dawes received the Nobel Peace Prize for his work in 1924 as chairman of the international committee that organized Germany's rebuilding and the restructuring of its war reparation payments. In 1924, he was nominated and became Calvin Coolidge's vice president. From 1929 to 1931, he served as United States ambassador to England. Dawes was the last Illinois politician elected to a federal executive office.

Dawes remained at the house until his death in 1951. It was owned by the Dawes family until the death of his wife in 1957. Following the dictates of Dawes' will, the house and its contents were bequeathed to the Evanston Historical Society. The society has kept it open to the public as a house museum since 1960.

Root–Badger House

Kenilworth, 1896

One of the first houses to be built in the center of Kenilworth, the Root-Badger house was named after Frank Root, the original owner, who only lived in the house until 1900, as well as the second owner, Alpheus Shreve Badger. Root was a music publisher whose uncle, a composer, was known for his popular Civil War songs. He took over his father's firm, E. T. Root and Sons, and later became secretary-treasurer of the McKinley Music Company. Badger was in the lumber business. He built the stables, which were later converted into a garage, and added a wing to the back of the four-square classical house in 1905.

Street facade

Living room

Living room with view toward stair hall

Dining room

Stair

Child's room

Root hired as his architect Daniel H. Burnham, who had risen to national prominence as the chief architect of the 1893 World's Columbian Exposition in Chicago. Burnham, along with his friend Charles Follen McKim, of the New York firm McKim, Mead, and White, assembled the roster of architects invited to design buildings for the fair. More importantly, he was responsible for the decision that all of the principal buildings at the fair would be classical in style. The centerpiece of the fair, which was referred to as the White City, was an ensemble of classical buildings called the Court of Honor. The impact of the World's Columbian Exposition was to popularize a classical revival in American architecture. Civic, institutional, and to a much lesser extent, residential buildings would be built in the classical style. The overall planning scheme for the fair and the formal grandeur of the Court of Honor are generally acknowledged as having been the impetus for the City Beautiful movement that brought Burnham important urban design and planning commissions for Chicago, Washington, D.C., Cleveland, San Francisco, Baltimore, and Manila. Perhaps the best known of these is the 1909 Burnham and Bennett plan for the city of Chicago. By 1910, enjoying enormous professional success, Burnham's architectural firm had become the largest in the world.

The white clapboard Root-Badger house appears two stories high from the front, concealing a full third floor behind its deep cornice and a classical balustrade running continuously around the top of the house. Sited in the center of a block, the house has the largest lawn and garden in the village of Kenilworth. The classical facade is distinguished by a half-round, two-story porch with four Ionic columns said to have come from the Court of Honor of the fair. The classical detailing of the front porch is repeated in the covered porch on the north side and in other details of the house at different scales. The first-floor urns that form part of the pedimented window trim reappear atop the driveway posts.

The plan of the house is organized around a central stair hall, which doesn't extend the full depth of the house. The entry and stair hall opens symmetrically into the library and dining room on the north and the living room on the south. The living room extends the full dimension of the side of the house and has a wide bay window projecting onto a large curving covered porch that stretches the full depth of the house. The porch gives access to the side yard and gardens by stairs from the front and the back. On the second floor, four bedrooms occupy the corners of the house around an open central hall, with a shared sitting room between the two front rooms. This fifth room has a door opening onto a small balcony projecting over the entryway under the two-story front porch.

Master builder Paul Starett constructed the house. Starett was a Kenilworth resident who had worked on the buildings for the 1893 World's Columbian Exposition. He went on to build Daniel H. Burnham's Flatiron Building in New York City (1901), the Lincoln Memorial in Washington, D.C. (1911), and is probably best known as the builder of the Empire State Building in New York (1931), then the world's tallest building.

EASTBANK

CHARLES COMSTOCK HOUSE

Evanston (1897)

CHARLES COMSTOCK was born in Oswego, New York, attended Northwestern University, and remained in Evanston after his graduation. In 1863, Comstock, then the president of the Traders Insurance Company and the western agent and a partner in the Onandaga Salt Company, bought the first brick house built in Evanston (1860). The Italianate structure, based on Andrew Jackson Downing's "Regular Italian Villa Type," was built by George Foster, one of the incorporators of Northwestern University and an Illinois state legislator.

Original structure, 1860

Porte cochere

The same year that he bought Foster's house, Comstock founded the Eclectic Club, which met in his new home for "intellectual improvement and social enjoyment." According to Comstock, the club, which lasted for fifteen years and included members of Evanston's most prominent families, was limited in its membership only by "the seating capacity of our parlors." The club met every Monday evening at the house of a different member, and the programs consisted of readings, music, and dramatic presentations. Comstock, who became a grain merchant and was a prominent member of the Chicago Board of Trade, soon had need of a larger house and turned to Jarvis Hunt to enlarge and remodel his.

Hunt, the nephew of well-known New York Beaux-Arts architect Richard Morris Hunt, had come to Chicago in 1893 to supervise the construction of the Vermont State Building at the World's Columbian Exposition. After the fair, Hunt stayed on in Chicago and set up an architectural practice. The classicism of the Chicago fair had great impact on the architectural taste of the time, becoming a fashionable style for institutional, commercial, and residential buildings. Hunt transformed the main

EASTBANK

Living room

Study

Sun porch

block of Foster's original house by extending it in three directions. An enormous two-story curving porch faced the side yard and was balanced by a two-story wing added to the opposite side. The house was extended to the front with a two-story addition and a one-story open porte cochere with tall windows serving as a wind break. The additions were tied together by a deep cornice with both dentil blocks and projecting brackets. Like the fair buildings, the exterior was finished in white stucco, and the new window lintels were carved with a Greek key design. On the interior, the living room spanned the entire length of the original structure, no doubt providing ample seating capacity for Comstock's Eclectic Club.

Known as "Eastbank" after Hunt remodeled it, the Comstock house was one of Evanston's grandest mansions until it was demolished in 1941.

RAGDALE

HOWARD VAN DOREN SHAW HOUSE

Lake Forest (1897)

RAGDALE, ARCHITECT HOWARD VAN DOREN SHAW'S Lake Forest home, was built in 1897 as a summer house for Shaw's family and his parents. Shaw was 28, had two small daughters, and had been in practice for only three years at the time. Like Frank Lloyd Wright's house in Oak Park, the house functioned to advertise Shaw's practice as well as gaining him entry into the society of wealthy Chicagoans who lived or summered in Lake Forest. In 1897, Lake Forest was becoming a suburb of large country estates, following the Onwentsia Country Club's first season. Shaw would become a

Front facade

RAGDALE

Rear facade

Barn and cottage

Entrance hall

prominent member of the community, designing many of the great houses as well as the gracious civic gateway, Market Square, a green surrounded on three sides by shops and apartments just opposite the train station.

Shaw had opened his architectural practice in 1894, working from the attic of his father's house in Chicago's Hyde Park. His first employee was Robert G. Work, who later became David Adler's partner, and his first commission was for two party-wall houses, one for himself and his wife Frances, and one for her sister and her husband. The houses were paid for by Frances' father. In 1896, Shaw's father Theodore, owner of a successful dry goods business, gave him the money to buy property for a summer house in Lake Forest. Shaw bought 53 acres of land on the west side of Green Bay Road which is located along the edge of a glacial ridge that once formed the shore of Lake Michigan. Shaw divided the acreage into thirds, selling two parcels to friends and keeping the larger southern portion of the property that had an old apple orchard on it.

Ragdale was clearly influenced by the Arts and Crafts movement and by the work of the English architect Charles F. A. Voysey. It would be difficult to overestimate the influence the Art and Crafts movement had on architects who at this time were concerned about the development of an American architecture. Without being stylistically eclectic, the architecture of the Arts and Crafts movement offered a freedom from the formal axial planning and architectural design principles taught at the French Ecole des Beaux-Arts. Arts and Crafts architecture was picturesque, suggesting an informal comfort and

Living room alcove

domesticity, which gave it great appeal. It also had a theoretical underpinning that called for the revival of craftsmanship, handwork, and the use of high-quality materials. The movement began in England with John Ruskin and William Morris and his circle, who strove to revive the craft guilds. Their work was well known in America through its publication in magazines. In December of 1896, *House Beautiful* magazine began publication in Chicago, an important city for American Arts and Crafts where the craft shops of Jane Addams' Hull House served as the movement's center. The work of William Morris, Walter Crane, Charles Robert Ashbee, and Charles Francis Annesley Voysey was illustrated in its first issue. Ragdale was built the following year, coinciding with the founding of the Chicago Arts and Crafts Society.

Ragdale's light-colored stucco exterior, blue-green painted trim, and slate roof are particularly reminiscent of the work of English architects C. F. A. Voysey and Mackay Baillie Scott, both of whom were Shaw's contemporaries. The cut-out heart motif in the window shutters and the back of the bench Shaw designed and built himself for Ragdale's south porch is also a typical Arts and Crafts motif. Ragdale's widely-spaced double gable at the front of the house is similar to that at the Orchard, the country house Voysey built for himself in 1899, two years after Shaw's house was completed.

Dining room

Ragdale also exemplified the Arts and Crafts–style interior. The front hall has the barrel-vaulted ceiling that characterized many of Shaw's later houses, oak paneling, and built-in benches. Leaded glass interior windows visually connect the dining room to the front hall. The dining room's raised hearth has tall andirons designed by Shaw and arched niches to either side, with built-in serving shelves. The walls were covered with William Morris wallpaper. The trim and beamed dining room ceiling were painted blue-green. The living room has an inglenook with built-in benches on either side of the fireplace.

Shaw was known as a perfectionist, not only in matters of design, but also craftsmanship and construction. He spent a great deal of time on his construction sites, and was often seen admonishing a workman for sloppy work or instructing a workman on how to properly execute a task. Shaw was himself a skilled carpenter and mason, and loved working on Ragdale. Francis Shaw wrote that "he and the gardener built the sleeping porch off our bedroom at Ragdale. When he got to the tin roof, he sent for a roofer. The union questioned the job, and the next day three men stood in the drive and watched him. He never looked up, and they sent a tin man that afternoon."

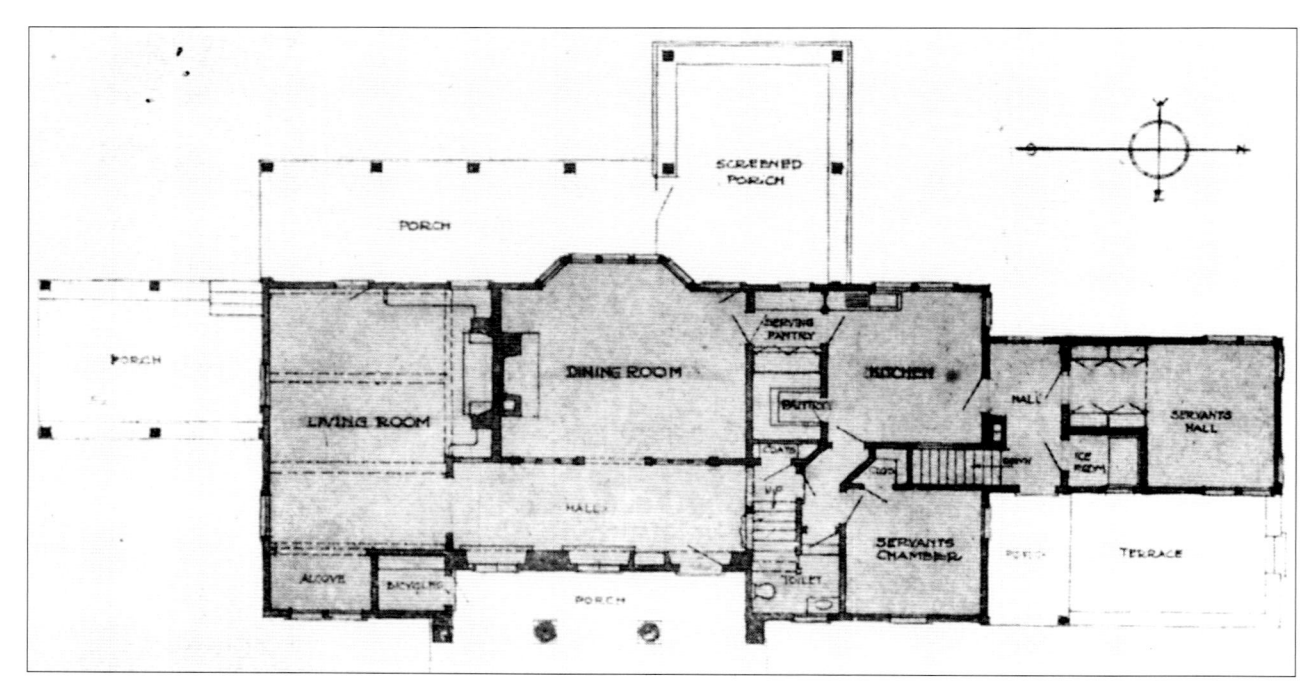

First floor plan

The garden and grounds at Ragdale were also designed by Shaw and reflect the influence of Gertrude Jekyll, the famous English garden designer. Shaw built a writing studio for his wife Frances, who was a published author, patterning it after an Irish cottage. Part of the grounds was the "Ragdale Ring," a much larger version of the "council rings" that Jens Jensen included in his naturalistic landscapes. The Ragdale Ring was used for theatrical performances and seated audiences of up to 200 on benches designed by Shaw. Noted poets Carl Sandberg, Harriet Monroe, founder of *Poetry Magazine*, and Vachel Lindsey were all friends of the Shaws and attended performances of plays written by Frances Shaw.

Ragdale proved to be unusual in Shaw's oeuvre. Its style was far too unassuming to suit his wealthy clients. Was the house named for Ragdale Hall in Leicestershire, England, to which it bears no resemblance? Was it named for the ragweed that grew in the fields? Or, was it named to suggest a 19th-century version of "Shabby Chic"? In any case, the association of the Arts and Crafts movement with a socialist agenda would have made the style unacceptable to Chicago's wealthy captains of industry. Ragdale was, however, an important work in Shaw's architectural development. Lake Forest author and historian Arthur Miller, Jr., wrote that "the same elements that characterize . . . later Shaw buildings show their roots in Ragdale: playful irregularity, eclectic architectural imagery drawn from different times and places, a spirit of domestic tranquility and community, use of natural materials . . . and decoration created by individual craftsmen."

Ragdale was given to the city of Lake Forest by Shaw's granddaughter, Alice Ryerson Hayes, who created the Ragdale Foundation, a community for artists and writers.

1900–1909

WARD W. WILLITS HOUSE

Highland Park (1901)

Frank Lloyd Wright's Ward W. Willits house, designed and built in 1901, is his most significant North Shore residence. It is universally recognized for its influence on Wright's later work, as well as the Prairie School architects who followed his lead. It was also important for the development of 20th-century European modernism. Noted architectural historian Vincent Scully succinctly summed it up in 1960, calling the Willits house "the first great masterpiece among the Prairie houses."

Wright was the father of Prairie School architecture, but what makes the Willits house so important architecturally? For the first time, Wright had a client with sufficient means to fully develop his ideas about what domestic architecture ought to be. The Willits house hugs its flat prairie setting, with four wings radiating from a central brick fireplace core, becoming progressively more open as they extend out into the landscape. The prairie's most insistent natural feature—horizontality—dominates. Low-slung hipped roofs with broad sheltering overhangs are reinforced by ribbons of art glass windows and thin dark wood bands encircling the house. Where there are vertical accents, they don't reflect structure as half-timbering does in Tudor architecture. Instead they serve as counterpoint to

Street facade

Porte cochere

Coach house

Living room

Staircase

Dining room

Bedroom

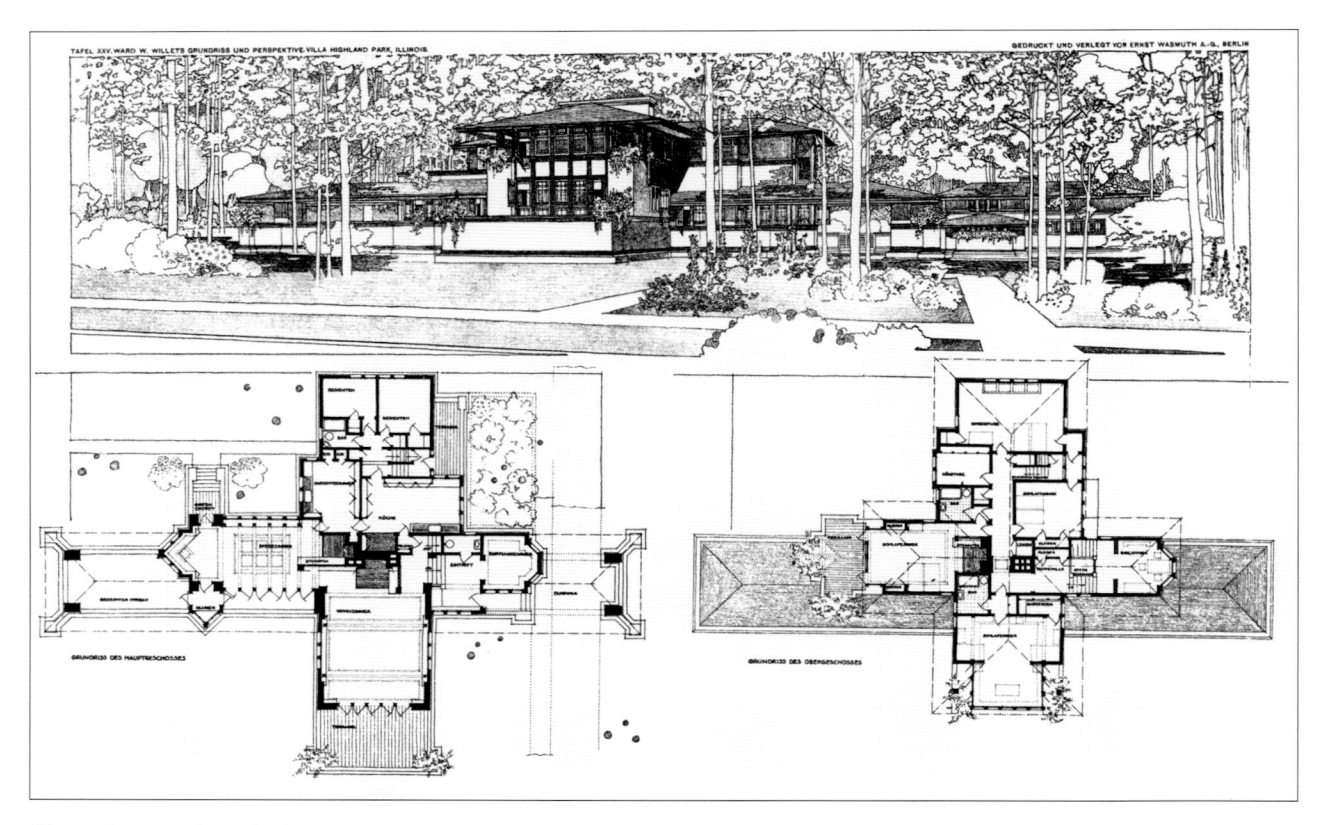

Floor plans and rendering

the horizontals, geometrically grouping together first- and second-floor windows to integrate the horizontal layers of the house. The significance of the Willits house lies in its abstract geometric simplicity and the invention of a vocabulary of architectural forms that were largely devoid of specific historic references. This was a radical notion in 1901, when most architects were trained in the eclectic academic tradition of the Ecole des Beaux-Arts.

Wright claims to have rejected historical architectural forms. He even denied any indebtedness to Japanese architecture, although he admitted being influenced by the simplicity characteristic of the Japanese prints that he collected. The Willits house bears a resemblance to the Ho-o-den Pavilion at the World's Columbian Exposition of 1893. This half-scale representation of a wooden temple was the official exhibit of the Imperial Government of Japan. Wright would have known the structure since he worked on the fair's Transportation Building for Louis Sullivan. A strong case could be made for the pavilion's influence on the Willits house, for it had wide, overhanging shallow sloped roofs, walls made up of rectangular panels accented by slender wood verticals and horizontals, and a cross-shape plan. Wright had not yet been to Japan when he designed the Willits house, yet he traveled there for the first time in 1905, accompanied by Mr. and Mrs. Willits.

Wright's understanding of architectural space grew out of his familiarity with large Queen Anne– and Shingle Style houses such as those designed by his first employer, J. L. Silsbee. These houses had stair halls opening vertically and horizontally, connecting the central rooms of the house. The spaces are visually connected, but individual rooms retained their definition and identity. In Wright's design for the interior of the Willits house, the spaces are visually connected in an even more continuous way. By the manipulation of abstracted geometric elements, spaces are created within spaces. The dining room, for instance, has been subdivided into a secondary space created by ceiling beams forming a grid containing panels of stained glass. These are centered over the Wright-designed table, visually locking its location into place and defining, with the aid of Wright's high-backed chairs, an intimate dining space within the larger room.

Throughout the house, ornamental decorative moldings like those found in traditional houses have been abstracted into flat boards that function spatially. They define the edges of rooms or continue from one room to the next, emphasizing the continuity of space. Other common residential elements have also been abstracted and reinvented, like the sconces that Wright simplified into cylindrical globes set in rectangular brass fittings.

Ward W. Willits was typical of the entrepreneurial businessmen who hired Wright. Leonard Eaton, who compared Wright's clients with those of Howard Van Doren Shaw, observed that Wright's clients were not looking for houses as statements of their social status or their Colonial or English heritage. According to Eaton, those who hired Wright tended to be risk-takers, successful but independent-minded corporate executives who forged ahead, marching to a "different drummer." Willits met this profile. After his birth in a small Illinois town in 1859, his family moved to Chicago to ensure better schooling. When Willits was 20 years old, he went to work for the Adams and Westlake Company, a brass foundry that manufactured railway and auto supplies. By 1891, he was vice president; by 1905, just after his new home was completed, he had been made president. He belonged to the Exmoor and Old Elm country clubs, and served on the boards of several companies, including the Harris Trust and Savings Bank.

Willits lived in the house until his death in 1951, at age 92. It is being carefully restored by its current owner.

JAMES PATTEN HOUSE

Evanston (1901)

THE DEMOLITION OF THE JAMES PATTEN HOUSE, designed by George Maher in 1901, was one of the North Shore's most tragic architectural losses. Exquisite wrought iron gates are all that remain to remind those driving down Evanston's Ridge Avenue that a monumental granite mansion, its stable, and expansive lawns once occupied the entire block. Today the gates open onto a housing development.

George Maher is usually identified as a member of the Prairie School, because like Frank Lloyd Wright, his typical work is geometric in composition and goes beyond the traditional historic sources

Street facade

Porte cochere

Detail, front entrance

Entrance hall

that dominated residential design. He and Wright were contemporaries, and Maher's architecture was equally original, but with its own character. Rather than emphasizing horizontality, complex massing, and a picturesque footprint as Wright did, Maher designed houses that emphasized solidity, continuity of wall treatment, and symmetry. He sought, and believed he was creating, a method of visually unifying the parts of his houses through the "motif rhythm theory," which was based on the repetition of a single design motif applied at different scales and for different elements throughout the house. These motifs were abstracted patterns inspired by a plant indigenous to the area. Maher often also repeated a specific geometric shape, usually the segmental arch, which can be found over door openings and fireplaces and topping capitals and balusters. This was a shape he favored in his designs for more modest residences than the Patten house.

Maher set out to create an "indigenous" architecture, one that was highly original and "American," when he designed the Patten house. Adhering to his motif rhythm theory, he adopted the native thistle as the governing motif, but with an engulfing intensity, repeating it in stenciled wall and ceiling treatments, carved woodwork, draperies, furnishings, and stained glass. Through the repetition of the thistle motif, Maher accomplished the design unity he was striving for in his architecture. He also achieved it through scale. The sheer massiveness of the house—inside and out—expresses a sense of

Dining room

Dining room hutch

Music room

weight that is only slightly relieved by the linear delicacy of the spiky thistle pattern and other small and complex decorative treatments. Crisply carved deep openings reinforce the solidity of the building. Although there are many Maher-designed houses on the North Shore, especially in Kenilworth where he lived, none compares with the Patten house in scale, spatial variety, or degree of commitment to the motif rhythm theory.

George Maher's Patten house, though hardly mainstream, is somewhat reminiscent of earlier buildings. Its basic rectangular shape transforms the ubiquitous four-square plan. Its heavy, rough-faced granite exterior recalls H. H. Richardson's 1886 John J. Glessner house located on Chicago's once-chic Prairie Avenue. Its ornamentation, incorporating dense foliate patterning, is similar to Louis Sullivan's decorative treatment of the 1886–89 Auditorium Building. Maher's inspiration for ornamentation comes straight from nature, as did Sullivan's. Interestingly, his design borrows ideas from architects who were at the forefront of progressive practice 15 years earlier, but evinces a synthesis that is unique.

Maher's client, James Patten, was as extraordinary as his house. Born in 1852 in Freeland Corners, a small town in Dekalb County, Illinois, he first worked in a country store, then on his grandfather's

Stable

farm. Upon arrival in Chicago, he took a job with the State Grain Inspection Department. Shortly afterward, he went out on his own, becoming immensely successful as a speculator in wheat, corn, and oats. The *Chicago Tribune* reported that on May 29, 1909, he cornered the wheat market, making at least $2 million in a single day. Between 1901 and 1905, he served as mayor of Evanston. In the late 1910s, he was president of Northwestern University's board of trustees. At the time of his death in 1928, Patten left a fortune estimated at $19 million. With earnings from his profits in the commodity markets and his substantial real estate holdings, Patten donated over $1.5 million to Northwestern and other Evanston institutions, including the Y.M.C.A. and Evanston Hospital. But James Patten, "capitalist" and "philanthropist," will always be remembered as the "Wheat King."

WESTMORELAND

A. B. Dick House

Lake Forest (1902)

IN 1884, ALBERT BLAKE DICK, founder of A. B. Dick and Company, had a successful lumber business in Chicago. As a result of the volume of his business correspondence that year, he devised a process he called "autographic stencils" that he used for duplicating form letters quoting prices for his customers. Dick met Thomas Alva Edison and approached him for help with his invention. The two men became friends, and Dick went into the duplicating business using a device designed by Edison, a pointed steel rod with a vibrating needle powered by an electric motor that could make 8,000 perforations per minute in a sheet of paper. This stencil was the basis of the A. B. Dick Mimeograph machine. Dick, who was born in Schenectady, New York, in 1856, lived with his parents in

Front facade

Rear facade

Entrance hall

Library

Stable and water tower

Westmoreland County, Pennsylvania, before they moved to Illinois. A trustee of Lake Forest College, Dick had five children, naming his third son, Edison, after the friend who had so generously allowed him to make use of his invention.

Westmoreland, built in 1902, was the name A. B. Dick gave to his Lake Forest estate and home. It was composed of the main house, stables, a coach house, and a water tower. Westmoreland was the largest house architect James Gamble Rogers designed before moving to New York in 1905. Rogers had built in Lake Forest for his father-in-law, Albert Morgan Day, president of the Chicago Stock Exchange, and for the Farwells and the McCormicks. Albert Day was related through his wife to the McCormicks, who owned the McCormick Reaper works. Rogers' older sister Anne was married to Francis C. Farwell. The Farwells were one of Chicago's oldest families, and one of the earliest to move to Lake Forest. John V. Farwell had gone into the dry goods business, starting a store with Marshall Field. John V. Farwell, Jr., served as chairman of the committee responsible for Yale University's campus plan. After Rogers moved his practice to New York City, many of his most important commissions were for Yale.

Both Albert Blake Dick and his architect James Gamble Rogers were avid golfers. Dick belonged to both Shore Acres Country Club in Lake Bluff, designed by David Adler, and the Onwentsia Club in Lake Forest, designed by Harrie T. Lindeberg. It is possible that they knew Grey Walls, the country house Edwin Lutyens built in 1900 for Lord Lyttelton on the 18th hole of Muirfield Links, one of Scotland's oldest golf courses. Westmoreland, like Grey Walls, has a curving entry front, an oval entry hall, and a similar relationship in plan between the main rooms of the ground floor and the service spaces. Lutyens' work was well known to an American audience through its publication in *Country Life* magazine, which featured country homes of the English aristocracy, and the *Studio*, which documented the work of the English Arts and Crafts movement. While Grey Walls may have been one source for Westmoreland's unusual floor plan and its curving front, the most prominent planning features are also to be found in 18th-century French architecture. Rogers, who worked as William Le Baron Jenney's chief draftsman before attending the Ecole des Beaux-Arts in Paris, would have known the house plans illustrated in J. F. Blondel's *Architecture françoise* (1752), with their curved facades, oval rooms, and complex internal planning.

Westmoreland's curving front facade acted to define a space of arrival in the prairie landscape. The simple brick facade with its regular grid of shuttered windows and classical entryway gives the house a decidedly Georgian feeling, except for the round "bull's eye" dormer windows, which are French in origin. Inside, the entry hall, an oval rotunda with French detailing, uses the length of its oval space to establish the main circulation of the first floor as the cross axis of the plan. This also differentiates the public spaces on the main floor from the service wing.

In 1941, Lake Forest Hospital was built on 24 acres of the Westmoreland estate that were donated to the city of Lake Forest by Mrs. A. B. Dick, Sr. Westmoreland was demolished after World War II and only the gates and the coach house remain today.

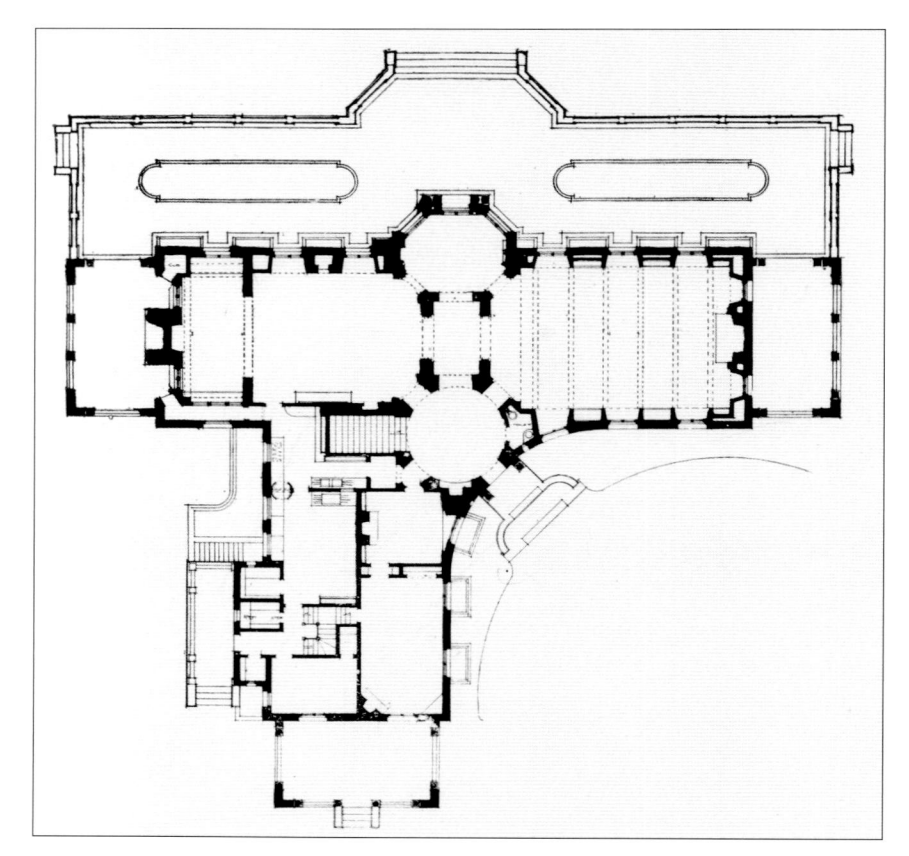

First floor plan

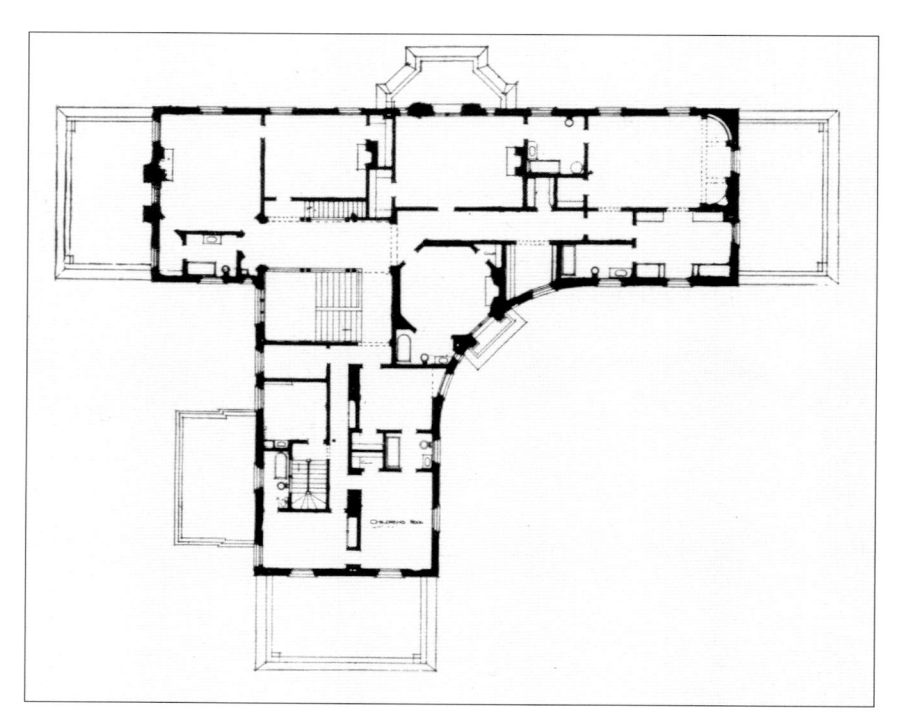

Second floor plan

Harry Rubens Estate

Glencoe (1903)

The Harry Rubens estate, built by George W. Maher and landscaped by Jens Jensen between 1901 and 1903, was published frequently in early architectural journals. Because its design was so extreme, the house and stable buildings aroused considerable controversy in *American Architect* and the *Architectural Record* in the context of debates over what constitutes "indigenous" architecture.

Like other Chicago-area architects whose work is identified with the Prairie School, Maher created buildings that were based on geometry. What sets him significantly apart in his endeavor to create an

Front facade and grounds

Front facade

Porte cochere

Entrance hall

indigenous American architecture was the system he developed to unify his designs. Calling it the "motif rhythm theory," his stated intent was to draw inspiration from native plants. For the James Patten house in Evanston, he selected the thistle; for the Emil Rudolph House in Highland Park, he chose the Tulip tree; for the Ernest J. Magerstadt house in Chicago, he picked the poppy. The motif that unifies the Rubens estate is the hollyhock. Highly abstracted, it may be found on ironwork, piers, screen walls, balconies, light fixtures, art glass, stair balustrades, and fireplace mantles. Maher believed that these decorative motifs, although a form of applied ornament, had the power to visually integrate all the elements of the building.

Maher's design for the Rubens estate is unique among his work. The simplicity of exterior forms that characterizes his architecture is rejected here in favor of a very mannered design. Tall brick walls buttress the ends of the house and the exterior walls of the porte cochere. Each wall surrounds a pair of attenuated columns that ignore classical proportions. Windows assume a variety of shapes. Some of the exterior walls, semi-circular in plan, are reflected in microcosm in the omnipresent abstracted circular hollyhock flower.

Main stair

The interior of the house is in the Arts and Crafts style. The Chicago Arts and Crafts Society was founded at Hull House in 1897, and the movement influenced Maher's design of the interior woodwork, articulated brick fireplaces, and chandeliers. Maher's expression of the forms various materials can take, his respect for retaining natural finishes, and his use of geometry to tie exterior and interior forms together reflect ideals shared by the Arts and Crafts movement as well as the Prairie School. This is one reason he is often considered to belong to the Prairie School of architects.

Maher's stable building is more radical in design than the house. Its vocabulary—the brick end walls, thin paired columns, and screens with circular patterns—is clearly derived from that of the house. But its plan, composed of two rectangular sections that form diagonals flanking an entrance drive topped by an over-scaled clock tower, is unlike anything in Maher's architectural repertoire.

Jens Jensen was proud of the landscape he designed for Rubens, and it was indeed among his best. Robert Grese, a Jensen biographer, notes that "it was the first of his creations to give a true reflection

Stables

of his principles." With its prairie-like meadow, sun openings, gardens with native plant material, and wetland plantings surrounding a pool area, Jensen's design mimicked the midwestern landscape's most characteristic natural features. Its beauty was recognized in Marian White's *Book of the North Shore* (1910), which presents a photograph of the grassy meadow with a caption calling it "The Park at Residence of Mr. Harry Rubens."

Harry Rubens was one of George Maher's wealthiest clients. Born in Vienna in 1850, he emigrated to the United States, settling in St. Louis in 1867. For the next several years, he had interesting jobs, including working as city editor of the *Westliche Post*, founding the comic journal *Puck*, and serving as private secretary to United States Senator Carl Schurz. In 1873, he moved to Chicago, where in 1877 he was admitted to the Illinois Bar Association. His wealth likely stemmed from having served as director and general counsel to the United Breweries and other large corporations. Remaining connected to his Germanic heritage, Rubens served as counsel to the consulates-general of Austria-Hungary and Germany, as well as president of the Germania Club. He was decorated by the emperor of Germany with the Order of the Crown in 1902, and by the emperor of Austria with the order of the Iron Crown in 1906. Rubens was one of many German American North Shore residents who commissioned the German-speaking Jens Jensen as landscape architect. Others of Jensen's clients included lumber magnate Hermann Paepcke and brewer Edward G. Uihlein, as well as Julius

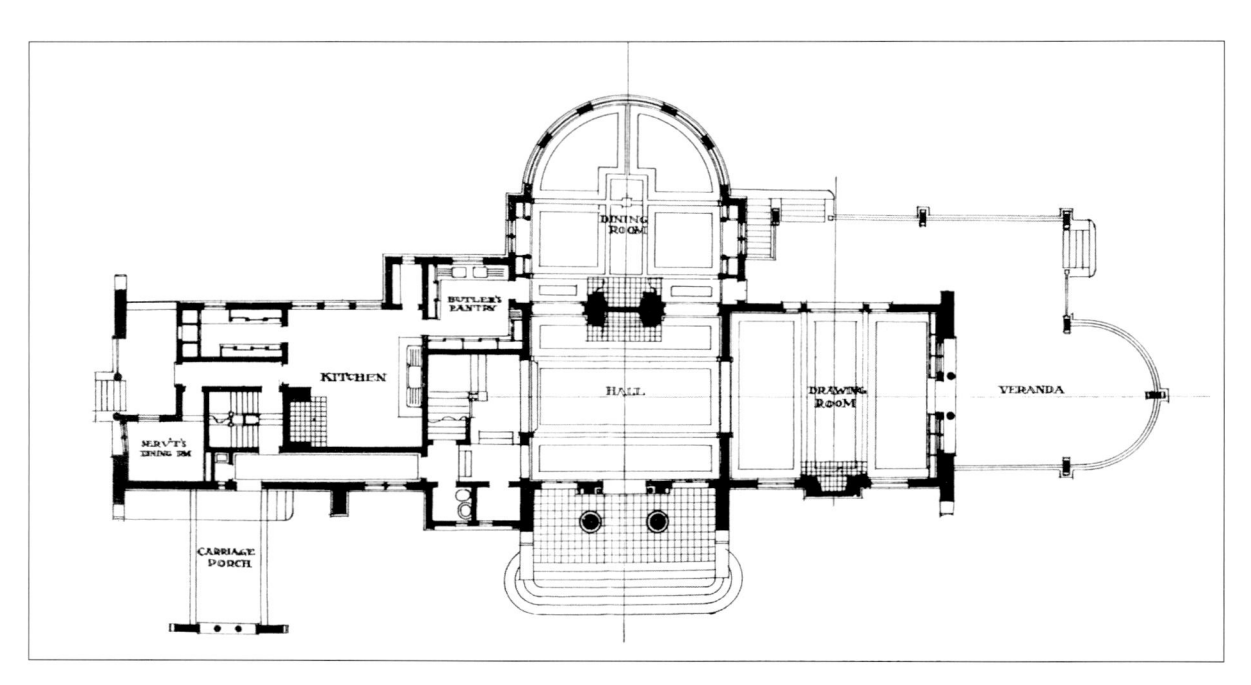

First floor plan

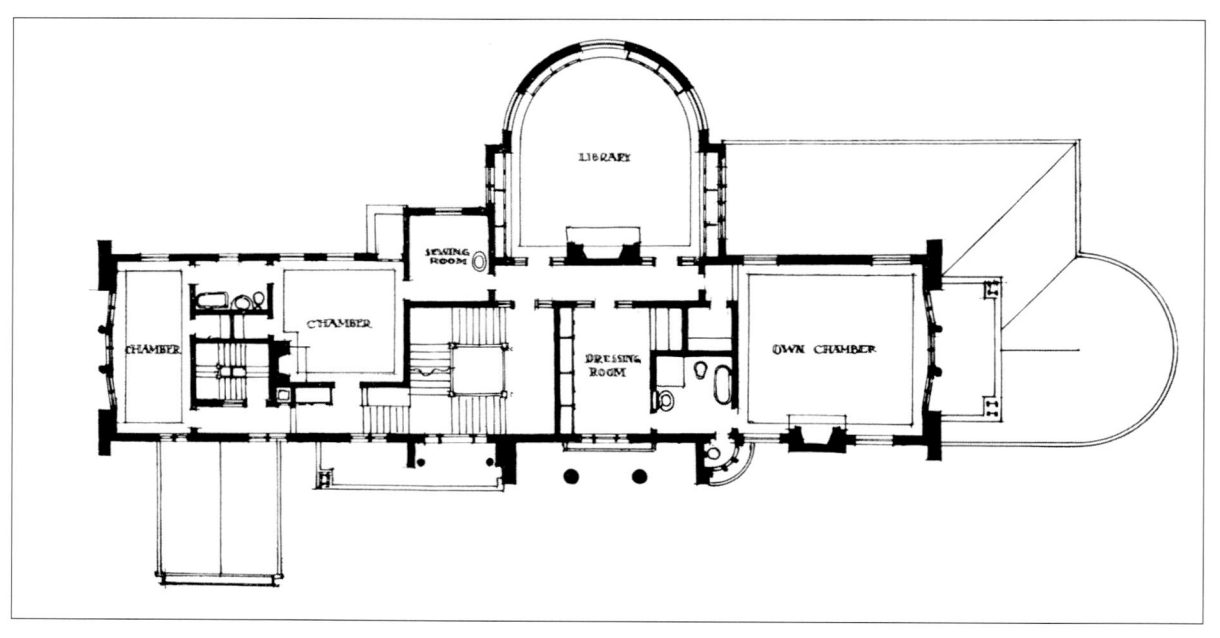

Second floor plan

Rosenwald, philanthropist and president of Sears Roebuck, shoe manufacturer Harold Florsheim, and A. G. Becker, founder of the brokerage company that bore his name.

The Rubens estate, purchased for $300,000 in 1960, was subdivided by the buyer into eleven lots. The house was demolished, and only a concrete wall at the edge of the property, distinctly Arts and Crafts in design, serves as a reminder of the elegant home that once occupied the site.

INDIANOLA

HERMANN PAEPCKE ESTATE

Glencoe (1903)

INDIANOLA IS THE NAME OF THE GLENCOE ESTATE on which Hermann Paepcke built a Queen Anne house a decade after the style ceased to be fashionable. Perhaps lumber magnate Paepcke thought that Queen Anne architecture would showcase the use of wood, which adapts well to the complex structure and variety of roof shapes and surface textures associated with this style.

The popularity of the Queen Anne style in America dates to about 1876, when the British commissioner's building was constructed for America's Centennial Exposition. With its picturesque form and multitude of gables, window types, and wall treatments, the exposition building prefigured the imposing homes that Americans would build throughout the country during the 1880s and 1890s. Many examples, like Indianola, were set at the water's edge. Queen Anne was the style favored by McKim, Mead, and White for their seaside cottages in Newport. It was widely published in architectural

South facade and bluff

House from southwest

periodicals and pattern books of the time. Ironically, historians note that the name of the style had nothing to do with the reign of Queen Anne (1702–14), but instead borrows from 15th- and 16th-century architecture. Stylistically, the Paepcke house has striking Queen Anne characteristics, including an irregular footprint, a variety of decorative wall surface treatments including half-timbering, shingles, and slender clapboards, multiple porches, and three very different-looking towers: one that is cylindrical with a pointed conical top; another that is polygonal with a flared roof; and a third that is rectangular with a bracketed double-sloped pointed roof. The steeply-pitched roof shapes of the towers stem from the German architectural tradition.

Hermann Paepcke was born in Mecklenburg-Schwerin, Germany, in 1851. Recognizing the opportunities America offered, when he was 21, Paepcke moved to Indianola, Texas, and went into the export business. While there, he married Paula Wagner, whose parents were also German. Perceiving that a better future awaited him in Chicago, Paepcke and his wife moved and he set up a planing mill and lumber company. The business prospered, and at the dawn of the 20th century, he diversified, investing heavily in timber lands in the South, where he established mills to manufacture lumber from the timber. He also built or purchased large paper mills. His most important decision, however, was to establish the Chicago Packing Box Company. Walter, Hermann's son who became head of his father's various businesses when Paepcke died in 1922, later founded and served as chairman of Container Corporation of America. With a committed interest in the arts, Walter Paepcke and his wife Elizabeth "Pussy" Hilken Nitze Paepcke helped to put Aspen, Colorado, on the map. They were two of the

Garden facade

Jensen landscape

Guest cottage

Stable

founders of the Aspen Skiing Corporation, and in the 1950s founded the Aspen Institute of Humanistic Studies to create an alliance between business and the arts.

The Hermann Paepckes selected the architectural firm of Frommann and Jebsen, who had many German clients, to design their new home in Glencoe. In 1896, Frommann and Jebsen had designed a stable building that resembled an old German country house, with Queen Anne detailing, in Chicago's Humboldt Park. However, they were best known for the many saloons they built in German neighborhoods throughout the city for Edward G. Uihlein, Chicago agent for the Joseph Schlitz Brewing Company and a friend of the Paepckes.

Jens Jensen was selected to landscape the Paepcke's 20 acres of Lake Michigan property. In 1900, Jensen had just been dismissed as superintendent of Humboldt Park for railing against political patronage, and did very few public projects until 1906, when he was appointed superintendent and landscape architect for Chicago's West Park System. With few social connections and little academic training, Jensen had not yet developed a residential clientele. Hermann Paepcke and Harry Rubens were willing to give him a chance, and between 1901 and 1903 they commissioned him to landscape their large suburban estates. These jobs not only kept Jensen solvent, but they also launched his career of designing private landscapes with meadows, curving drives, and exquisite vistas such as that enjoyed by the Paepcke family. Sadly, the house at Indianola was destroyed by fire, and its landscape has been subdivided.

Augustus Magnus Estate

Winnetka (1906)

Robert C. Spencer, Jr., architect for the Augustus C. Magnus house, combined Prairie School and Tudor architecture to design his most impressive residence. By the time it was completed, Spencer had absorbed the progressive influence of Frank Lloyd Wright and his colleagues. H. Allen Brooks commented in his book, *The Prairie School* (1972), that during the late 1890s, Spencer was Wright's best friend. They shared space, along with Dwight Perkins and several other architects in Steinway Hall, and both belonged to a group of architects referred to by Wright as the "18" that included the diverse talents of Howard Van Doren Shaw, Arthur Heun, and Myron Hunt.

Spencer was never a slavish follower of Wright. By 1902, the Steinway Hall group had begun to disperse, and Spencer was practicing on his own. He was particularly enamored of English architecture, as well as the work of his British contemporary, Charles F. A. Voysey, who like Spencer was incorporating but simplifying more traditional English sources.

Front facade

Lake facade

In the Magnus house, the Prairie School influence can be seen in the building's strong horizontal emphasis. Topped by a shallow-pitched hipped roof with shingles laid in a linear pattern, the horizontality of the house is reinforced by slender bands of wood located above and below the second-floor ribbon of casement windows. Its picturesque massing, leaded windows, and half-timbering, however, recall Tudor architecture, even if the dark half-timbered trim forming abstract geometric patterns of verticals and horizontals exists to integrate the design. Warm woodwork and pared down design treatments are also used on the interior, notably in the handling of the graceful spiral staircase.

Jens Jensen's naturalistic landscaping design approach always incorporated native plant material like redbud, maple, and hawthorn trees. Spencer's decorative leaded window treatment was inspired by the hawthorn tree's leafless winter appearance for the first-floor windows, and its leafy summer appearance for those on the second floor. Casement windows were specified by Spencer to maximize light and Lake Michigan breezes. Convinced of their benefits, in the 1920s he founded the Chicago Casement Hardware Company.

Augustus Charles Magnus was born in 1862. He served as president of a bottlers and brewers supply company founded by his father. Magnus was a member of the Indian Hill Country Club in Winnetka as well as the Montecito Country Club in the Santa Barbara area, where many of Chicago's most prominent families spent the winter. The Magnus house, which was frequently published in contemporary architectural journals, has been demolished. Its gate house, which was stylistically integrated with the main house, remains standing on Sheridan Road, and has been converted into a single-family residence.

Detail of entrance and stair tower

Stair

Coach house

Estate from Sheridan Road: Spencer rendering

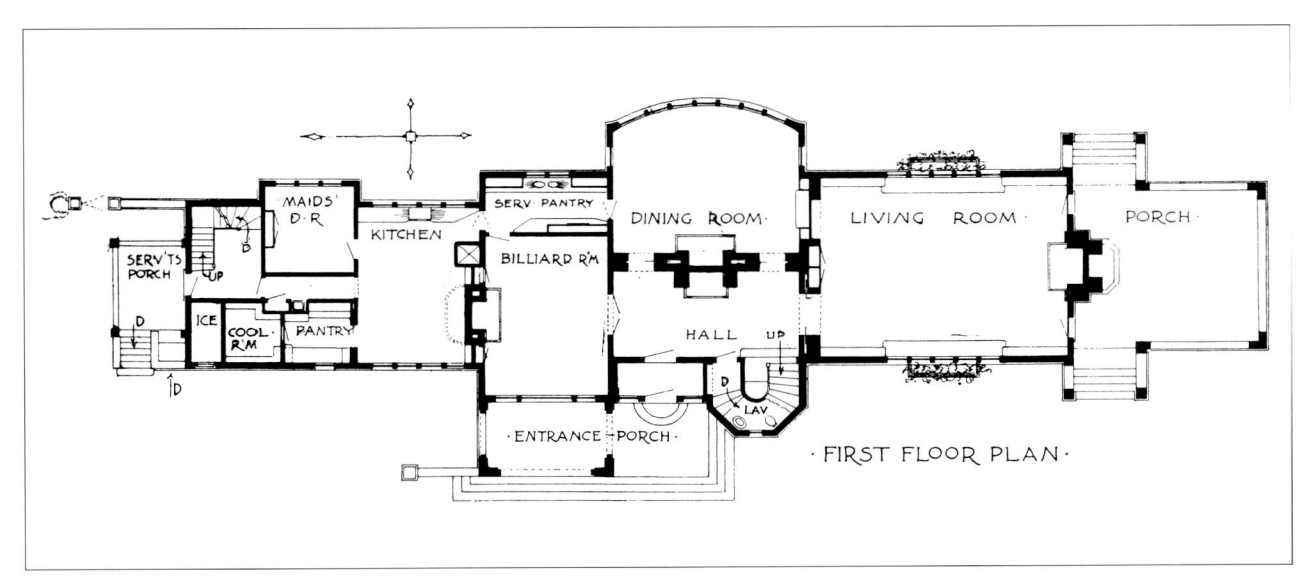

First floor plan

CHARLES FERNALD HOUSE

Lake Forest (1907)

Howard Van Doren Shaw's colonial-style residence for Charles Fernald is perhaps the most elegant of Shaw's houses with wood-clad exteriors. The entryway, centered in the main block, is flanked by pairs of two-story giant order Tuscan pilasters. These extend through the roof and are topped by decorative urns, a device adapted from Italian Renaissance precedents for 19th-century English architecture in the classical style. Dormers with arched windows also give the blank wall between the pilasters vertical extension. A projecting balcony shelters the double-door entry. The landing of the main stair opens out onto this balcony through French doors surmounted by an arched

Front facade

Entrance detail

Screen porch

Entrance hall and staircase

Gun and trophy room

transom window, with a keystone draped with painted decorative wooden garlands. These elements act to give emphasis to the center of the facade and to provide a monumentality that scales the entrance to the rest of the house. Two-story-high pilasters topped by urns were used again by Shaw in the Thomas Donnelley house built in Lake Forest in 1911. However, the pilasters at the Donnelley house subdivide the front facade of the main block into bays, resulting in a far less original treatment. The main block of the Fernald house, which projects slightly forward, is flanked by a service wing to one side, and on the other, a screen porch with a sleeping porch above. These provide an asymmetrical balance to the house from the front. Living and sleeping porches, stacked one above the other in this way, were an element Shaw used in a number of the houses he designed as summer residences. For houses built prior to the introduction of air conditioning, outdoor living and comfortable sleeping accommodations were an important concern.

Inside the house, the entrance hall and stairway were flooded with light from above through the French doors at the stair landing. The unusual stair railing seems to echo the Gothic muntin pattern in the arched stair window and dormers at the front of the house. A photo of the stair published in the *Architectural Record* in 1909 shows a bearskin draped over the railing at the stair landing. The skin may have been a souvenir from Fernald's 1898 trip to the Klondike as a representative of C. E. Whitney and Company, San Francisco wholesalers. Fernald was a hunting enthusiast, and Shaw also designed a gun and trophy room for the house with a vaulted ceiling featuring bands of delicate decorative plasterwork.

Chares Fernald was born in Santa Barbara, California, in 1873. He worked in San Francisco for three years during the 1890s. In 1903, when he met and married Bessie Swift of Lake Forest—daughter of Louis Swift, the prominent meatpacker—Fernald was in the cattle business in Sonora, Mexico. In 1908, Swift hired Shaw to design a house for his daughter Bessie in Lake Forest. That year Fernald went into banking, first with Drover's National Bank, Chicago, and then with the Fort Dearborn National Bank and the Continental Bank and Trust Company where he was made a vice president in 1924. By 1909 the Fernalds had rented the house to Cissy Patterson, who had returned to Lake Forest from Europe as the divorced Countess Gizycki. Howard Van Doren Shaw had built Westwood Farm, the Lake Forest estate of Cissy Patterson's father Joseph Medill Patterson, who in 1910 became editor of the *Chicago Tribune* along with his cousin Robert McCormick. The Fernald house still stands today in Lake Forest.

MELLODY FARM

J. Ogden Armour Estate

Lake Forest (1908)

J. Ogden and Lolita Sheridan Armour's thousand-acre country home, Mellody Farm, was elaborate even by Lake Forest standards. Built over a period of four years, between 1904 and 1908, the Italian villa designed by Chicago architect Arthur Heun was constructed at an estimated cost of $10 million. The grounds contained numerous outbuildings including a stable, orangerie, greenhouse, orchards, tennis courts, a 20-acre man-made lake, and extensive formal gardens terminating in a small structure called a casino, the Italian term for a small house.

Front facade

Mellody Farm

Porte cochere

Garden facade

Main hall toward grand staircase

The main house, approached through a pair of monumental stone gates down a sweeping driveway and over a concrete bridge, was planned in an H-shape measuring 164 by 164 feet. Including the kitchen wing, covered walkway, and attached laundry, the entire building runs 419 feet from north to south. The spaces are huge, the materials are opulent, and the ornamentation is lavish. The central hallway, extending the length of the house, is 112 feet by 45 feet, and has Caen limestone walls, marble floors, and an ornamental plaster ceiling. The music room has a parquetry floor and contains a pipe organ. A light-filled winter garden running parallel to the hallway has a stone frieze of birds, trees, flowers, trellises, and a fountain. The second floor, approached by a monumental staircase, has three master bedroom suites—one each for Mr. and Mrs. Armour, and one for their daughter Lolita—opening off a large rectangular hallway. At one time, staff serving the Armours numbered 125. Their estate,

Living room

situated at the western edge of Lake Forest in the land of gentlemen's farms, is comparable to the grandest places on Long Island, in Newport, and along New York's Hudson River. Peter B. Wight, in a 1916 article for *Architectural Record*, called the J. Ogden Armour estate "a house and garden in the planning of which limitations of cost are not evident, and carried out on a scale that has seldom been equaled in any other country home in America."

Plans for Mellody Farm began in 1904, when Armour bought up several working farms, including that of Patrick Melody—a name that metamorphosed into Mellody when the Armours named their estate. Only a small portion of the estate was forested, and much of the undeveloped land was swamp that was drained to create the lakes. The railroad siding, built to bring in construction materials, was used to import vast numbers of plants, shrubs, and trees, as well.

The house Arthur Heun designed for the Armours was fireproof, concrete construction with steel beams to accommodate long spans. Its stucco-faced brick was painted pastel pink, and red tiles covered the roof. These features, along with arched loggias, towers, and balconied openings, all tie the design stylistically to villas of the Mediterranean region. The choice of Italian architecture was in fashion: Edith Wharton was just completing her book on Italian villas and their gardens. Heun, then a relatively young architect, developed a reputation designing distinguished historical revival residences like this one (though generally considerably smaller). In this case, however, he also drew from his experience sharing space with architects Frank Lloyd Wright, Dwight Perkins, and Pond and Pond at

Winter garden

Steinway Hall in Chicago. Although the house was clearly inspired by Italian Renaissance architecture, it has a horizontal emphasis that is expressed through bands of windows, a continuous string course, and broad eaves. These are characteristics of the Prairie School that Heun would have been exposed to during the time he spent with Wright and his contemporaries.

Jonathan Ogden Armour, born in 1863, was the second son of meatpacking magnate Philip Danforth Armour. At the turn of the century when his father died, J. Ogden Armour became president of Armour and Company, which was making hundreds of millions in profits. For years, he was rumored to be one of wealthiest men in the country. However, muckrakers and social reformers, such as the writer Upton Sinclair, challenged the excesses of the wealthy and railed against mistreatment of workers by them. Sinclair, for instance, directly attacked Armour in his novel *The Jungle*. To counteract his critics, Armour defended himself and his company in the book, *The Packers, the Private Car Lines, and the People*.

By the 1920s, the phenomenal success of Armour and Company came to a grinding halt. During World War I, the United States government purchased huge supplies of meat from Armour, but at the end of the war the government unloaded its surpluses on the market, dramatically driving down the price of pork and beef. The company no longer enjoyed huge earnings. J. Ogden Armour's personal business affairs were in equally poor shape because of a series of unwise investments. By the end of 1922, he and the company were deeply in debt and creditors compelled Armour to relinquish control

Water garden

of his company. These financial setbacks forced the Armours to abandon living at Mellody Farm. After J. Ogden's death in 1927, his wife, determined to clear his debts, sold the farm to a group of Chicago investors led by utilities magnate Samuel Insull, who intended to turn the property into a prestigious golf resort. Insull's construction team completed an 18-hole golf course, began work on a locker room addition, and laid out an airport. The Depression of 1929 put an end to these grandiose plans.

A miraculous turn of events revived the Armour family fortune. Years earlier, Lolita Armour had given her husband $1.5 million and took in return 400 shares of stock in Universal Oil Products, a company that held patents for producing gasoline from crude oil. Lolita's investment had looked so foolish to the Armours' creditors that they had never claimed what they believed to be worthless stock. Her creditors' inattention proved to be Mrs. Armour's good fortune. The explosion in automobile sales created a demand for gasoline. Lolita Armour sold her shares of Universal Oil Products to Shell Union and Standard Oil of California, earning her $25 million on the $1.5 million investment. By 1934, she was rich enough to hire society architect David Adler to design a new Lake Forest estate for her.

Since 1947, portions of the house at Mellody Farm, later additions, and many acres of surrounding property have served as home to Lake Forest Academy, a private secondary school. The rest of the Armour estate has been either developed with single-family homes or preserved as open space. Lake Forest Open Lands, an environmental group, redeveloped one Mellody Farm gatehouse off Waukegan Road as a nature center.

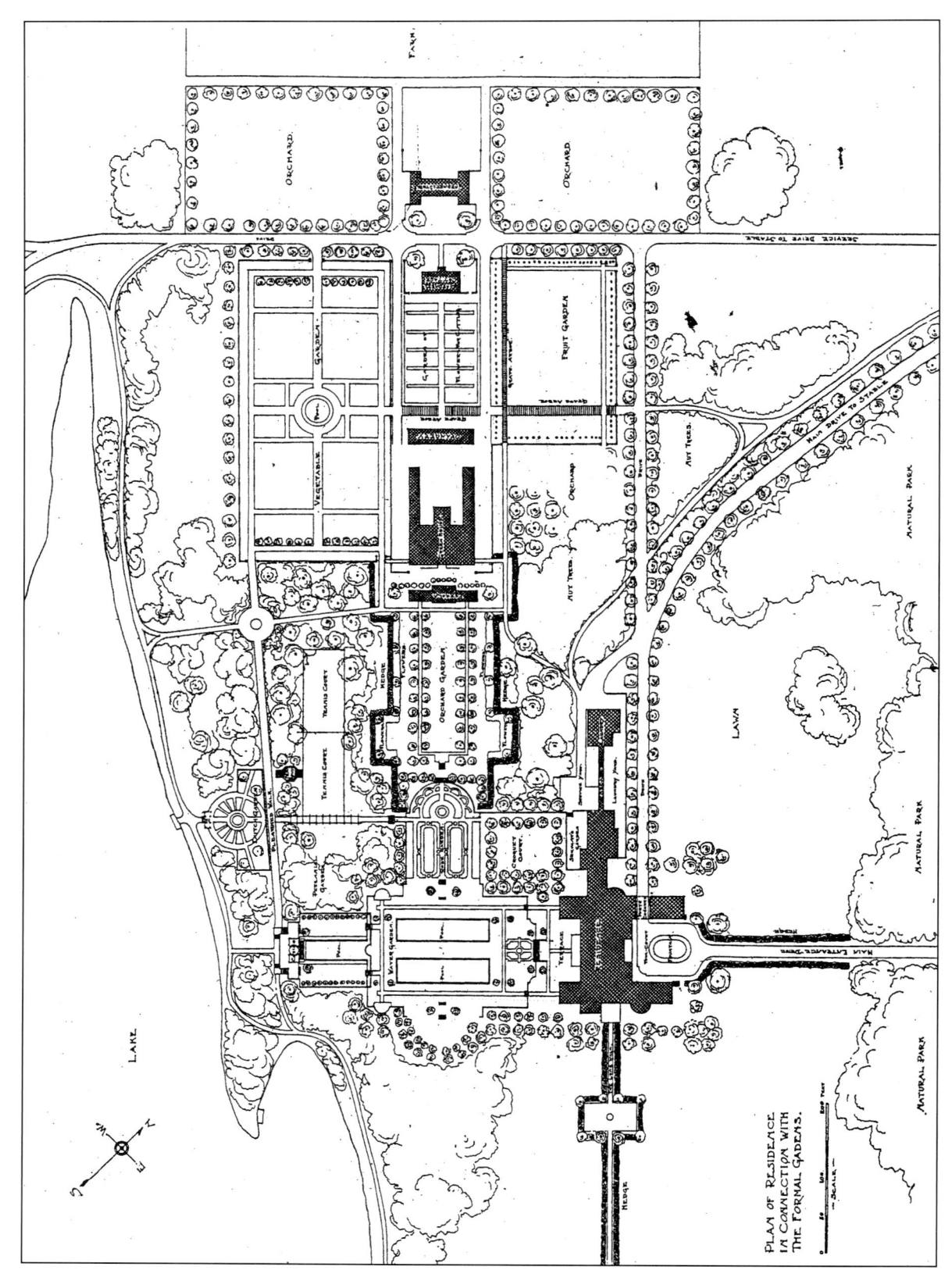

Site plan of house and formal gardens

HOUSE OF THE FOUR WINDS

HUGH J. MCBIRNEY HOUSE

Lake Forest (1908)

IT IS LIKELY THAT THE HUGH J. MCBIRNEY HOUSE prompted architect and historian Thomas Tallmadge to write that Howard Van Doren Shaw "was the most radical of the conservatives and the most conservative of the radicals." While the McBirney house has been described as being Arts and Crafts in style, and more recently, as having Iberian-Moorish influences, it has more in common with the forms of the hipped roof houses of Wright and the Prairie School, and should be compared to Myron Hunt's double-house for Catherine White in Evanston. Except for the very English arched entry canopy, the house is almost devoid of specific stylistic elements. Named the "House of the Four Winds" by the McBirneys, perhaps because of the porches facing in all four directions, the house is only one room deep, which promotes good cross ventilation. The entry porch opens into a cross-vaulted loggia-like entry hall-gallery that runs through the narrow house from front to back. The plan is brilliant in its

Front facade

Rear facade

simple spatial organization, with the living room open to the gallery and axially open to the morning room as well as an enormous covered porch with steps leading out into the garden. The formal garden and reflecting pool are laid out to the side of the house, and the house's central axis extends through the *en suite* sequence of rooms out into the landscape in a way that Wright's Prairie houses promise but rarely deliver. The garden has as its main feature a long, thin rectangular pool, and is loosely based on the Generalife garden at the Alhambra in Granada, Spain. The McBirney's garden was conceived by Shaw, who had visited the Generalife in 1892 and written enthusiastically about it to his wife, Frances. The strolling garden on the cross axis of the main garden was designed by Rose Standish Nichols, who also added the upper water channel.

Like Shaw, Hugh McBirney was a graduate of Yale University and a member of the Yale Club. McBirney also served as president of Chicago's University Club from 1901 to 1903. Born in Cincinnati, Ohio, in 1853, McBirney came to Chicago in 1880. He was assistant manager and treasurer of the McBirney and Johnson White Lead Company, and was later president of the National Lead Company, McBirney and Johnson's successor. Hugh McBirney was also an artist, interested in the Arts and Crafts movement. He designed decorative metal articles of wrought brass for his house. As an explorer, McBirney led a research expedition to China and the Far East in 1917. He and his wife Mary Campbell McBirney were residents of Chicago's posh Prairie Avenue on the near south side, where Shaw lived briefly after he moved from Hyde Park. The House of the Four Winds was built as their summer house.

Entry hall

HOUSE OF THE FOUR WINDS

Living room

Dining room

Sun room

Water garden

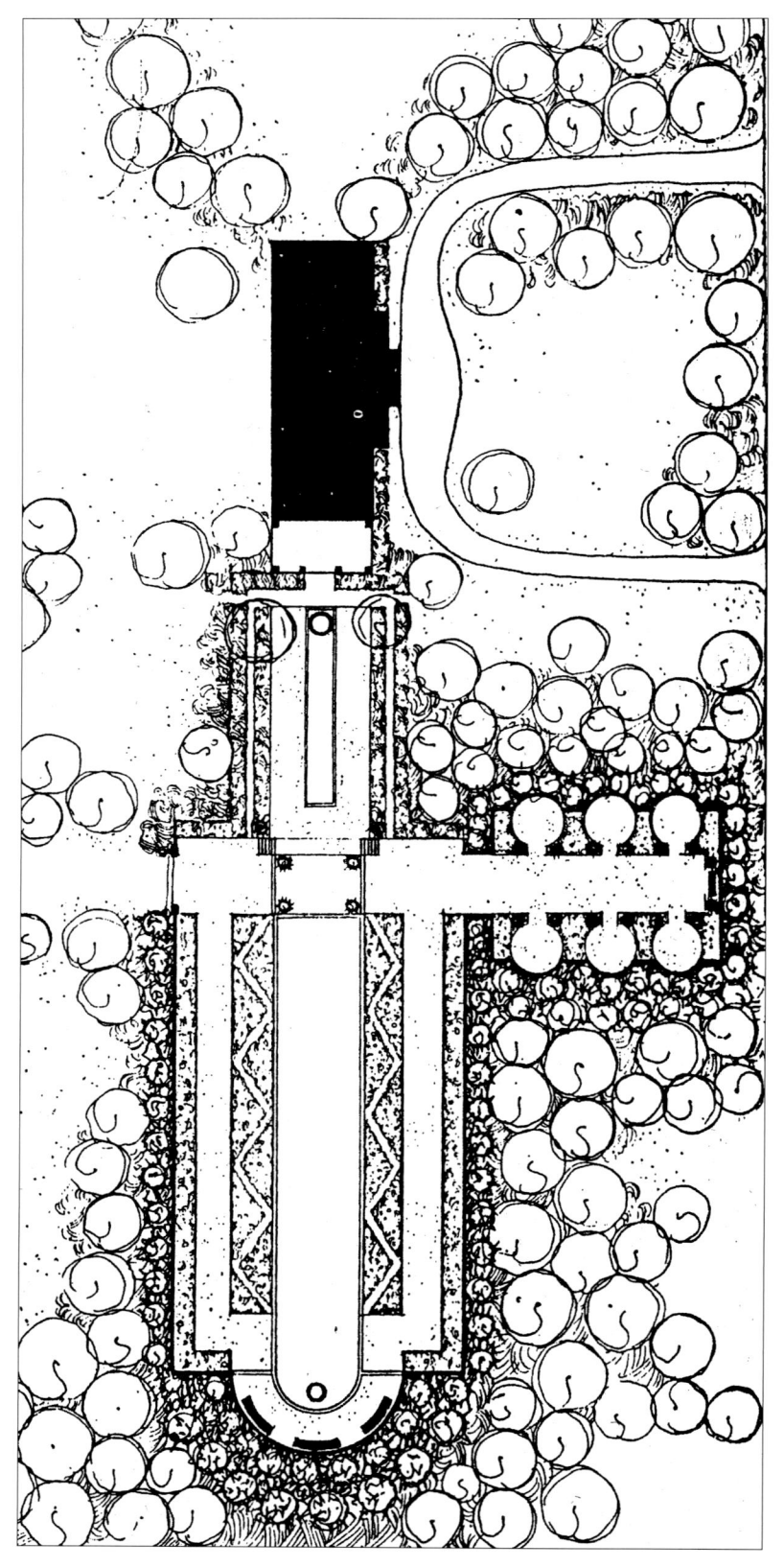

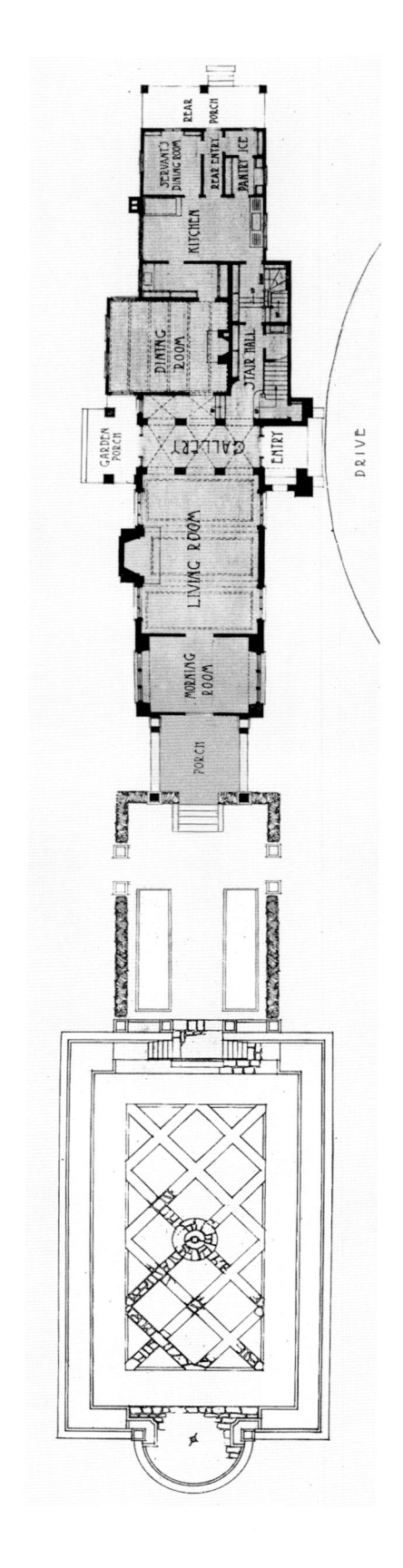

Site plan (left); garden and first floor plan (right)

VILLA TURICUM

HAROLD AND EDITH ROCKEFELLER MCCORMICK HOUSE

Lake Forest (1908–11)

One of the largest of Charles Platt's country houses, the Harold and Edith Rockefeller McCormick estate, was situated on 300 acres of lakefront property in Lake Forest. The house was designed in three sections, only two of which were built, between 1908 and 1911. The 1908 portion was U-shaped around a courtyard opening toward the lake; the 1910–11 portion extended the building to the west, creating two interior courtyards; the third and unbuilt portion would have added two wings to the front of the house, forming an entry court. The villa presented an opportunity for Platt to merge his dual talents as architect and landscape designer in creating one of Lake Forest's finest estates.

Aerial view

Frank Lloyd Wright design

Harold Fowler McCormick was born in Chicago in 1872. He was a son of Cyrus H. McCormick, Sr. (d. 1884), the inventor of the reaper, and of Nettie Fowler McCormick. He graduated from Princeton University in 1895 and married Edith Rockefeller that same year. Heir to the Rockefeller fortune, Edith was one of the wealthiest women in America. Harold McCormick served as treasurer, vice president, and then president of the International Harvester Company, which was founded in 1902 and included the McCormick Reaper Works, the company founded by his father. Harold was a trustee of the University of Chicago and the McCormick Theological Seminary. Along with Edith, he was active in the Chicago Orchestral Association and the Chicago Civic Opera Company. McCormick was a member of the Commercial Club, which sponsored the Burnham Plan for Chicago, the Chicago Athletic Club, and the Onwentsia Club of Lake Forest. Edith was a founder of the McCormick Institute of Infectious Diseases and the Chicago Zoological Garden.

Though they eventually hired Charles Platt, the McCormicks first invited two other well-known architects to make plans for their lakefront house. In 1906, they hired James Gamble Rogers, a Chicago architect. Rogers, who had recently opened an office in New York, had designed several very large houses in Lake Forest, and his wife Anne Day Rogers was related to the McCormick family through her mother. Rogers had also designed the McCormick Reaper Works Men's Club in Chicago in 1904. In their correspondence with Rogers, the McCormicks were very specific about wanting an Italian villa. Rogers, who later became known for his Collegiate Gothic buildings designed for Yale University, proved to be the wrong man for the job. In 1907, Harold McCormick asked Frank Lloyd

Entrance facade

Wright to make a plan for the house. Wright's design would have organized the bulk of the house in a long rectangle parallel to the water's edge, terraced down the bluff with a series of tall retaining walls. Like Rodgers, Wright, who had achieved prominence as a residential architect, seemed the wrong choice given Edith's desire to build an Italian villa. Mrs. McCormick particularly disliked houses with overhangs like those found in Wright's work, believing they made the interiors dark. In his book *Frank Lloyd Wright to 1910, The First Golden Age* (1958), Grant Manson wrote of the commission:

> The story of the rejection of the McCormick design has never been fully revealed. It has been suggested that it was Mrs. McCormick who refused it, saying that her mode of life simply could not be suited by a Prairie House. In any case it was she who suddenly went to New York in August, 1908, and placed the commission for the house which she eventually occupied in the hands of a master of traditional architecture, Charles Augustus [sic] Platt, who gave her a handsome Italian villa that is as knowing a piece of archeology as can be seen in the Middle West. That it was erected upon the ruins of the Chicago School was, for him, unimportant.

Garden facade

Loggia

VILLA TURICUM

Entrance hall

Library

Pompeian room

Mrs. McCormick had seen photographs and plans of Platt's 1891 Cornish, New Hampshire, house for his next-door neighbor Annie Lazarus, the daughter of a New York banker. The house, called "High Court," was published in the *Architectural Record*, and Edith McCormick asked Platt for a house similarly planned. The first phase of the McCormick's house, which they named "Villa Turicum," was loosely based on High Court, particularly the U-shaped disposition of rooms gathered around a colonnaded courtyard.

Villa Turicum, as finally built, was approached down a long allée, past the stables, service buildings, kitchen and flower gardens, and a greenhouse. Located to the north of the approach drive, these were accessed by a separate service road. In front of the house, a long grass mall with semi-circular ends formed a grand turnaround. The west front, with its wide projecting central bay and Tuscan simplicity, focused the monumental approach on a modest entry porch supported by two Ionic columns. This feature was based on the south entrance into the central courtyard of the Villa Mondragone in Frascati, photographed by Platt on a trip to Italy in 1892. (This photograph is reproduced in Keith Morgan's essay accompanying the 1993 reprint of Platt's book *Italian Gardens*.)

Inside Villa Turicum, an archway in the east wall of the entry hall led to a wide, vaulted corridor, mirroring the main entry with its arched transom window and establishing the main axis of the house. The corridor provided a channeled vista through the house from the front door to the lake, while con-

Water stairs

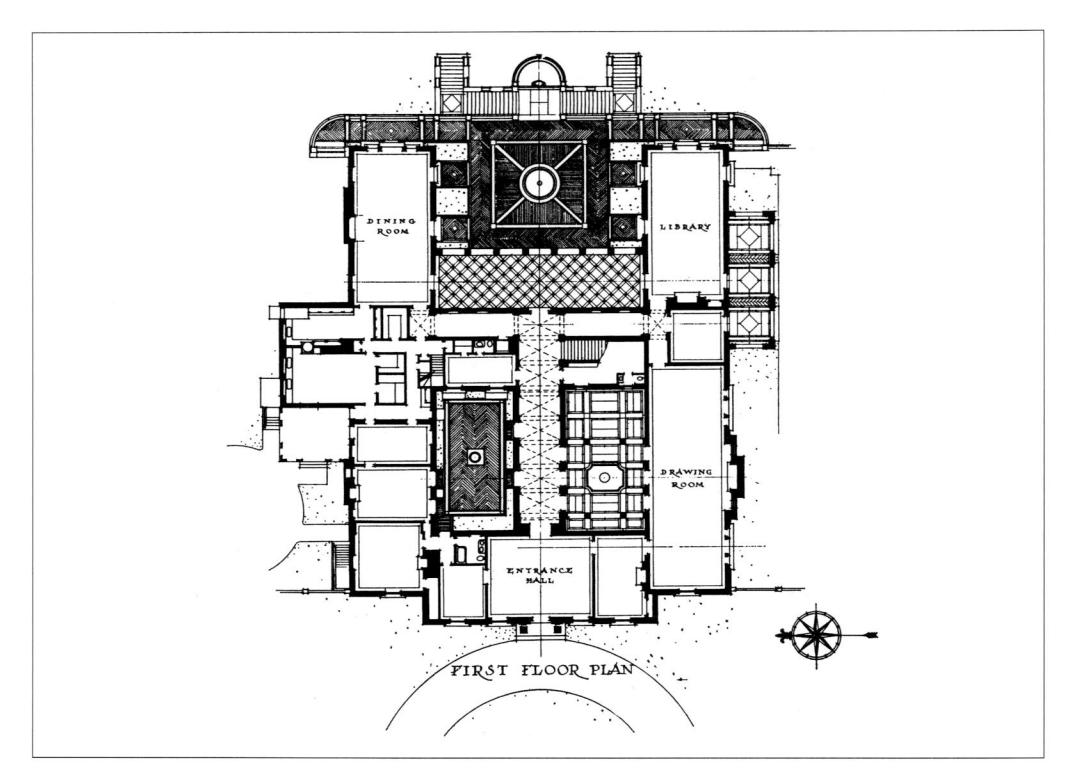

First floor plan

necting the main rooms of the first floor. This hallway was flanked on the north side by an open courtyard and on the south by a glass-covered atrium. The two courtyards provided natural light to the interior side of the rooms that comprised the central block of the house, giving each of the rooms windows on two opposite walls. At the end of the central corridor a north-south hall connected the dining room and library. These projecting wings formed a terrace, enclosed on three sides and open to the lake. This space overlooked a series of landscaped terraces, grand staircases, and water features leading down to the shore.

In addition to being an accomplished artist and Beaux-Arts-trained architect, Charles Platt also practiced as a landscape and garden designer. Platt's book, *Italian Gardens*, published in 1894, was the first publication on the subject in English. It was also the first book on the subject to be illustrated with photographs, all taken by Platt. The book helped popularize formal gardens in America and launched Platt's career as a garden designer. For Villa Turicum, Platt developed the bluff leading down to a swimming pool overlooking Lake Michigan as a series of stairs, terraces, and a water cascade modeled after the one at the Villa Lante at Bagnaia. Platt's rendering of Villa Turicum from below should be compared to his photograph of the Villa d'Este in his garden book, which was clearly the source of this image. On top of the bluff, to the south of the house, he planned a formal garden and bowling green, and the path extending the main axis of the formal gardens led to a polo field.

The McCormick house was torn down, and the property was subdivided for a residential development. Some of the garden elements remain intact on the site, as does a part of the water cascade.

Finley Barrell House

Lake Forest (1909)

Howard Van Doren Shaw's house for Chicago stock broker Finley Barrell is set on a large wooded lakefront estate in Lake Forest. It was famed for its rose garden and water lily ponds. The design of its courts, terraces, and gardens makes it one of the most fully realized of Shaw's English Arts and Crafts–style country houses.

Street facade

Stair hall

Gallery

Library

Finley Barrell, who was born and educated in Chicago, founded Finley Barrell and Company in 1890. His company grew rapidly, gaining membership in both the Chicago and New York Stock Exchanges, and became one of the country's leading stock and grain commission traders. Finley and Grace Barrell had only one child, John Witbeck Barrell, who graduated from Yale in 1915 and went to work in his father's firm. Tragically, he drowned the following year at the Barrells' summer house on the Illinois River in Havana, Illinois. Barrell, who claimed to have built his business for his son, was devastated by the loss, and in November of 1916 withdrew from his company, turning over control of it to his partners, who reorganized the firm as Block, Maloney and Company. Suffering a nervous breakdown, Barrell never recovered from his son's death. The Barrells sold the house Shaw built for them, supposedly because living in it reminded them of their son, and built a second house in Lake Forest designed by Frederick Perkins. They donated the money for the construction of the Gothic-style gray stone entrance gate to the Lake Forest Cemetery as a memorial to their son. Finley Barrell lived only nine years after his son's death. He died in Lake Forest at the age of 61.

Sun porch with view of formal garden

Formal garden from porch

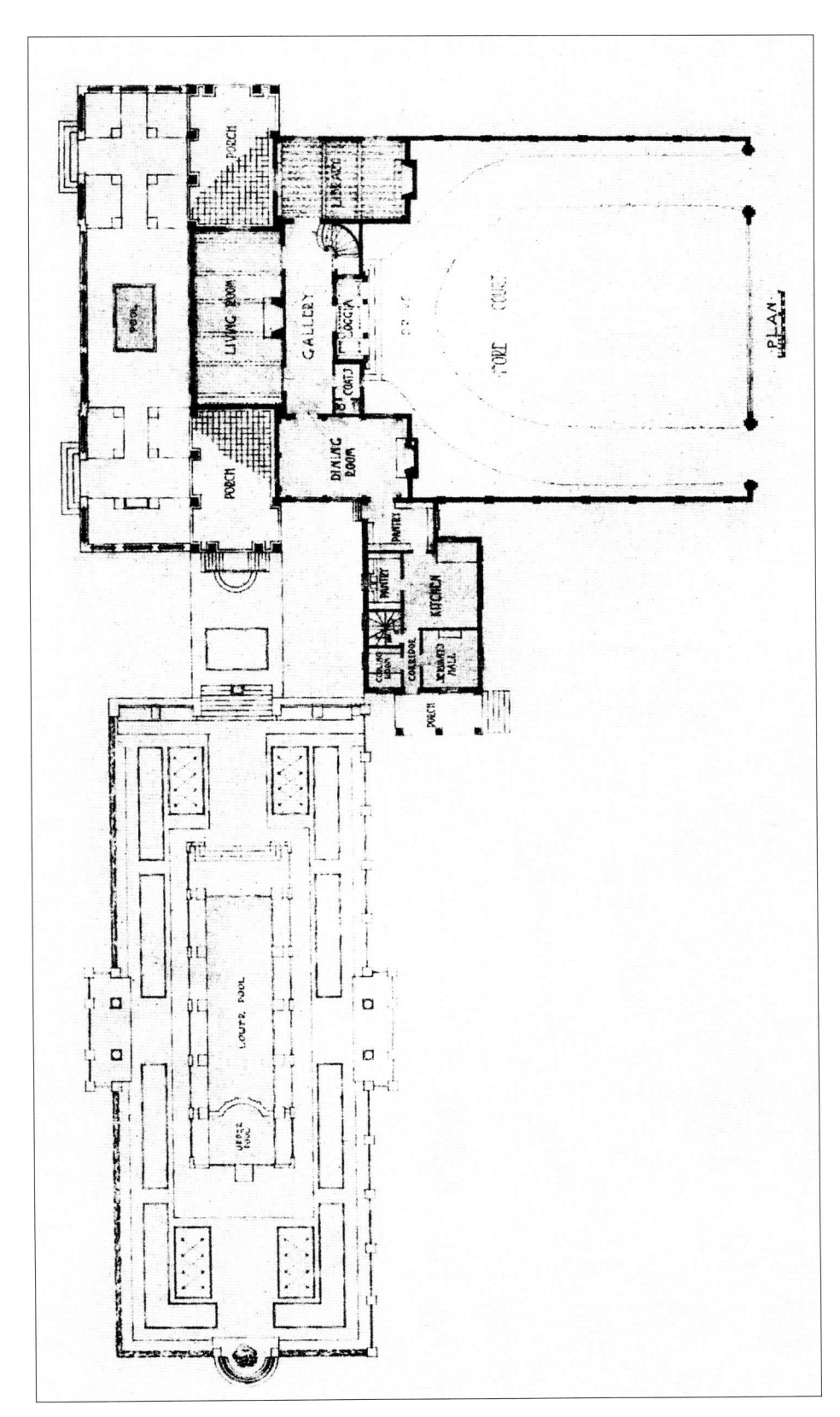

Garden and house plan

The house Shaw designed in 1912 of brick and cut stone has an unusual triple gable on the main block, and a recessed classical entry loggia with four simple Tuscan columns. The recessed loggia used as an entry porch was a favorite motif in Shaw's houses. The recessed classical entry is an Italian Renaissance device, most dramatically illustrated by the Villa Medici at Poggio a Caiano, where the entire entry porch looks as if it had been pushed into the body of the villa. The use of a triple gable on the Barrell house to emphasize the center of its facade may have been inspired by C. E. Mallows' triple-gabled house with a recessed loggia, which was published in Hermann Muthesius' highly influential book, *Das Englische Haus* (1908). Shaw's design is also reminiscent of Edwin Lutyen's Tigbourne Court (1899) in Surrey, with a triple gable and recessed classical loggia. Like Tigbourne Court, the central block of the Barrell house is flanked by gable-ended wings with prominent, paired chimney breasts. The garden walls extend to the street, forming an entry court and screening the service wing. Whereas Tigbourn Court maintains the symmetry of its front facade, exhibiting quirky asymmetries in its plan, Shaw created a visual quirkiness by breaking the symmetry of the front facade. A tall stair window centered under the gable to the right is balanced against two single-story windows stacked one above the other on the left. The stair window acts to visually establish a secondary center for the facade.

The plan of the house skillfully arranges the principal ground floor rooms to maximize their connections to the exterior and to the rear porches. At the front of the house, the recessed loggia has a projecting glass canopy with a French balcony above that opens off the intermediate stair landing. The loggia opens into a long vaulted gallery running parallel to the living room, and connects to the library and dining room. Both rooms open through French doors to porches at either end of the living room. Above these are sleeping porches for the corner bedrooms. As part of the volume of the main block of the house, the porches are situated under one roof. This arrangement of the rooms and of the two-story porches, a reoccurring design feature in Shaw's houses, ensured good cross-ventilation in hot weather. Like Shaw's McBirney house (1908), the living room of the Finley Barrell house opens axially to a sun porch with steps leading out to a formal garden. Laid out along this same axis, the garden extends the interior spaces of the house laterally into the landscape. The garden, like the one at the McBirney house, has a multi-level water feature with Islamic influences. Warren Manning was the landscape architect, but Shaw, no doubt, had a say in the design of the Barrells' garden.

RAVINE BLUFFS DEVELOPMENT

Glencoe (1909–16)

THE RAVINE BLUFFS DEVELOPMENT, designed and built by Frank Lloyd Wright between 1909 and 1916, is unique. There is nothing like it in Wright's extensive body of work. Wright's client was his attorney and friend Sherman Miller Booth II, who commissioned the subdivision. It consisted of five small houses built on speculation at a cost not to exceed $7,500 each, a large home for Booth and his wife Elizabeth, a reinforced concrete bridge spanning a ravine leading to the subdivision, and three poured-concrete entrance sculptures. Each sculpture contained a spherical planter, vertical electric lamps, and a bronze plaque displaying with the name "Ravine Bluffs." Booth also asked Wright to

Booth house from road

Railroad waiting station

design a Ravine Bluffs railroad waiting station for the North Shore Line, an electric railroad that once extended north from Chicago roughly paralleling the Chicago and North Western Railway.

The designs Frank Lloyd Wright generated for Booth belong to his Prairie School period, dating from the early 1890s through about 1917. During this time, he designed houses that were highly original—characterized by low horizontal lines, low-pitched or flat roofs, ribbons of windows, horizontal banding, and broad sheltering eaves. In the Ravine Bluffs Development, no reference to traditional historical styles was evident.

Each of the small Wright-designed houses in the development was to be two stories high and dimensioned like the others (51 feet across the front, 36 feet deep, and 32 feet high), with a flat roof and stuccoed walls. Frank Lloyd Wright scholar Susan Solway (a former resident of one of the homes in the development, who today lives in Wright's E. E. Brigham House in Glencoe) has suggested that Booth, who was known to have speculated in real estate, afforded Wright the opportunity to realize his lifelong interest in creating attractive low-cost housing. The plans for the houses at Ravine Bluffs, excluding their porches, are almost identical to those for the $5,000 Fireproof House published in the *Ladies' Home Journal* in 1907.

The house that Wright designed for the Booths, 108 feet across the front, 50 feet deep, and 34 feet high—considerably larger than the subdivision houses—is frame and stucco, with a gravel roof. It was built at a cost not to exceed $16,000. Wright's plans linked an existing barn and gardener's cottage situated at

Entrance sculpture

right angles to one another with a new, vertical four-story block. The barn wing, with its Wright-designed ventilator, became the kitchen and dining room. The cottage was transformed into a study and bedroom area. The new portion consisted primarily of a large living room, second-floor bedrooms and balcony, a third-floor sleeping porch and roof garden, and a fourth-floor open tower over a stairwell.

After 1909, during the years he was working on this housing development for Sherman Booth, Wright's commissions slowed considerably, and he was undergoing great turmoil in his personal life. In 1909, he had departed for Europe to oversee the German publication of his work, *Ausgefuhrte Bauten und Entwurfe von Frank Lloyd Wright*. Although enjoying great professional recognition, his practice was declining. He had fallen in love with Mamah Borthwick Cheney, the wife of one of his clients, and closed his studio, taking her to Europe with him. He found on his return that he had only five or six remaining small projects in his office, the most important of which was the Booth subdivision. His practice picked up with the commission for Midway Gardens in Chicago and the Imperial Hotel in Tokyo, but Mamah Cheney and her children were murdered in 1914 by a deranged servant at Taliesin, their Wisconsin home. By the time Wright's work for the Booths was completed, he was spending most of his time either at Taliesin or in Japan. He had abandoned the pure Prairie style he initiated, and both architecturally and personally, his life took a new direction.

Although the railroad station has been demolished, the houses all remain. Because of infill housing, though, the original relationship of the houses to their landscape and to each other has been lost.

[139]

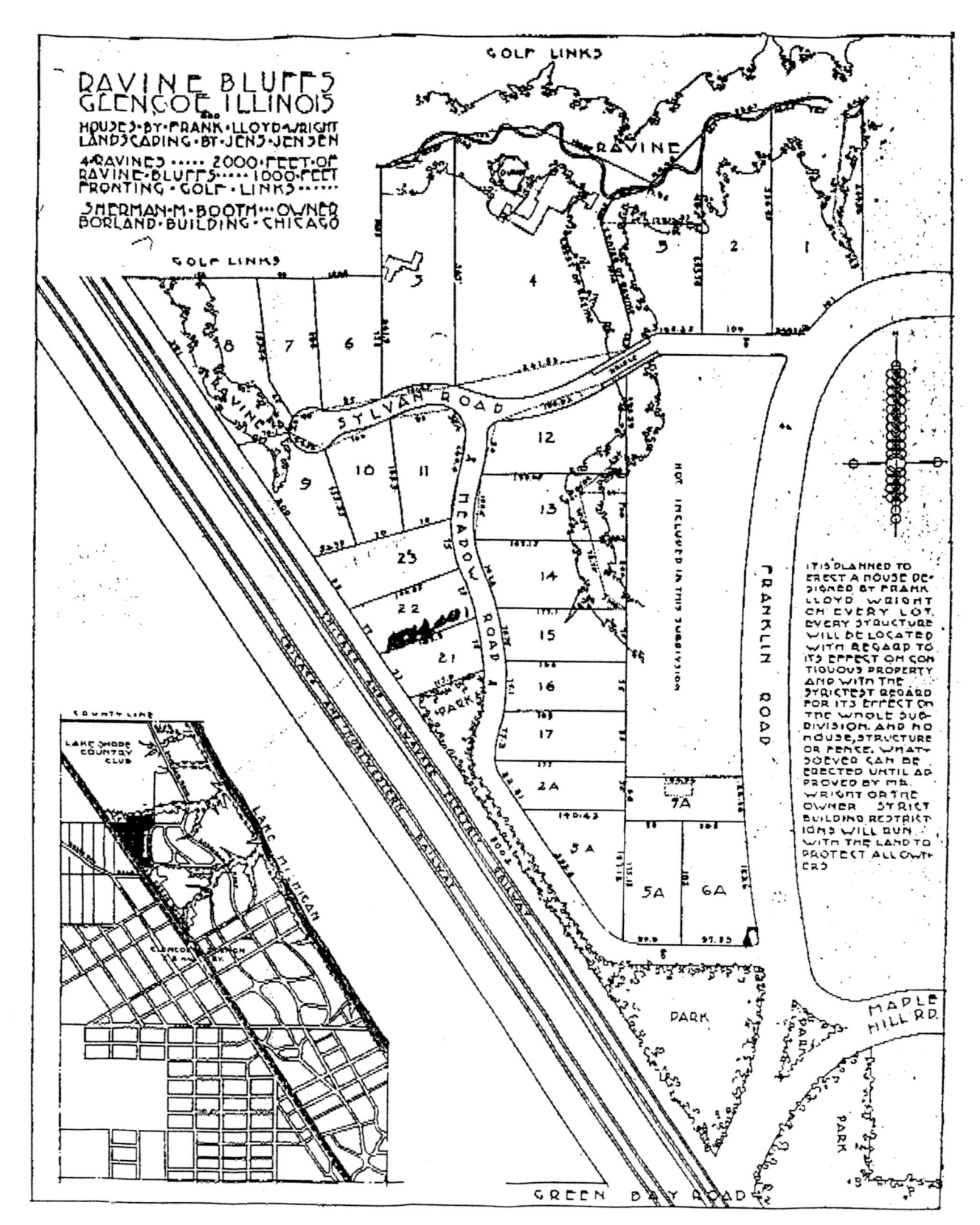

Plat of development

1910–1919

HAVENWOOD

EDWARD RYERSON HOUSE

Lake Forest (1912)

Howard Van Doren Shaw designed two houses in Lake Forest for Edward L. Ryerson, one in 1906 and the second in 1912. Both were Italianate villas of similar size and internal organization. Ryerson, who was interested in architecture and took an active role in the design and construction of his houses, built the second house because he felt the first had insufficient property for landscaping and grand formal gardens—he claimed that he sold his first house because it "was too near the railroad tracks." An avid garden enthusiast, Ryerson formed a foundation to provide fellowships for

Front facade

students of landscape architecture. Ryerson imported garden statuary from Italy and commissioned Rose Standish Nichols and Howard Van Doren Shaw to design his formal gardens. For the landscape design he hired Jens Jensen, the famous landscape architect, well known for his naturalistic designs. Havenwood was the largest landscape project Jensen had created on the North Shore and its formality was probably at the insistence of his client. Jensen had a difficult relationship with the dictatorial Ryerson, and at one point threatened to quit. According to Leonard K. Eaton's *Two Chicago Architects and Their Clients* (1969), of all of Shaw's wealthy and powerful clients, Ryerson was the only one who actually frightened him. There is no question that Ryerson had his way on the design of both the gardens and his new house. The design for Havenwood, with its severe Tuscan front facade, is certainly atypical of the English-style country houses for which Shaw had become famous.

Edward L. Ryerson was born in Chicago in 1854. His father, Joseph T. Ryerson, who opened a hardware and iron goods store in 1842, went into steel manufacturing. After attending Yale University's Sheffield Scientific School, Edward returned home to go into the family business. Succeeding his father in 1883 as head of Joseph T. Ryerson and Son, Edward built the business into one of the country's largest steel companies. Ryerson sat on the executive committee of the Illinois Merchants Trust, was president of Chicago's Newberry Library from 1914 until his death in 1928, and also served as a trustee of the Chicago Historical Society. He was a member of many social clubs,

Motor court

HAVENWOOD

Rear facade

Rear terrace

Entrance hall

among them Lake Forest's Onwentsia Club, of which Shaw was also a member, and Shore Acres Country Club in Lake Bluff.

Havenwood was approached from the east by a curving drive that brought the visitor into a three-sided entry court. The approach allowed for the development of a lawn laid out perpendicular to the front facade and bordered by flowering plants and trees. The first of Shaw's houses for Ryerson had an unusual, fully-recessed two-story entry porch with classical columns on the first and second floors, similar to Palladio's Villa Pisani-Placco near Padua. The second house had a much more modest one-story entry porch. This may have been at the request of the client, and could have been based on the entry porch of Charles Platt's Lake Forest house for Harold and Edith McCormick, Villa Turicum. Like the first Havenwood, the entry opened into a well-lit vaulted gallery opposite the back of the living room fireplace. Where the gallery of the first house opened at one end into the library and at the other into the dining room, the gallery space in the second house led to an east-facing stone terrace. Raised exterior terraces wrapped around the east, south, and west sides of the house, with the east and south

Living room

terraces connected through the covered porch off the library. The second floor also had south-facing exterior spaces. These were covered, loggia-like porches over the living room and first-floor porch adjacent to the library. While the exterior of the house has none of the signature elements that came to typify Shaw's work, the interior was a different matter. The vaulted gallery is a Shaw trademark. The wood paneled library with its ceiling vaulted in two directions is reminiscent of early 19th-century work by English architects such as George Dance and Sir John Soane, who made elaborate use of vaulting in their designs. The chimney pieces in both the library and the dining room are also English Renaissance in style.

The second Havenwood is no longer extant. The property was sold to the Franciscan Order and used as a monastery until 1979, when it was demolished and the land was subdivided. Ironically, all that remains today of Ryerson's second Italian villa is the stucco garage with part of the servants' quarters that Shaw was allowed to build in the English Arts and Crafts style.

HAVENWOOD

Garage and servants' residence

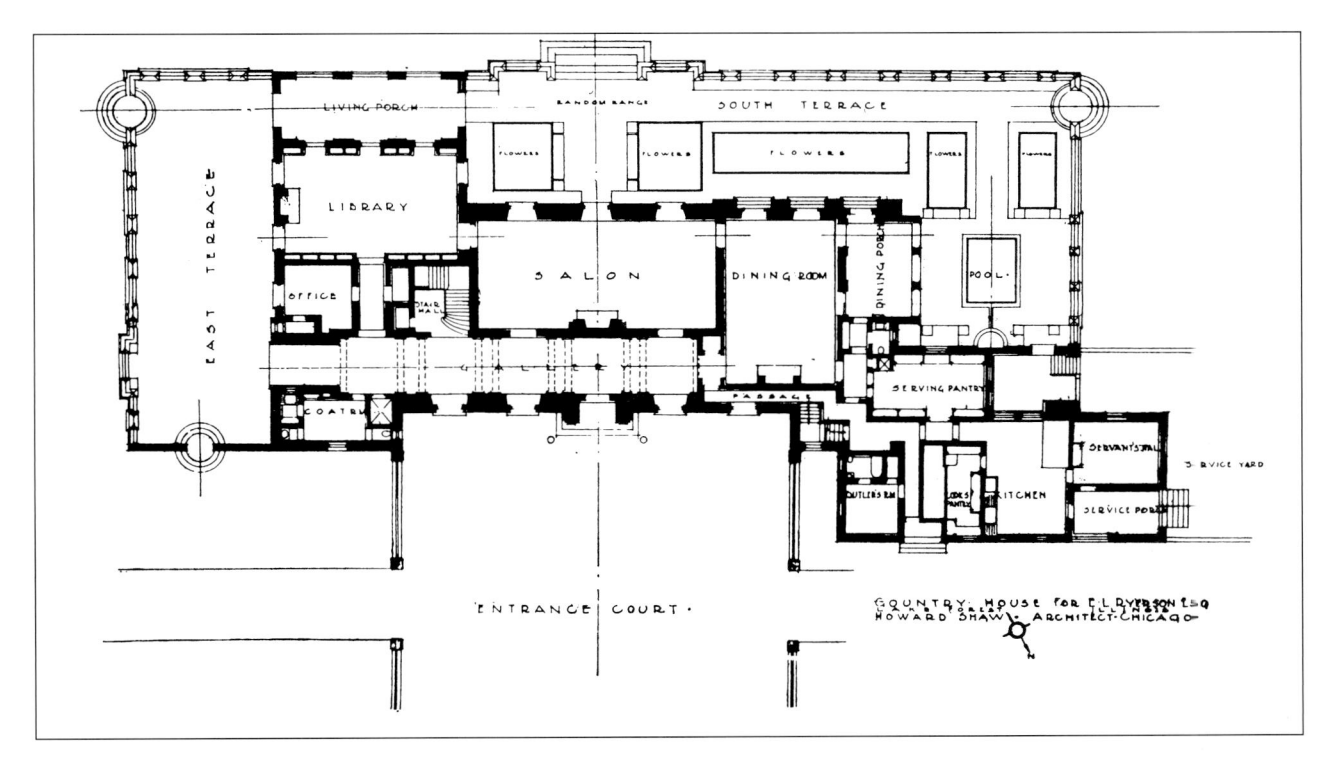

First floor plan

NATHAN WILBUR WILLIAMS HOUSE

Evanston (1912)

ROBERT SPENCER'S HOUSE FOR NATHAN WILBUR WILLIAMS, built in Evanston in 1912, represents the popularization of Prairie School ideas about residential architecture. Writing about the Williams house in the April 1914 issue of the *Western Architect*, William Gray Purcell, a well-known Prairie School architect, quipped: "How could one belong to that crowd on the top floor of Steinway Hall for so many years and not show it in his work?" He was referring to the studio space Spencer shared with Frank Lloyd Wright, Myron Hunt, and Dwight Perkins, and he was suggesting that Spencer had somehow gotten the house all wrong.

Front facade from Sheridan Road

South facade

Lake and garden facade

Entrance hall

Living room fireplace

Living room

Prairie Tudor in style, the Williams house has large overhangs at the gable ends, like Wright's Warren Hickox House (1900) in Kankakee, Illinois, and his Dana House (1904) in Springfield, Illinois. Spencer used Tudor half-timbering as a compositional device to group together the windows in the gable end of the house. These windows extend up all the way up to the underside of the plaster soffit and visually allow the plane of the underside of the roof to slide from the inside to the outside, much like two houses Walter Burley Griffin built in Evanston for banker Hurd Comstock at about the same time. With the Williams house, Spencer may have been trying to move away from Wright's influence, which can still be seen clearly in his Magnus house (1905), with its low hipped roof and horizontally banded windows. The clear expression of the Williams house stair in a series of tall casement windows that step down the front facade is an interesting feature not found in either English Tudor or Prairie-style architecture. Not only do these windows mark the presence of the stair on the front of the house, but they also bring light into the stair and flood the upper stair hall with afternoon sun. The brick exterior has cut-stone sills and column capitals. The capitals were carved with a hollyhock motif that appears on the exterior and is carried throughout the house as a decorative theme. The interior, with its simple, somewhat heavy geometric forms and hollyhock motif, is far more Prairie in flavor than the exterior, and is close to the sensibility of George Maher, who frequently used repeated plant motifs in his designs.

Dining room detail

The Williams house is L-shaped, with a projecting garage and high brick wall to the north, creating an enclosed motor court in front of the garage. The main elevation of the house faces Sheridan Road, with the principal rooms facing to the rear and providing views of the lake and gardens that were once extensively landscaped. The living room alcove, the dining room, and the entry hall all open onto a sun porch with brick walls, a tiled floor, and symmetrical fountains at either end. This porch opens onto a raised terrace that originally abutted a rose garden. Steps from the terrace led down to a tennis court and lawn. The landscaping also featured a fountain built as part of the brick wall at the north edge of the property and a trellised teahouse with brick piers at the corners and an open wood arbor for its roof.

Williams had been a long-time Evanston resident when he built his home on Sheridan Road. He was born in 1867 in Chicago, where he grew up attending public schools. He went into the real estate business, and later was principally engaged in the management of his family's holdings. Williams was a member of both the Exmoor and Onwentsia country clubs. His house still stands, but the open entry porch, originally approached from the south, has been enclosed with a cut-stone arched Tudor surround for the new front door that faces Sheridan Road. The gardens, landscaping, and tennis court are no longer extant, as the property was subdivided and a new house was built to the east.

C. Percy Skillin House

Wilmette (1914)

John S. Van Bergen, architect for the Skillin house, had an excellent background in the Prairie School. He worked for Walter Burley Griffin, Frank Lloyd Wright, and William Drummond, before beginning his own private practice in 1911. His house for C. Percy Skillin in Wilmette, just west of Sheridan Road, provides a compelling argument for Frank Lloyd Wright's architectural accomplishment in the development of the Prairie house. As with the 20th century's two other most influential modern architects, Le Corbusier and Mies van der Rohe, Frank Lloyd Wright developed a language of residential forms and spatial planning strategies that was internally consistent and transmittable as a style. The Skillin house, which illustrates this, was based on Wright's cross-shaped or cruciform-plan houses, most notably, the Ward W. Willits house of 1901 in Highland Park. The fireplace, located at the

Street facade

Living room

Library

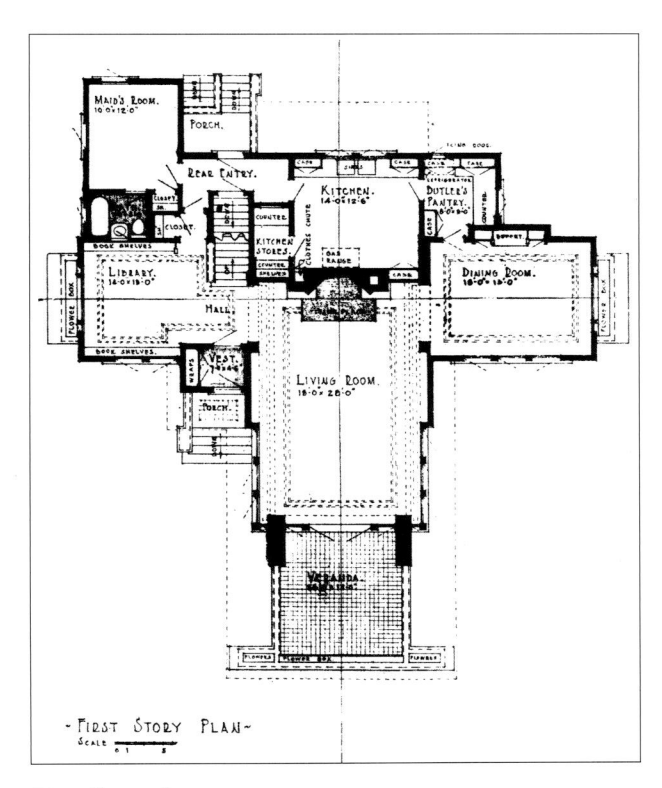

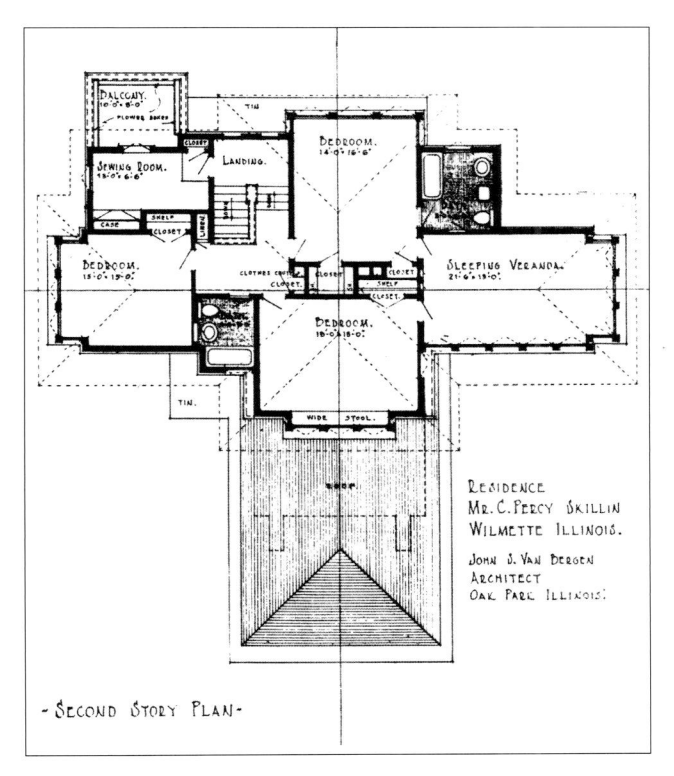

First floor plan　　　　　　　　　　　　*Second floor plan*

center of the Skillin house, anchors its three-dimensional masses. It forms a back edge to the living room at the point where it connects to the entry hall on the west side, and the dining room on the east. On the exterior, the low-pitched roofs, stucco walls, continuous bands of windows, and careful proportions make the house almost indistinguishable from Wright's work of the early 1900s.

In the design for the Skillin house, Van Bergen's most interesting addition to the vocabulary of the Prairie house was his use of windows with simple horizontal muntin divisions instead of art-glass casements. These further emphasized the horizontal lines of the house. Where Wright's Willits house used vertical trim boards to visually tie together groupings of first- and second-story windows, here, the windows and horizontal trim emphasize only the horizontal extension of the house. Unlike the Willits house, where the three wings facing front all are extended by porches, only the living room of the Skillin house projects, through French doors, into a south-facing sun room that that forms a porch-like space.

C. Percy Skillin was born in 1884. He pitched baseball as a student at Dartmouth, and was a renowned player, receiving several offers from major league baseball teams. Instead, Skillin elected to go into business, and became an investment broker in the city of Chicago. He only lived in his Van Bergen–designed home a short time before dying of kidney disease in 1924 at 39. Skillin grew up in Oak Park, and it is highly likely that he knew of Van Bergen, who was an Oak Park resident and built many houses in that suburb. Van Bergen later moved to Highland Park, where he was equally prolific.

Rosemor Lodge

Edward L. Glaser House

Glencoe (1916)

The Edward L. Glaser house, known as Rosemor Lodge, is an extensive remodeling of a much smaller house. In 1916, Benjamin Marshall, of Marshall and Fox, took a simple rectangular house with only four rooms on the first floor and expanded it into one that is large and impressive, with several large family living rooms and eight service spaces—including four servants' bedrooms—on the first floor. Said to have once been located on 50 acres, the house is a typical Tudor Revival manor house, with an irregular footprint, stuccoed walls with half-timbering, and gabled roofs. This belies the more lavish Tudor interior.

The house is entered from a glass-walled vestibule opening into a large hall, with the major living spaces opening from it. A men's club look characterizes Mr. Glaser's study, tucked away adjacent to the stair landing. The feeling of the stair hall, located across from the front entrance, is baronial. The stair

Front facade

balustrade is carved walnut, and the baseboards are marble. The most surprising room, however, is the "court," a large square space with latticework walls surrounding a fern-filled pool. Throughout the room are references to classical architecture interpreted in lattice: pilasters with vertical slats topped by Ionic capitals, and latticework door lintels in the form of slanting jack arches with centered lattice keystones. The ceiling, composed of wood strips in a geometric pattern, recalls the plaster strapwork on the ceiling of the library. The stair hall, dining room, and breakfast room all open onto this screened court.

E. L. Glaser was a member of one of many prominent German Jewish families who settled in the village of Glencoe. The attraction there was Lake Shore Country Club, the North Shore's first Jewish country club, designed by Howard Van Doren Shaw and built between 1908 and 1910. Glaser was born in Cincinnati in 1861. His family moved to Chicago when he was quite young, and he was educated in Chicago public schools. In 1893, Glaser married Etta Rosenbaum. He was employed by her family's grain commission firm at the Chicago Board of Trade, working his way up to be president, then chairman of the board. This firm was one of the oldest grain elevator operators in Chicago. Glaser served as a trustee of the Brookfield Zoo and in 1915 was elected a governing annual member of the Chicago Historical Society. He was made an honorary lifetime trustee of the society in 1931 for having given $10,000 to its new building fund. Locally, he served as president of the Glencoe School Board. Glaser died in 1935. The house is currently a single-family residence.

Study

STONEBRIDGE

WILLIAM V. KELLEY HOUSE

Lake Bluff (1916)

WILLIAM V. KELLEY, described in *Who's Who in Chicago* as a manufacturer and financier, retired at the age of 51. Wanting to move with his wife and three sons to the country, he bought 130 acres of wooded land at the southern border of Lake Bluff from a farmer, John Mines, who had failed financially and could no longer pay taxes on the land. Kelley began by having Jens Jensen create a one-and-a-half-acre pond and "prairie river," a signature Jensen feature, at the front of his new estate. The pond was fed by an underground spring, and was created to complement the existing natural three-acre lake at the back edge of the property. Over the narrow end of the pond, Kelley constructed a stone bridge, hence the name "Stonebridge" given to the estate. Stone gateposts, the

Front facade

STONEBRIDGE

Front courtyard

Rear facade

Living room

bridge, and the lagoon were all part of the long entry drive that curved through a large grove of mature oak trees leading to the manor house.

Howard Van Doren Shaw, who lived a half-mile south of the Kelleys' property on Green Bay Road, was not only the nearest neighbor, but also a close personal friend. He was chosen as the architect for Stonegate's manor house and gatehouse, both of which were completed in 1916. In many ways, Kelley's house was the most radically eclectic of Shaw's houses. It calls to mind the French philosopher and encyclopedist Denis Diderot's (1755) definition of an "eclectic" as "a philosopher who . . . from all philosophies which he has analyzed without respect to persons and without partiality, makes a philosophy of his own peculiar to himself." In this house, Shaw combined elements such as the arched entryway, suggestive of Italian villas, with English Tudor and French Gothic stone details. The roof gables and dormer window are English, as are the domed bay windows on the back of the house, which look Jacobean and could be based on Charlton House (1607) in Greenwich or Burghley House (1575) in Northants. A tall domed water tower, the dominant feature of the gatehouse, which contained stables

Library

and servants quarters, repeated the roof form of the bay windows. This tower and its dome also recall the towers built at the entrance to Market Square, the commercial center of Lake Forest Shaw designed while he was working on Stonebridge.

Inside the house, the finely-crafted detailing includes Gothic stone arches, leaded-glass windows with medieval-looking stained-glass insets, English Tudor linenfold carved wood paneling, and a distinctly French dining room with decorative plaster work. Part of Shaw's genius was that he was able to make original, often quirky compositions using historical elements. This set him apart from his Paris-trained Beaux-Arts contemporaries, for whom the use of specifically identifiable precedents for both a building and its details had been an educational and a philosophical requirement.

In its planning, Shaw's design cleverly balances picturesque asymmetries to produce an overall formality on the exterior. The center of the entry front and the center of the rear facade are shifted with respect to one another. This places the entry hall and entry porch off center of the main suite of ground-floor rooms at the back of the house, and allows the living room to receive light from both sides. On the

Dining room

front facade, the service wing balances a projecting wing that contained a billiards room and a guest suite. This keeps the entry porch centered on the mass of the front of the house. At the back the living room's bay overlooks a terrace, gardens, and an enormous meadow. At the front, windows open out to a three-sided courtyard with a small reflecting pool. At its north end, the living room opens to the French dining room, and on the south to an English library. The library and dining room each open, in turn, to sun porches that flank the rear facade like matching bookends. At the north end of the living room, a carved linenfold oak screen-wall covers the pipes for an organ that used to sit in the living room. The library is perhaps the best room in the house because of its mastery of architectural space. A vaulted plaster ceiling separates the oak paneled room from a series of bookshelf-lined alcoves. A carved wood cornice with articulated oak leaves helps tie together the alcoves and the space of the main room.

William Vallandigham Kelley was born in Ohio in 1861. After finishing high school, he took courses at a commercial college in Cincinnati. Kelley began his career as a clerk in a hardware store in Springfield, Ohio, and then worked for a company that manufactured steel springs for cars and locomotives. Enjoying enormous success, he served from 1905 to 1912 as president of the American Steel

Breakfast room

Foundries. He was chairman of the board of the Miehle Printing Press and Manufacturing Company, and held directorships of several banks, including the Continental Illinois Bank and Trust Company and the Lake Shore Trust and Savings Bank. Kelley was also on the board of Armour and Company.

Kelley died in 1932, and following the death of his wife Lillian in 1934, the estate was sold to Walter Patton Murphy. Murphy was a large donor to Northwestern University and upon his death in 1942, the property, including the house, was left to the trustees of Northwestern, who sold the property to the Servite Order of the Catholic Church. Renaming the house "Stonegate Priory," the Servites transformed it into a seminary. In 1955 they added a chapel, kitchen, refectory, classrooms, and dormitory rooms. These were built around a courtyard that enclosed the back of the house and the rear terrace. The three-story structure, built in buff brick with aluminum windows, is an awkward and unsympathetic addition that now blocks the view of the landscape from the main rooms of the house. In 1969, Stonegate was sold to Harrison Conference Services, Inc., which converted the property into a conference center and hotel. Remarkably the main features of the Kelley house have survived these changes.

STONEBRIDGE

Gatehouse, with servants' quarters, garage, and water tower

Front courtyard seen from entrance portico

Wyldwood

Clyde Carr House

Lake Forest (1916)

In 1913, Clyde Carr and a group of fellow members of the Onwentsia Club founded the Old Elm Club. Located just south of Lake Forest, it was exclusively a golf club and was organized because the Onwentsia Club closed its golf course on Sundays, which for many Lake Forest businessmen who worked six-day weeks—religion aside—was unacceptable. This didn't keep the Onwentsia Club from hiring Carr's East Coast architect Harrie Lindeberg to design their new clubhouse. Carr, who was born in Chicago in 1869, attended Lake Forest Academy, Princeton University, and Northwestern University. After college, he worked for People's Gas, Light and Coke Company, and then for W. S. Mallory and Company of Chicago, iron jobbers. Carr later became president of the Joseph T. Ryerson and Son steel company.

Front facade

Garden facade

Highly picturesque, with projecting curved bay windows, steeply pitched slate roofs, half-timbering with brick diapering (herringbone-patterned brick work on a vertical surface), the Carr house is a skillful assembly of materials and forms that blends English country house and Norman influences. The entry porch rises a story and a half in height, with a pattern of diagonal lines on its gable end made by projecting brick stretchers. The entry arch is composed of eight courses of brick with long, thin pieces of slate set radially, as if they were keystones. The contrast between these stones and the brickwork recalls the English Cotswold practice of setting small, dark stones into the mortar joints between brick courses to produce a beaded effect. Perhaps the most amazing element of this entryway is the ornate iron gate designed by Oscar Bach of New York, a well-known artist who worked in wrought iron.

Lindeberg's design cleverly separates the service wing of the house by angling it away from the main block and screening it at the ground floor with a brick wall that encloses a service court. This allows the living room to face not only the back of the house, but a lawn at the front of the house that is screened from the approach drive. An octagonal entry hall connects to a gallery that opens to the dining room and to a large stair hall. Off the stair hall, at the back of the house, lies a projecting oval

View from rear lawn

breakfast room facing the rear lawn. Here, again, a freestanding garden wall screens the outdoor space from the service wing.

Of Lindeberg's Lake Forest residential commissions, the Carr house is perhaps the best and the most typical from this period. Fortunately it survives unaltered in its original landscape setting, designed by landscape architect Warren Manning.

Entry hall

WYLDWOOD

Living room

Dining room

[169]

Wyldwood

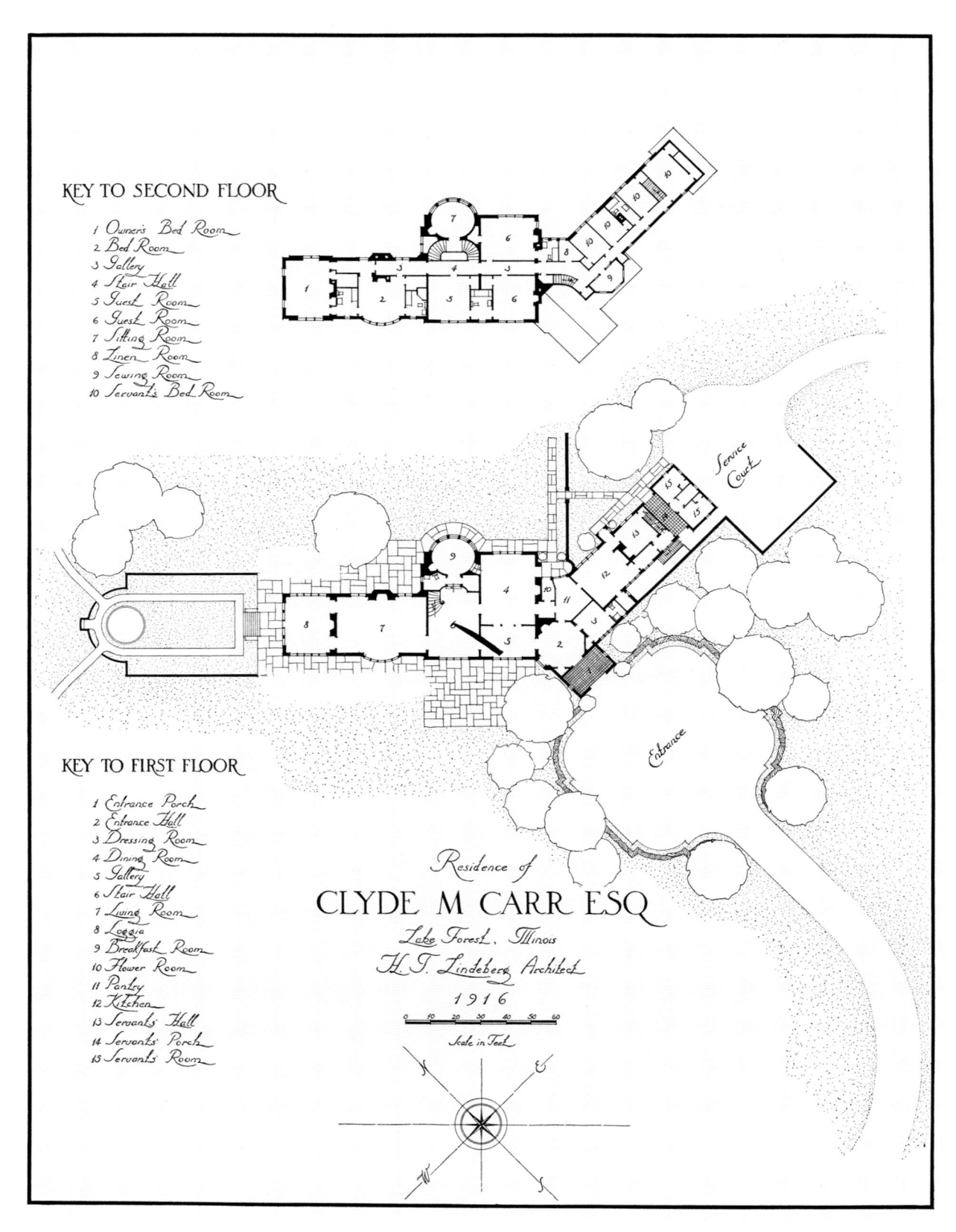

KEY TO SECOND FLOOR

1. Owner's Bed Room
2. Bed Room
3. Gallery
4. Stair Hall
5. Guest Room
6. Guest Room
7. Sitting Room
8. Linen Room
9. Sewing Room
10. Servant's Bed Room

KEY TO FIRST FLOOR

1. Entrance Porch
2. Entrance Hall
3. Dressing Room
4. Dining Room
5. Gallery
6. Stair Hall
7. Living Room
8. Loggia
9. Breakfast Room
10. Flower Room
11. Pantry
12. Kitchen
13. Servants' Hall
14. Servants' Porch
15. Servants' Room

Residence of
CLYDE M CARR ESQ
Lake Forest, Illinois
H. T. Lindeberg, Architect
1916

Site plan

House in the Woods

Mrs. Cyrus (Nettie) McCormick Estate

Lake Forest (1916)

"House in the Woods" lives up to its name. Tucked back in the forest, in an area known as the old south woods, and accessed by a long winding road, the Nancy Marie (Nettie) Fowler McCormick house was designed by well-known Chicago architect Dwight Perkins of the firm Perkins, Fellows, and Hamilton. As Cyrus Hall McCormick had died in 1884, the house was commissioned by Nettie's daughter Anita McCormick Blaine. In 1914, Anita had the idea of building her mother a home on the east side of Lake Forest, immediately next door to her other two children, Harold and Cyrus Jr. Located on land belonging to Cyrus Jr., the estate included a manor house, a gate house/gardener's cottage, a tea house, a garage with an attached power plant, and a walled garden that was part of the Jens

Front facade

Rear facade

Jensen–designed landscape. According to Anita, the house was envisioned as being "more modest and cheerier" than Harold and Edith Rockefeller McCormick's 44-room Villa Turicum. In 1916, Nettie celebrated her 80th birthday at her new home.

The name Cyrus Hall McCormick is often mentioned in the same breath as Henry Ford and Ely Whitney. In 1831, he invented the first machine for cutting grain, the "reaper" that revolutionized farming and foreshadowed the end of manual labor. Born in Virginia in 1809, McCormick recognized that Chicago was the center of grain trading and distribution and moved there in 1847. By the next decade he had become a millionaire and met and married Nettie Fowler, a schoolteacher 26 years his junior. When McCormick died in 1884, Cyrus Jr. assumed control of the business founded by his father and, aided by his mother Nettie, built the company that would become International Harvester. Nettie McCormick lived almost a half century longer than her husband, and received recognition for the progressive changes she initiated at McCormick and Company as well as for her philanthropy. In 1886, after the Haymarket Square labor riots, she advocated raising wages. Later she implemented profit sharing, pensions, and workmen's compensation. Her charity work included support of the Y.M.C.A. and schools in Asia, private gifts to missionaries, and donations of over $1 million to the McCormick Theological Seminary.

Living room

Dining room

Despite Anita Blaine's comments, the house cannot accurately be described as modest. Its characteristically Prairie-Tudor exterior is impressive, with front-facing gables, stone-framed windows with bands of leading, carved bargeboard, and massive chimneys supporting molded chimney pots. Patterned brickwork and crisp definition of wall edges reflect Perkins' commitment to the Arts and Crafts movement. Like his colleague Robert C. Spencer, who shared an office with him at Steinway Hall in Chicago, Perkins had no problem combining historic and more progressive Arts and Crafts features.

The house is entered through an arched loggia next to a landscaped pool. The home's floor plan befits its wealthy patron. The first floor contains large living and dining rooms, a sun room and breakfast room, all with landscaped vistas. The major living areas have rich carved wood paneling. On the second floor, Mrs. McCormick's "chamber" includes an adjacent sleeping porch and upstairs living room that opens onto a terrace. Her personal maid's room

Main staircase

is situated next to her own bedroom. There is a guest wing with four bedrooms that each have a private bath. The angled service wing contains the kitchen, pantries, laundry, sewing room, and five servants' bedrooms. Fireplaces are prominent features in most of the major living spaces and all of the bedrooms of the house.

Upon Nettie Fowler McCormick's death in 1923, the estate was valued at $11,778,000. Although its property has been subdivided and outbuildings have been converted into single-family residences, the house remains unaltered.

House in the Woods

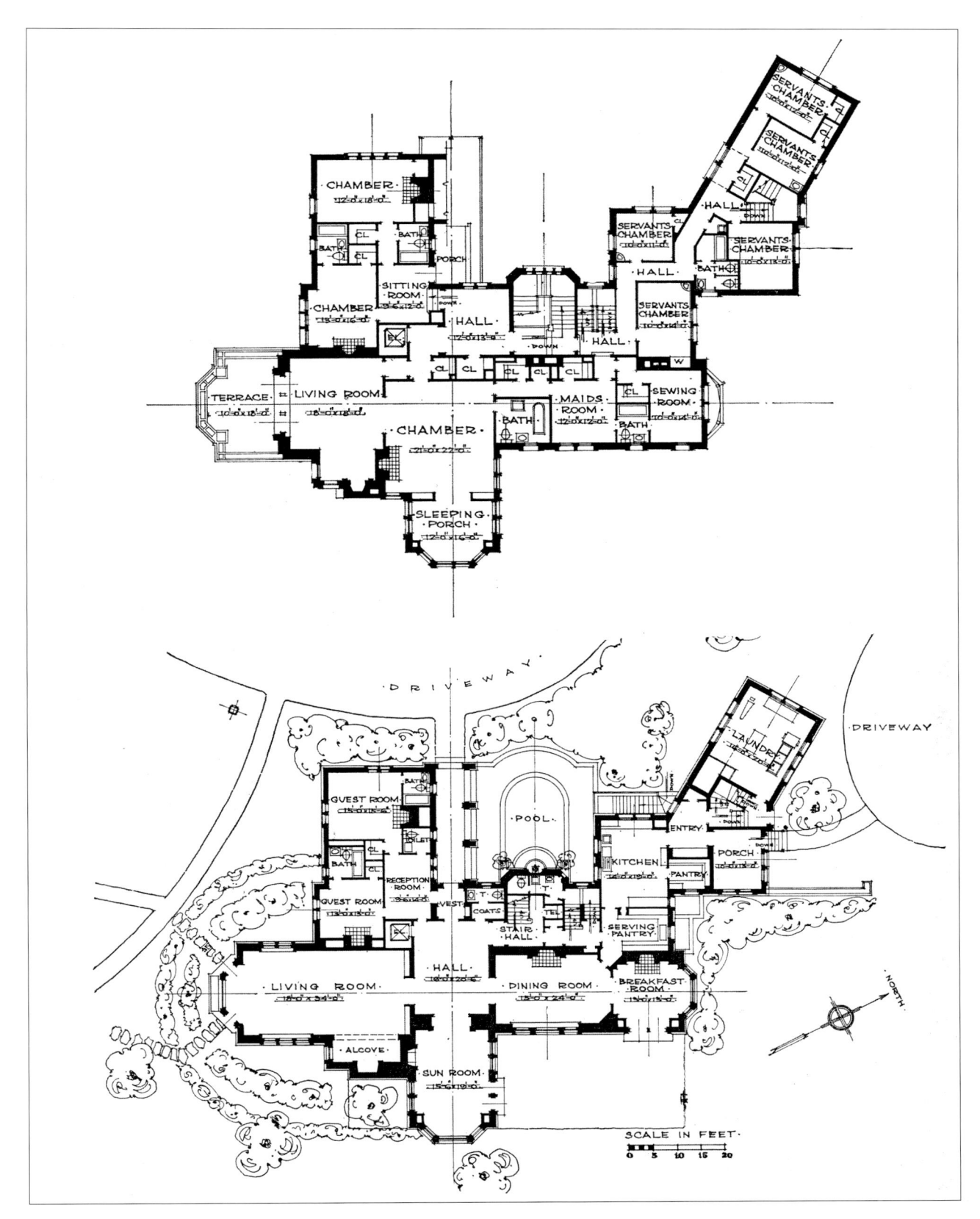

Floor plans

MRS. CAROLYN MORSE ELY ESTATE

Lake Bluff (1916–23)

T HE MRS. CAROLYN MORSE ELY HOUSE reflects David Adler's keen sense of artistry and passion for French architecture. Adler's signature design features—symmetry, rooms laid out enfilade, inset wall paintings, luxurious materials, exquisite crystal lighting fixtures, and above all, an intuitive sense of proportion and order—are everywhere in evidence. A formal, yet not extraordinarily large country house, it suited the lifestyle of a wealthy and sophisticated single woman.

 Adler was a devoted Francophile, especially early in his career during the teens and twenties, when he had just left the Ecole des Beaux-Arts and traveled extensively throughout France. Although French architecture never attained the degree of popularity that Tudor and Georgian Revival had on the North Shore, it received considerable attention nationally. All things French were very much in vogue

Garden facade

Garden facade detail

North wing of garden facade

Entrance court, service wing

Entrance hall

between the wars. Several books were published and circulated on French architecture, including the 1924 *French Provincial Architecture as Shown in Various Examples of Town and Country Houses, Shops and Public Spaces Adaptable to American Conditions*, by Henry Oothort Milliken and Philip Goodwin. Art magazine articles on French style were plentiful. An item in the September 1926 issue of *House and Garden* praised French design for its integrity, elegance, and tradition. Children of many fashionable families were taught French at home and frequently sent abroad to finish their studies at the Sorbonne in Paris.

The house that Adler designed for Mrs. Ely very closely resembles a particular French manor house, the 17th-century Pavillon de la Lanterne at Versaille. "Lanterne" refers to a building one looks through and appropriately applies to this house, which is only one room wide. The rooms are flooded with light streaming through French doors. Both structures were designed with a two-story center section flanked by wings that surround a court and have entrances topped by a triangular pediment

[179]

Living room

Stair, guest wing

containing an ornamental carved shell motif. Adler chose warm pink brick rather than cream-colored limestone, and added a tower in the north wing and a dog trot in the south, the servants' wing. By changing the proportions and fine-tuning the detailing, he transformed the French precedent into his own carefully wrought design.

Plans for construction on the 17 acres Mrs. Ely purchased in Lake Bluff began in 1914–15, when David Adler was hired. Her closest neighbors included three prominent Chicagoans who had commissioned highly acclaimed architects to design their country estates. Stanley Field, the nephew of Marshall Field I, built and managed the Field Museum of Natural History. The architectural firm for his 31 acres was Daniel H. Burnham and Company, which also designed many Loop skyscrapers. The Field house was demolished in 1967. Harry B. Clow, head of Rand McNally and Company, hired Benjamin Marshall, noted architect of estate homes, hotels, and luxury apartment buildings, to design his Georgian Revival house and engaged Jens Jensen to design the landscape. The third mansion, a large Classical Revival residence built for Albert A. Sprague of Sprague, Warner and Company, was designed by East Coast society architect Harrie T. Lindeberg. Mrs. Ely was the daughter of a wealthy steel magnate. By choosing Adler, this 54-year-old divorced, single woman was assured a home with cache equal to that of the other estate owners.

Plans were first drawn up in 1916 for the estate and its landscape. The buildings were to rest on formally-landscaped property with a gravel entrance court, symmetrically placed trees, and broad allées. Two gate house cottages flanking the driveway were built, and the orangerie shortly thereafter. Mrs. Ely lived in one of the cottages until 1923 while the main house was being constructed. During this period, Adler's landscape was visited by the Garden Club of America on its trip to the North Shore.

Adler's design was tailor-made for Mrs. Ely. The house was geared to the lifestyle of a woman. It contained an elegantly appointed women's coat room, and only a minimal men's toilet that was tucked under the staircase. Although there were no special rooms for men, there were a card room and a flower-arranging room, both associated with women's activities. The upstairs contained a single master bedroom, Mrs. Ely's boudoir, a personal maid's room, and a guest room. The towered wing, with its classical porch and library, had an upstairs bedroom. This area functioned as a guest wing, unconnected to

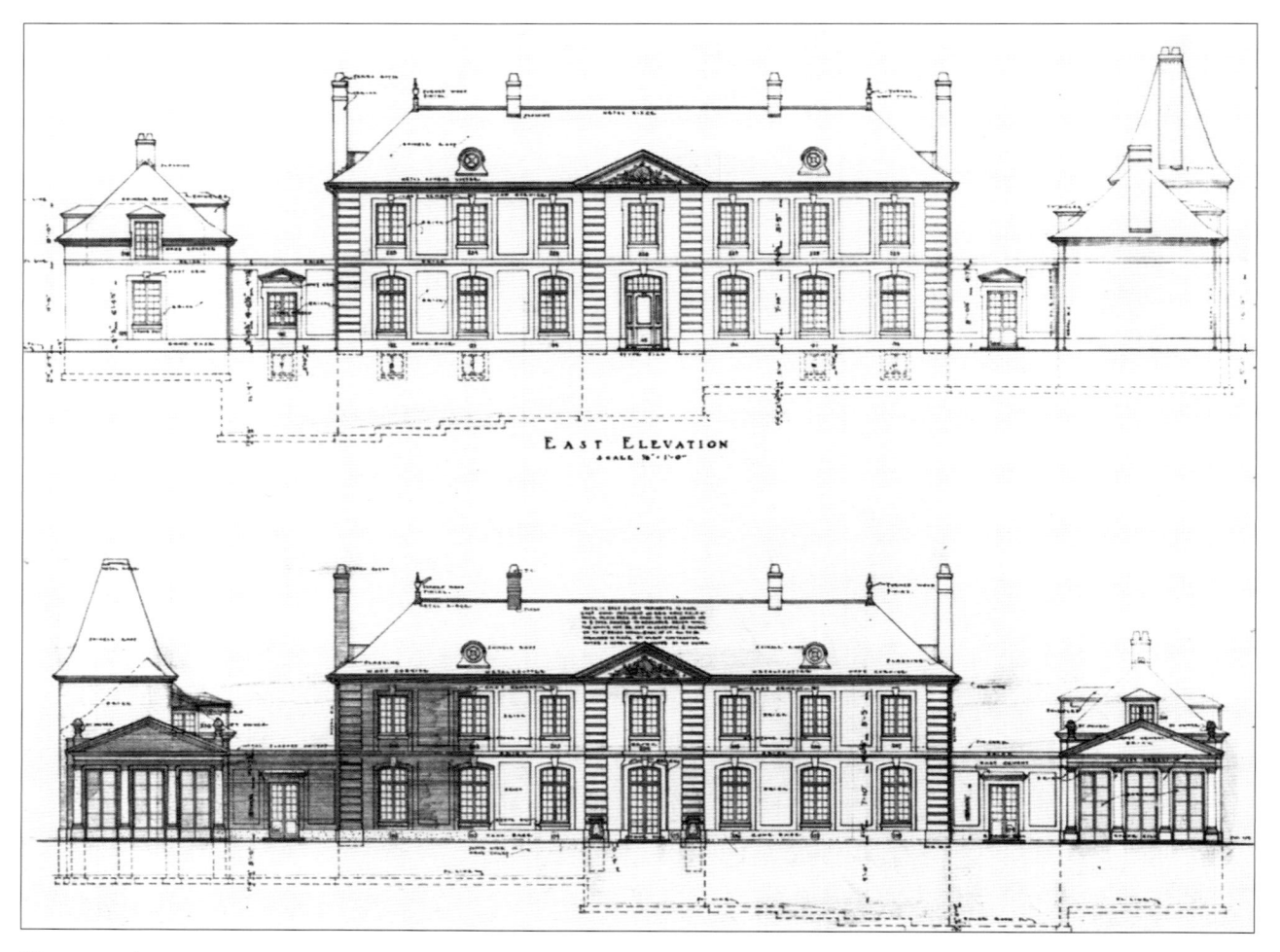

Elevation drawings

Mrs. Ely's private quarters on the second floor. With a serving pantry as large as the kitchen, a silver vault, and five bedrooms for female staff in the service wing, Mrs. Ely could live well and entertain graciously served by her own private staff.

She did not live in her beautiful house for long, moving in 1928 to an apartment Adler designed for her at 1301 Astor Street in Chicago. For 28 years the house was occupied by Mr. and Mrs. DeForest Hurlburd. In the 1950s, they had the tower wing removed and relocated across the lawn. This was done at the urging of their friend George Charney, art director of the *Chicago Daily News*, who later moved in and added two wings. The rest of the estate house has recently been thoughtfully restored. The outbuildings have been remodeled and enlarged into single-family homes.

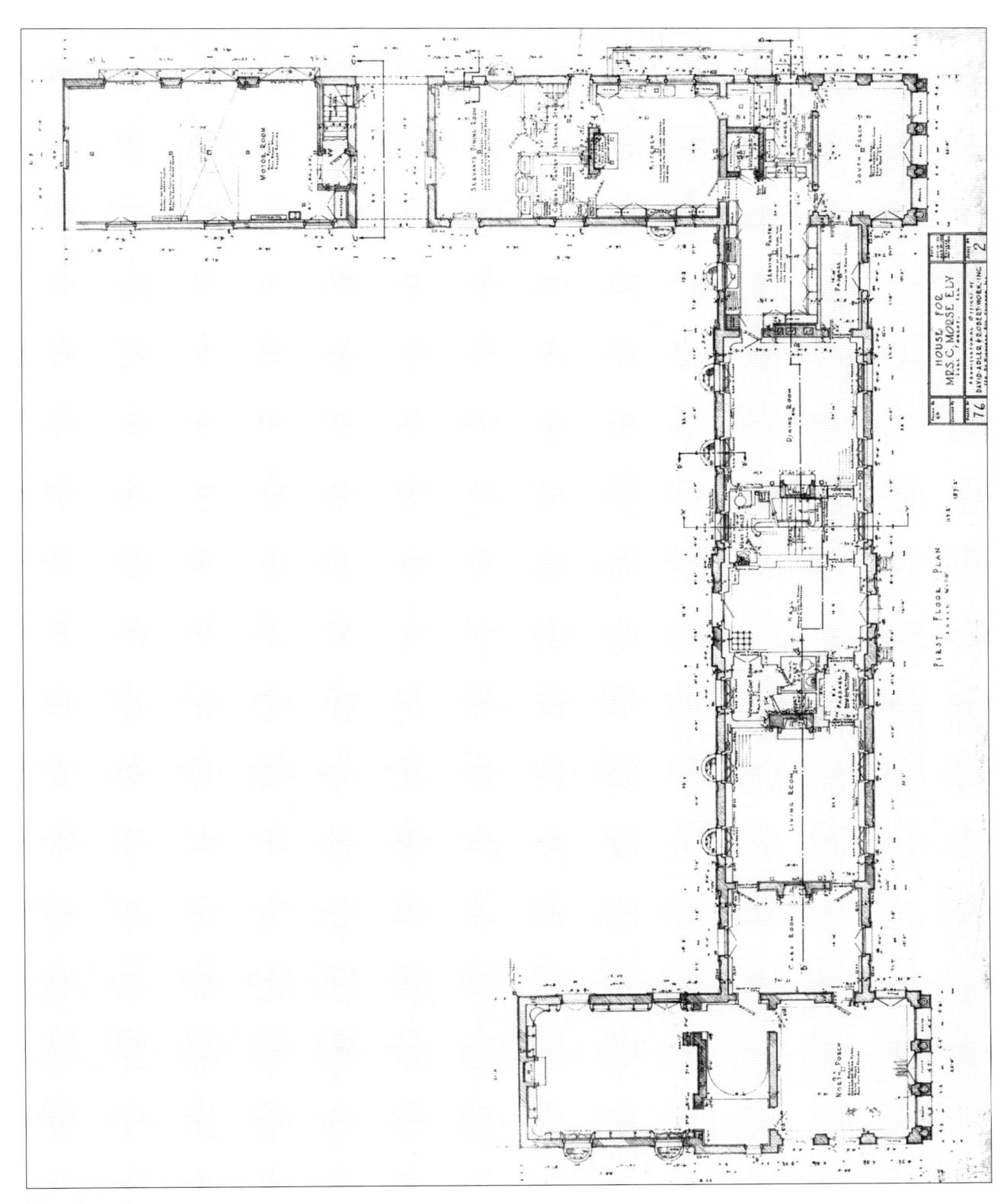

First floor plan

DAVID ADLER ESTATE

LIBERTYVILLE (1918–41)

David Adler, who established a reputation as Chicago's premier eclectic architect of the 1920s and 1930s, used his own home to experiment with features upon which he would later elaborate in far grander country residences for his wealthy North Shore clientele. Adler began to design the house in 1918 by remodeling and expanding a modest 1864 farmhouse and adjacent barn, adding handsome classical and Colonial Revival detailing. He designed an L-shaped addition to the barn to create a servants' cottage, attaching the two structures by a stair tower. All the wood buildings were whitewashed to resemble a simple grouping of French farm buildings, with the house and the servants' building connected by intimate courtyards. In this way, Adler created a comfortable atmosphere without abandoning the formal elements of historical architecture.

Garden facade, c. 1920

Front courtyard, c. 1920

Oblique view of garden facade, c. 1920

The houses Adler designed were characterized by several architectural features he first used in the remodeled farm buildings on the estate. Creating his own unique synthesis, on the exterior Adler combined Colonial Revival detailing, including shuttered double-hung windows, classical elements such as the dining porch topped by a Greek pediment, and a Norman French tower. The colonial elements he used are repeated in the Mr. and Mrs. William McCormick Blair house (1926), a classical porch may be seen in the Mrs. Carolyn Morse Ely house (1915), and the tower is repeated in the home he designed for Mr. and Mrs. Robert Mandel (1926). In each case his impeccable sense of detail, proportion, and symmetry is apparent. On the interior of his own home, Adler employed faux finishes for the fireplace surrounds, designed entrances to his bedroom, second-story, and dining room in a Palladian configuration, and decorated the walls of the 1918 dining room with scenic wallpapers made by the famous French wallpaper company Zuber et Cie. He later used these and many other design elements in projects for clients.

Over the course of his 38-year career, during which he designed more than 60 important country houses, David Adler continually enlarged his home and expanded his property from 17 acres to 240 acres, with formal gardens extending east toward the meandering Des Plaines River. The Architecture Department of the Art Institute of Chicago has in its collection thousands of drawings by Adler, including over 300 sheets of material dating from 1918 to 1948 pertaining to Adler's estate house and outbuildings. Strictly speaking, the house is not located along the North Shore, but rather farther west,

Living room

Dining room

Dining porch

in Libertyville. However, because his client base was predominantly from the area along the lake, and because his home was just a short distance from Lake Forest, the architecture of Adler's house is tightly linked to the North Shore.

There are several reasons why Adler built in Libertyville. His wife enjoyed riding, and this was horse country. She also was a published author, and living in the countryside offered her the solitude and quiet she needed to write her two novels. Adler's close friend, William McCormick Blair, who commissioned him to design his own Lake Bluff home, offered a different explanation. Blair was quoted in a Libertyville newspaper as saying that "The Adlers did not want an elegant home. They did not have the money to build a great home and didn't want to live that type of lifestyle." There is very likely yet another explanation. Adler was Jewish, and would probably not have been entirely welcome in the exclusive social setting of Lake Forest, despite the enormous respect he commanded and his many friendships there. Although Libertyville is some distance from Chicago, Adler commuted daily to his office in Chicago's Orchestra Hall designed by Daniel H. Burnham (1905).

Adler never stopped devoting personal creative attention to his Libertyville home. He added a garage topped by a cupola in 1926. And, even though he was despondent over the tragic death of his wife in an automobile accident in France in 1930, he kept fine-tuning the estate, connecting the house

Coach house of 1926

and servant's cottage in 1941 to create a large sitting room. He drew up plans to build out a large second-floor bedroom area in the attic. The discipline that Adler devoted to his clients' houses and gardens originated with the meticulous attention he bestowed on his own property. Today, his house is owned by the Village of Libertyville and occupied by the David Adler Cultural Center. It is open to the public.

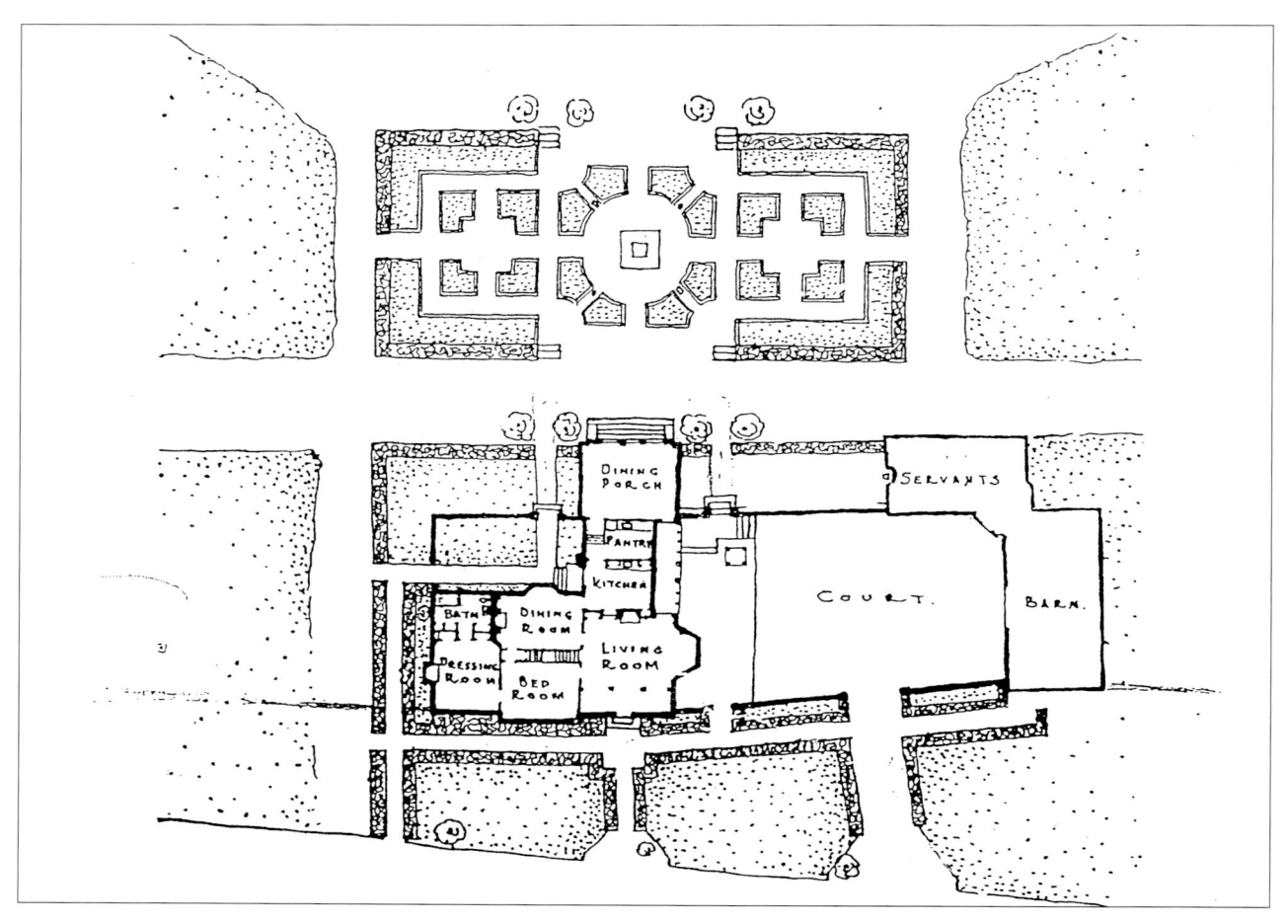

Site plan, 1918

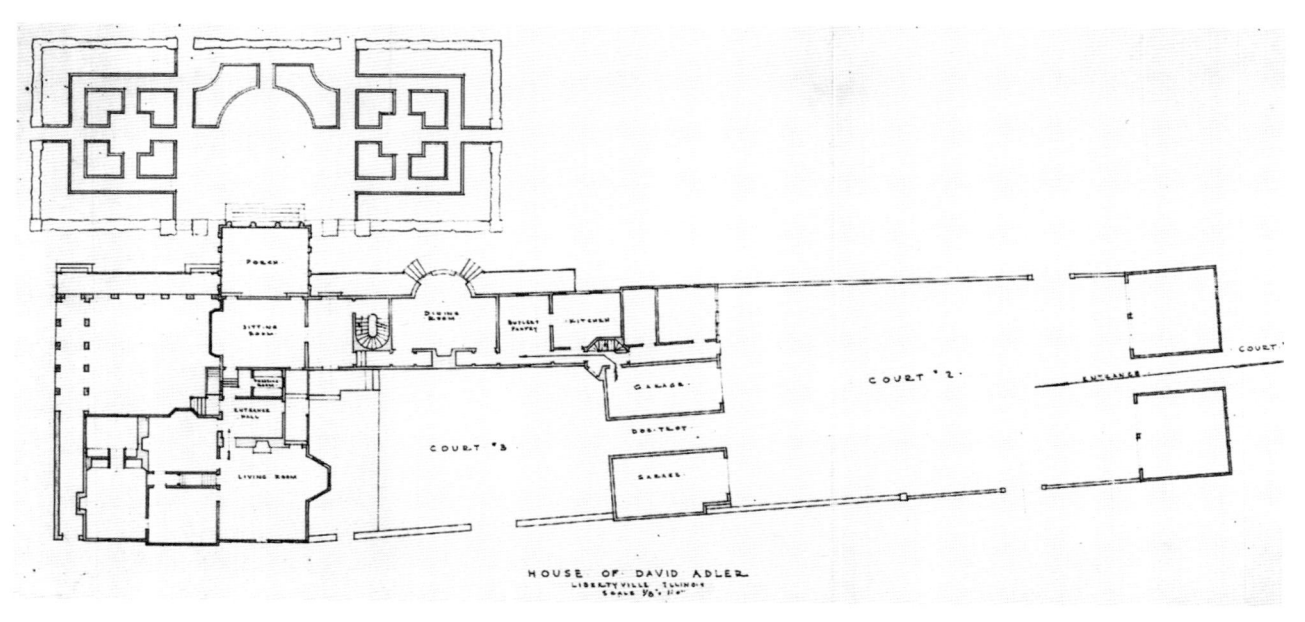

Floor plan, 1941

1920–1929

BENJAMIN MARSHALL
HOUSE AND STUDIO

Wilmette (1921)

FEW, IF ANY, significant Chicago architects compare with Benjamin Marshall for his exotic lifestyle. Whereas his residential designs for clients generally had more subdued interiors, signs of Marshall's flamboyant tastes are found throughout the interior of his own Spanish villa. Built on the shore of Lake Michigan, beginning in 1921, the house served as Marshall's residence and studio, and also provided drafting space to accommodate 45 architects. Said to have cost anywhere from $500,000 to $1 million, the house had 40 rooms.

Entrance court

Yacht harbor

Porch overlooking yacht harbor

Loggia leading to tropical garden

Indoor swimming pool

Benjamin Marshall's architectural talent has earned him an important place in the history of Chicago architecture. With exuberant historic detail not often found in Chicago's canonic office buildings, his luxury hotels and apartments along Lake Shore Drive and Michigan Avenue set the standard for those that followed. He is particularly well known as the designer of elegant hotels including the Drake, the Blackstone (which was converted into condominiums), and the Edgewater Beach (which was demolished). Most of the grand, older apartment buildings along East Lake Shore Drive were designed by Marshall. A prolific architect, who built over 200 Chicago buildings, he designed theaters, banks, private clubs (including the restored South Shore Country Club), and over 60 country estates. Marshall's elite residential clientele included Samuel Insull, the founder of Chicago's electric company, Commonwealth Edison; Francis Stuyvesant Peabody, the coal company magnate; and John T. Pirie, a partner in one of Chicago's foremost department stores, Carson Pirie Scott.

While living in Lake Forest, Marshall became enamored of a beautiful piece of Wilmette property forming a small peninsula. He hoped to build a large home there that would also accommodate his architectural office. The village, however, would not issue a building permit because the land was zoned for residential use only. In order to get his permit, Marshall made a deal with the sailors who moored their boats north of the land he wanted. He said that if they could talk the village into issuing a permit, he would allow the Sheridan Shore Yacht Club to use the basement of the office he wanted to build as their clubhouse. A permit was soon issued for "a studio-clubroom," and Marshall's

Chinese temple

new home was completed in 1924. The Sheridan Shore Yacht Club occupied the basement space until 1936.

Although the house stood three stories high, from its front facade on Sheridan Road only one story could be seen, and the Spanish Revival studio/house appeared relatively modest. Consisting of a fireproof steel-frame structure, the house was sheathed in pale pink stucco and sheltered by a red tile roof. Above the arched entrance appeared an indication of the intriguing ornamentation that became increasingly exotic on the interior: a salmon-colored plaster frieze decorated with rondels containing portrait heads of the sculptor Augustus St. Gaudens and architects Daniel H. Burnham and Stanford White. Marshall made it very clear who were his artistic heroes.

The decor of the interior could be described as eclectic, opulent, and somewhat bizarre. Marshall gathered decorative elements from all over the world. Inside the arched entrance fitted with a pair of old wrought-iron Roman gates was a large entrance hall. To the north was his drafting studio. To the east the space opened onto a loggia with stairs leading down to a glass-enclosed two-story garden with tropical palms, hanging ferns, and Spanish jasmine surrounding a free-form swimming pool lined with turquoise tiles from Algiers. Three large windows in this 75-by-110-by-50-foot-high space lowered at the touch of a button. By pushing a second button, a glass roof opened and the room became an outdoor garden. A brick path along the south side of the pool led to a Chinese temple, where everything—a pagoda, dragon portal, and a Buddha enshrined by embroideries—was brought from China. The floor was covered in quilted satin. A passageway along the south side of the pool led to Marshall's studio. This room contained a hand-carved stone fireplace similar to one in the Doge's Palace in Venice, chenille wall hangings, and a stage with modern lighting equipment. From an elaborately carved ancient pulpit, plans and sketches could be flashed onto a screen on the stage to entice potential clients. Tables to accommodate seventy-five guests were stored under the stage to create an instant café. An elaborately decorated old French sedan chair was used as a telephone booth.

Other rooms in the house included a tiny ship's cabin, set under the staircase, with a porthole that viewed a rocking diorama of the sea, showing a tossing ship or bathing mermaids. This room inspired a nautical bar he designed for the Edgewater Beach Hotel. A pair of ebony doors led to the floor above with bedrooms overlooking a tropical garden and a Turkish bath. Facing the harbor and Lake Michigan was the Egyptian porch, with furniture, including a 20-foot-long divan designed after those found at Luxor. Sofas piled high with pillows of red and yellow were designed to re-create the atmosphere of the Nile. The stellar feature of the room was a canopied dining room table that rose, completely set, from the service pantry below. Two terraced roof gardens opened off Marshall's Egyptian room. Dwarf fir trees and a bent grass lawn marked the upper, formal garden. A glass-bottomed goldfish bowl served as a skylight for the Pompeian rotunda below, and that opened into the Egyptian porch. The lower, informal garden contained a wrought-iron grille from a home in the New Orleans French Quarter.

Benjamin Marshall's guests were legendary. In 1924, the Prince of Wales, who for a short time was King Edward VIII and then the Duke of Windsor, visited the house. The prince signed his name into a wood table as did actors Ethel Barrymore, Beatrice Lilly, playwright Noel Coward, and conductor Leopold Stokowski. When entertaining, Marshall's dress included elaborately ruffled shirts. When greeting clients, he wore colorful ties with a matching handkerchief in his breast pocket.

During the Depression, Marshall ran into serious financial difficulties. The bank foreclosed his credit, and in 1936, his grand villa was sold to Nathan Goldblatt, secretary-treasurer of the Goldblatt Brothers Department Store, for $60,000. When Goldblatt and his wife had both died, the estate made fruitless attempts to sell the property, and in 1948 offered it to the Village of Wilmette for $125,000. Because of the high cost of maintaining and operating it, the village turned down the offer, and a wrecking permit was issued. The land was sold to the Baha'i Temple, with only an elegant pair of wrought iron gates opening off Sheridan Road left to serve as a reminder of Benjamin Marshall's lavish home.

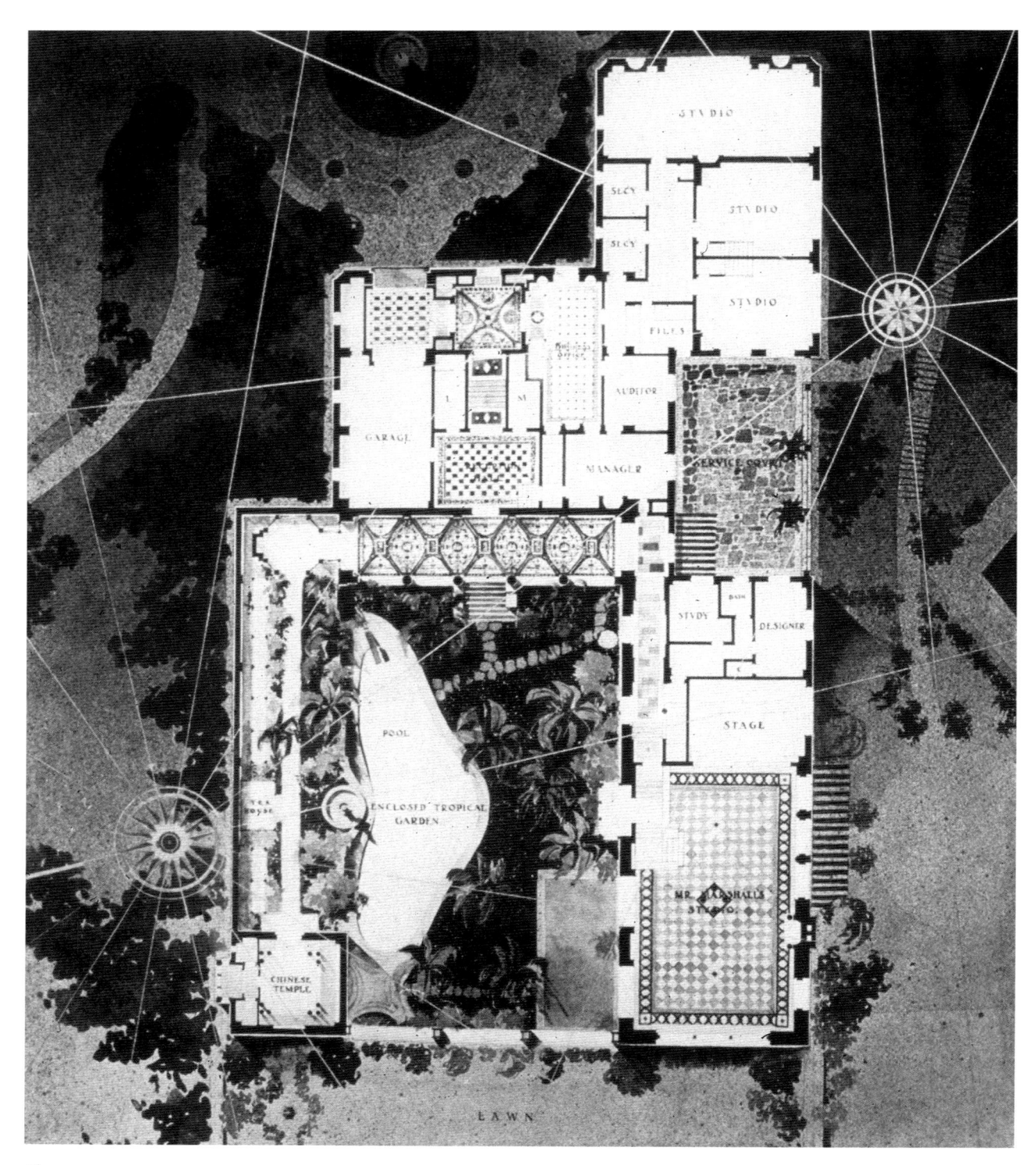

Plan

FAIRLAWN

ROBERT AND GRACE FARWELL McGANN ESTATE

Lake Forest (1921–23)

FAIRLAWN IS ONE OF TWO NORTH SHORE HOUSES designed by the New York firm of Delano and Aldrich. Typically, North Shore homes were designed by local architects. Houses by the likes of Howard Van Doren Shaw and David Adler often received national recognition, but Fairlawn stands among the finest of North Shore residences built by "out-of-town" architects.

In 1921, Grace Farwell McGann commissioned a garage pavilion, where she and her husband lived until their house was finished in 1923. Fairlawn was comparable in quality and stature to the many elegant estates that Delano and Aldrich were designing for New Yorkers in suburban Westchester County and on Long Island. It epitomizes classically inspired American residential architecture. The fireproof structure is concrete sheathed in brick, with centrally positioned doorways on both the front

Aerial view

[199]

Entrance facade

and the garden facades. Inside, the rooms are laid out symmetrically. Door openings linking the main hall to the dining room and the stair hall are enfilade. The arched front entrance is grand, raised by several steps, flanked by tall pilasters, and topped by a swan-neck broken pediment. A large triangular pediment is set over the center block of the house. On the garden side, the central three-bay block projects in three dimensions, forming a temple front with Ionic columns supporting a second pediment.

Stylistically, the McGann house is modeled after a variant of American Georgian architecture. Its massing, recalling 16th-century Palladian villas, consists of a hipped-roof rectangular center block linked by lower, two-story sections with pedimented side dependencies. The red brick exterior is punctuated by double-hung multi-pane windows with shutters. With its elegant classical detailing, the house is one of Lake Forest's finest Georgian Revival residences.

Like David Adler's North Shore designs inspired by colonial architecture, the McGann house is simple, elegant, and artfully thought out. Interior finishes include exquisite Baccarat crystal chandeliers, marble floors, and an elliptical staircase. Yet, ornament is quite spare, controlled, and consistent with the massing of the house, which feels considerably larger in scale than any that Adler designed. For its size, the public rooms are few and the ceilings are high. The two-story-high living room takes up the entire east pavilion wing, and is often referred to as "the big room."

Garden facade

The house, originally sited on an eight-acre estate, was connected by terraced, formally landscaped gardens to a long rectangular brick coach house. This outbuilding also had a central temple front containing the arched openings Delano and Aldrich favored. The firm's biographers, Peter Pennoyer and Anne Walker, point out that Delano and Aldrich very carefully sited their houses, and considered landscape an extension of the architecture. In the early 1950s, the property was subdivided, with Fairlawn resting on three and a half acres. The exquisite formal gardens connecting the two structures, however, have remained intact.

This Delano and Aldrich–designed house was the second Fairlawn. The first was an 1870 Italianate structure, with grounds landscaped in a picturesque manner by Frederick Law Olmsted. Built for the family of Charles Benjamin Farwell, Grace McGann's father, it was destroyed by fire in 1920. Charles Farwell had made a fortune from the three-million-acre, oil-rich XIT Ranch, which he owned with his brother, John V. Farwell, in the Texas Panhandle. Charles gained prominence as a political figure. He served in Congress between 1871 and 1876 and in the United States Senate between 1887 and 1891. Grace was a landscape painter and founding president of the Chicago Arts Club. She warranted a separate listing in Chicago's *Who's Who*. Robert McGann, who was also listed, owned an engineering firm.

Coach house

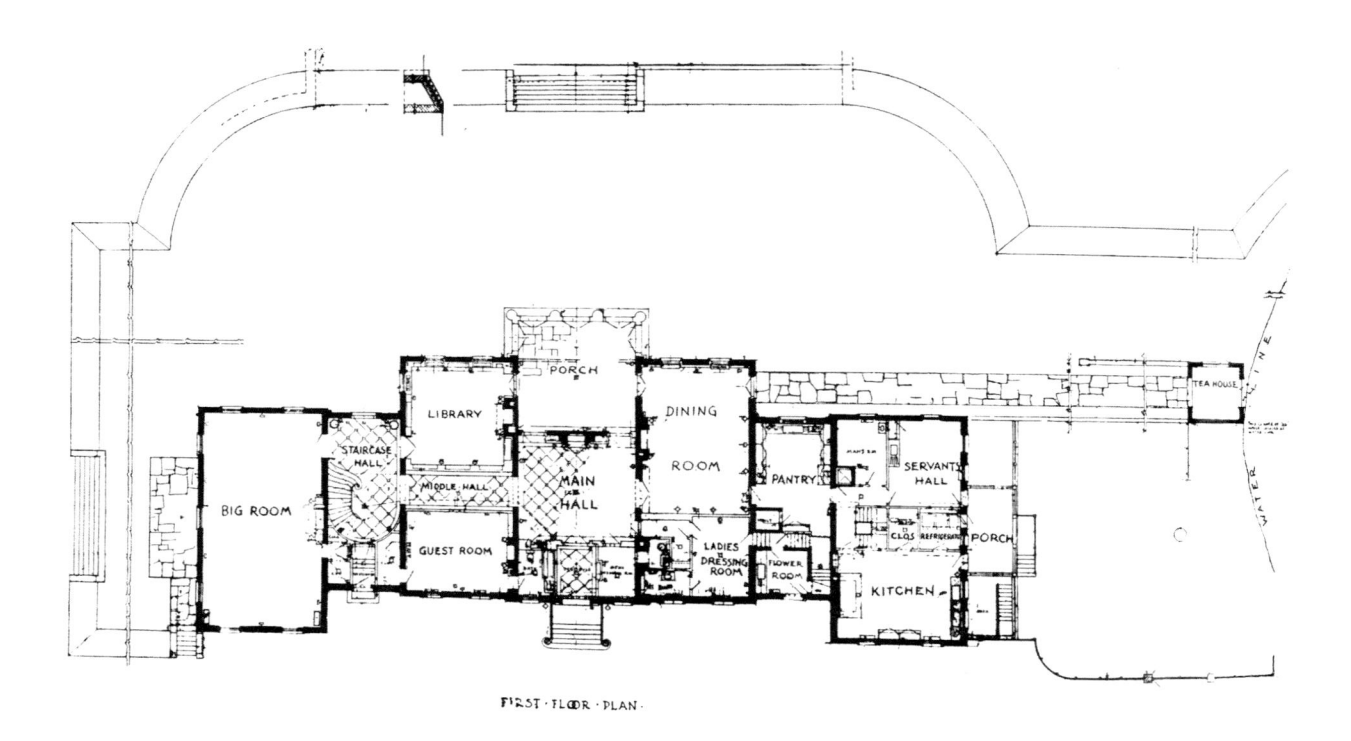

Plan

Gerard and Helen Bichl and Edward J. and Dorothy Schager Houses

Wilmette (1923)

Although it is not uncommon for siblings to live next door to one another in homes designed by the same architect, this pair of Italian palazzi is highly unusual in that together they form a small compound. Located on one of Wilmette's most gracious streets, the two large homes are located well back from the street. Accessed by a common drive through pairs of brick entrance posts set on a diagonal, the Bichl and Schager houses were designed to share a swimming pool and sunken formal Italian gardens connected by a bridge, beneath which a stone grotto was created. Symmetrically composed, the estate grounds include tennis courts for each daughter's family at the rear corners. The garden is still there, but the swimming pool, originally approached by separate paths leading from each house, was taken out.

The two houses were designed for Helen and Dorothy, the daughters of Wendelin and Agnes Seng, who immigrated to Chicago from Germany in 1856. Seng built on his experience as an upholsterer and mattress maker, becoming an inventor of swivels, hinges, and springs and creating an enormously

Houses from street

Garden looking toward Bichl house

Bichl house from street

successful furniture hardware business in the 1870s. Both husbands, Gerard Bichl and Edward Schager, worked for their father-in-law, as did many other members of the family. As they were a religious family, in the Schager house, one of the bedrooms functioned as a family chapel visited by bishops and priests during the Eucharistic Congress in 1926. A theater-size Aeolian pipe organ was installed in the living room.

The architect of record for the houses was George Maher and Son, but the designer was Philip Brooks Maher, who had joined his father's Chicago office in 1914 after graduating from the University of Michigan and traveling extensively throughout England, France, and Italy. He would open his own office in 1924. Although Philip Maher's practice concentrated on apartments and commercial buildings, he designed several North Shore residences, and built his own International Style house in Lake Bluff in the late 1930s (demolished).

The residential architecture Philip built for his North Shore clientele was not quite as progressive as his father's, but tastes had changed by the 1920s, and the Prairie School was out of fashion. In the

Rock garden

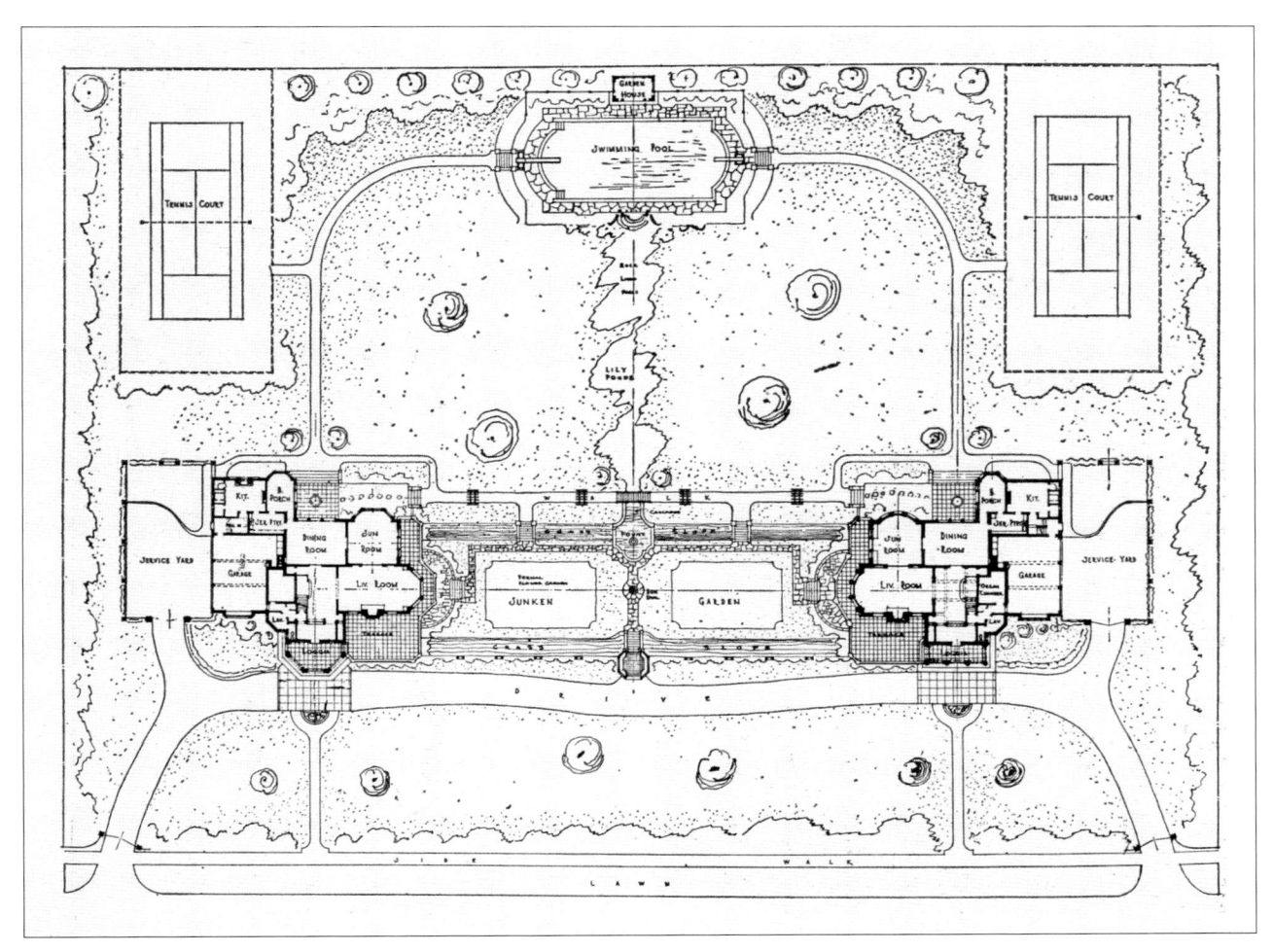

Plan of both houses

Bichl and Schager Houses, Philip embraced historic architecture, yet transformed it, abstracting and simplifying many details. Both houses designed by Philip Maher have features reminiscent of 16th-century Italian Renaissance villas, including arched loggias, glazed tile work, and terraces extending into the gardens. However, Philip employed a more modern approach to design, drawing upon the years he had spent traveling as a young man and his experience working in his father's office. The Bichl and Schager houses were each fitted with many modern conveniences, including six-tone dinner chimes that were electronically controlled from the butler's pantry, and concealed outlets in every room for a vacuum cleaner powered by a permanent high-speed motor in the basement.

Both the Bichl and Schager houses are being restored. They continue to complement each other and the more traditional historical revival houses on the street.

Felix Lowy House

Winnetka (1925)

Ernest Mayo was among the North Shore's most successful residential architects. Like Jarvis Hunt, Mayo came to Chicago to work on the 1893 World's Columbian Exposition and chose to remain. A resident of Evanston, where he built 38 houses, Mayo focused his practice on large residences for wealthy businessmen and professionals such as Felix Lowy. Lowy was born in Baltimore in 1888, but grew up in Chicago. He went to work for the Colgate-Palmolive-Peet Company in 1908, and in 1924 was made vice president. Lowy's promotion may have prompted him to commission Ernest Mayo and his son Peter to design a new house on Sheridan Road in Winnetka, just across from the lake.

Ernest Mayo, who was born and grew up in England, seems to have had a natural affinity for the ever-popular "Banker's Tudor" style. The Lowy house is remarkably similar to the Tudor-style house Mayo built for Ernest Reckitt on Forest Avenue in Evanston (1909). It is possible that Lowy admired

Sheridan Road facade

Garden facade

Entrance hall

Living room

Dining room

Master bedroom

this house and asked Mayo for one like it. In Mayo and Mayo's handsomely bound self-published office brochure, Peter Mayo wrote of the Lowy commission that "the house is Tudor in style with impressions of Haddon Hall at Derbyshire, the one-time home of Queen Elizabeth."

The Sheridan Road facade features a pair of two-story-high bay windows flanking the front doorway and bringing light into the entry hall. The symmetry of the facade is maintained throughout, down to the pairing of the garage and south-facing sun porch at opposite ends of the house. The circular drive that passes by a sunken garden continues to the north so that the garage can be entered from the back allowing the garage to have windows that match those of the sun porch. These garage windows had curtains sandwiched between double operable windows to protect them from dirt. While the property extended only 300 feet along Sheridan Road, it was deep enough to permit the development of formal gardens with pools, a rose garden, an arbor, a bird sanctuary, and a large greenhouse where flowers were grown year round.

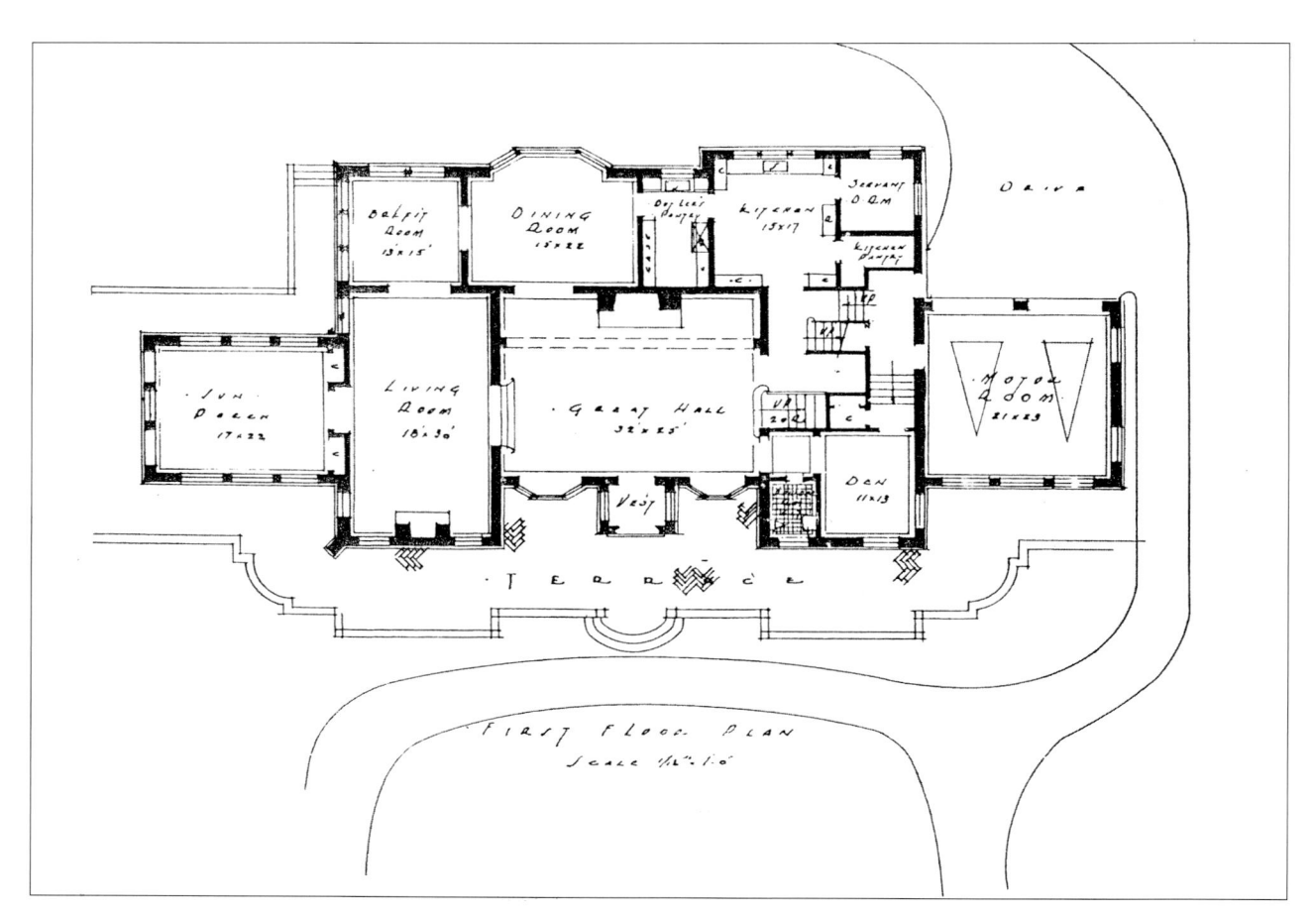

First floor plan

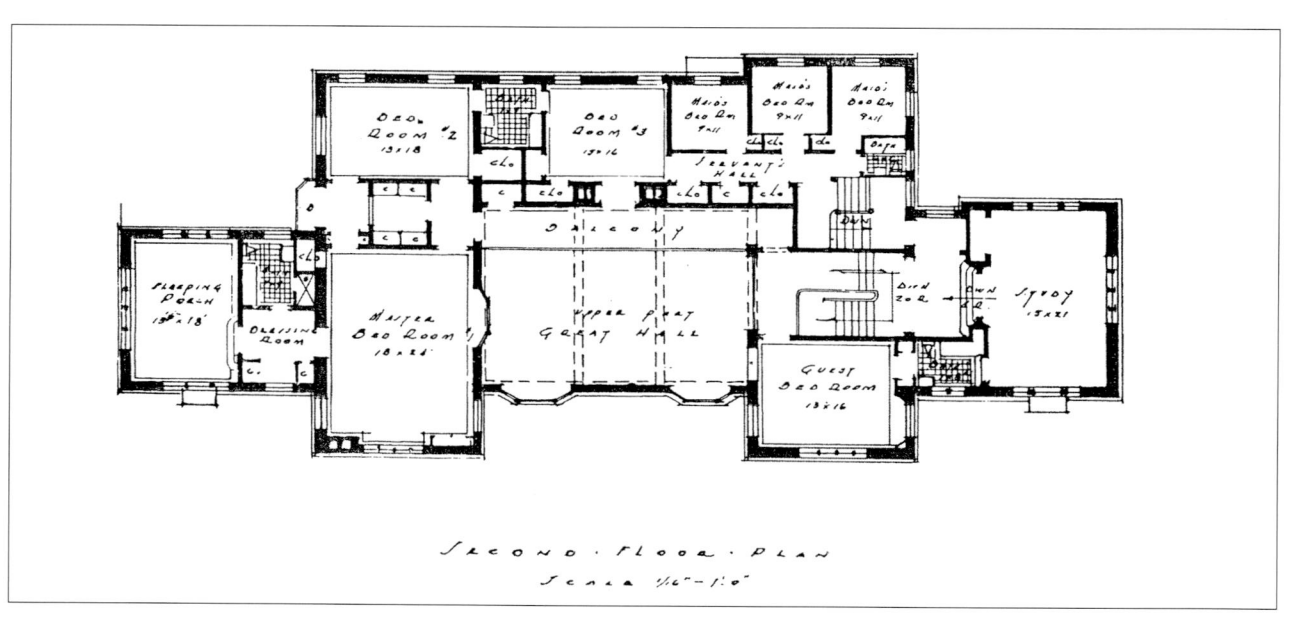

Second floor plan

From the entry vestibule, the cross-axis of the house is terminated by a large fireplace with a balcony above it running north-south along the back wall of the entry hall and connecting the main stair to the second-floor bedrooms. The spatial development of this "great hall," with its Elizabethan details and decorative stucco ceiling, is visually extended from the stair landing up four steps to a study, which enjoys an axial vista through much of the house. On the south wall of the great hall, centered over the arched entryway to the living room with its decorative iron gate, is an interior wood oriel window providing views out over the great hall from the master bedroom.

The planning of the Lowy house in part explains the popularity Mayo and Mayo enjoyed. The spatial sequences and vistas through the house, out to the garden along the north-south axis, and through the sun porch are skillfully conceived. In a nearly ideal arrangement, the living and dining room are entered directly from the great hall. Functionally, the strategy of balancing the mass of the living room against the stairs, service entry, kitchen, pantry, and servants' areas allows for a remarkably contemporary arrangement with respect to the garaging of motorcars, suggesting that it may have been the owners, not a chauffeur, who drove them. Although Lowy, as a modern businessman, may have driven his own automobiles, the house is nonetheless also perfectly planned with respect to spaces for the staff of servants. The back stair, three maids' rooms, and servants' hall are arranged so that all of the bedrooms, the kitchen, and the dining room may be reached without going through rooms or hallways reserved for family use.

The Lowy house still stands on Sheridan Road in Winnetka, although the land to the south, which originally belonged to the Lowy property, was sold and subsequently redeveloped.

NOBLE B. JUDAH ESTATE

Lake Forest (1925–28)

ORIGINALLY SITED ON 40 ACRES of formally landscaped grounds, the Noble Judah estate is dominated by one of Lake Forest's most elegant French Renaissance revival houses. Built between 1925 and 1928, its designer was New York architect Philip Lippincott Goodwin, although he wasn't the first architect selected. Work began in 1924, when Chicago's premier country house architect, David

Aerial view

Main drive

Gate

Southeast corner of house

West facade

House from swimming pool

Entry detail

Garden facade

Orangerie

Garden

Dining room

Adler, was hired to design a residential garage for Judah and his wife to live in while their main house was being built. The garage, containing an elegant interior salon as well as a motor court, was completed and published in the November 1925 issue of *Architectural Record*. Yet inexplicably, Adler was not invited to complete plans for the rest of the estate.

The entrance facade of the 24,000-square-foot main house is approached through a gate house that opens onto a rectangular, walled, cobblestone-lined courtyard flanked by a double row of linden trees. The house, faced in stone and half-timbering set in a variety of brick patterns, is topped by steeply pitched hipped and mansard roofs and surrounds an interior landscaped courtyard. To the west, beyond a formal terrace opening off the indoor swimming pool, were three grass allées: a wide lawn extending directly west, and two laid out on the diagonal to the property edges. To the south are formal gardens opening out from a broad terrace off the formal living spaces of the house. To the east is a walled, rectangular garden, a broad lawn sited between the garage and the house, and an orchard. The property, originally accessed through gates off estate-lined Green Bay Road, also contains an orangerie and a swimming pool with two pool houses.

View into living room

On a considerably smaller scale, the layout of the Judah property is reminiscent of the work of the acknowledged father of French Baroque landscape architecture, Andre Le Notre (1673–1700), who designed Versailles for Louis XIV. Characteristic French features include an axially-organized formal landscape composition extending out from the main house, clipped hedges, allées, fountains, sculptures, and various types of outbuildings that function to organize the landscape.

Goodwin's design for the Judah house is loosely based on a country inn in Dive-sur-Mer in Normandy, France. During the 1920s, the architect who, with Edward Durrell Stone, would design the

Bedroom

Sitting room

Museum of Modern Art in New York (1939) expressed his his displeasure with current architectural taste in a 1924 book he wrote on the adaptability of French architecture for "American conditions," stating:

> It is hoped that this book may be of influence in the U.S. where the pursuit of fashions in style and the imitation of strange foreign things in a cheap and hasty way has filled the land with curious sites. There is a style on which the best of any country's design is based and that is good proportion, simplicity and suitability. This book presents a few examples of this style to be found in France today.

Noble Brandon Judah was a Chicago attorney. Born in 1884 and educated at Brown University, he studied law at Northwestern. During World War I, he was exposed to the architecture of France, where he served as assistant chief of staff of the 42nd Division. He received the Distinguished Service Medal in the United States and the French Croix de Guerre with Palm and Legion of Honor. In 1917, Judah married National Cash Register heiress Dorothy Patterson of Dayton, Ohio. Shortly after their luxurious estate was complete, she went off to Long Island with her riding master, marrying him after her 1933 divorce from Judah. Although the property has changed hands several times and acreage has been sold off to allow other homes to be built, Goodwin's design remains intact, as does the pool and many of the formal gardens. The orangerie and garage both now serve as single-family residences.

CRAB TREE FARM

SCOTT S. AND GRACE DURAND ESTATE (1911),
AND WILLIAM MCCORMICK BLAIR AND HELEN BOWEN BLAIR ESTATE

Lake Bluff (1926–28)

IT IS UNUSUAL to find an important estate property with two equally interesting and significant histories associated with it. Crab Tree Farm was the location of a 265-acre dairy operation established by socialite Grace Garrett Durand, with buildings designed in 1911 by Solon Spenser Beman. In the early 1920s, the Durands sold 11 acres of the farm's wooded lakefront to William McCormick Blair for the construction of a country house. Designed by David Adler between 1926 and 1928, the Blair house was originally called "Port of Call." Today, the entire acreage is again under single ownership, with the original farm buildings housing the current owners' collection of Arts and Crafts furniture and decorative arts.

Durand farm buildings from Sheridan Road

Farm buildings

Blair house, front facade

Garden entrance

Lake facade

In the early 1900s, Grace Durand set up what became a flourishing dairy operation in the city of Lake Forest, selling as many as seven hundred quarts of milk a day before the end of April 1906. North Shore historian Michael Ebner has pointed out that the farm was a serious endeavor. Mrs. Durand took courses in agriculture at the University of Wisconsin, while her husband Scott remained at home to take care of their child. She won awards for her milk production and lectured on operating a model dairy. This was not the typical path for a woman whose husband's family members were pillars of the church and Lake Forest College.

Because her neighbors preferred not to live next door to cows, Mrs. Durand relocated her operation just north of the village of Lake Bluff in 1902, buying an existing farm. But in November 1910, the dairy suffered a disastrous fire. When she rebuilt, Mrs. Durand took no chances of a recurrence and had her architect, Solon Spenser Beman, design barns constructed of steel and concrete. In choosing Beman, the Durands selected an architect equal in stature to those that their friends hired to design farms that functioned only as a recreational pastime. Elegantly designed, the barns surround a courtyard, with the center building featuring a tower. They are French in their massing and symmetry, reflecting the architect's Beaux-Arts training and recalling the inspiration for the 1880s Pullman Administration Building and Clock Tower that Beman designed for railroad magnate George

Entrance loggia

Pullman's company town. Facing Sheridan Road, the farm buildings were a public statement that this was not merely a "hobby" farm but a serious agricultural operation.

The owners of the second important property were William McCormick Blair and his wife Helen Bowen Blair, both descendants of distinguished Chicago families. William was the grandson of William Blair I, who established Chicago's first and largest wholesale hardware dealership in 1842, and Ruby McCormick, the niece of Cyrus McCormick, inventor of the reaper. Helen was the daughter of Helen de Koven Bowen, who was one of the largest financial contributors to Hull House, Jane Addams' settlement house. William McCormick Blair was a civic-minded Chicagoan, serving as president of Chicago's prestigious Commercial Club as well president of the boards of the Chicago Art Institute and the Chicago Historical Society. In 1935, he co-founded William Blair and Company, which soon became the largest investment firm in the city. At age 96, in 1980, he helped found the David Adler Cultural Center, stewards of Adler's house in Libertyville.

The Blairs selected long-time friend David Adler as the architect for their country home. Sited at the end of a long private drive that passes a pond, a pair of cylindrical silos, and open pastures, the irregularly shaped house was designed to look like an early American colonial farmstead that grew over time, reminiscent of Adler's own house, which was sited on a large parcel of property and built over a period of many years. In a generously illustrated article in the January 1929 issue of *Architectural Forum*, Matlock Price commented that "many [early American farms] were remarkably individualistic and grew from generation to generation into structures of remarkable charm, with successive additions. Such a one this Blair house might well be." He suggested that the "unwhitened" rough stonework resembled old Pennsylvania houses and that the hand-split shingles were reminiscent of New England homes. The flared gambrel roofs recall New York's Dutch Colonial past. The front door, with its chevron pattern, is modeled after the design of the doors on the 18th-century Webb house in Orient, Long Island. Always the eclectic, Adler borrowed from a variety of sources, unifying them with the uncompromising sense of proportion and order that typifies the best of his work.

Although the Blair house, with its paneled rooms, human-scale spaces, casual living porch facing Lake Michigan, and Early American furnishings, conveyed informality, each room has a quiet dignity.

Main hall

Pine room

Dining room

Library

Tennis house looking into court

Classical details abound. Both the living and dining rooms have walls that are symmetrically composed. The dining room, inspired by the 18th-century Hewlett Room in the American Wing at New York's Metropolitan Museum, has arched cabinets flanked by pilasters surrounding a Delft tile fireplace. The library is a perfect 15-foot square, with a circular coved ceiling whose shape was mirrored in a carpet on the floor. This floor covering had a circular center surrounding a star—a signature motif often found in Adler's patterned floors.

Like most of Adler's houses, the Blair house is carefully sited. All of the principal public rooms face Lake Michigan. Because of its riparian location, the major landscaping is oriented to the front, where the door to the house is entered from a formal walled garden designed by the highly acclaimed landscape architect Ellen Biddle Shipman. Outbuildings are laid out in formal relation to one another. They include a Georgian-style tennis house, a Classical Revival folly with a temple front on axis with the main house, and a service court. The tennis house was a collaboration between Adler and New York architect James W. O'Conner. Like Adler, O'Conner attended the Ecole des Beaux-Arts. He had served as head draftsman for McKim, Meade, and White, and after establishing his own firm, designed several indoor tennis court buildings as well as homes for East Coast society families.

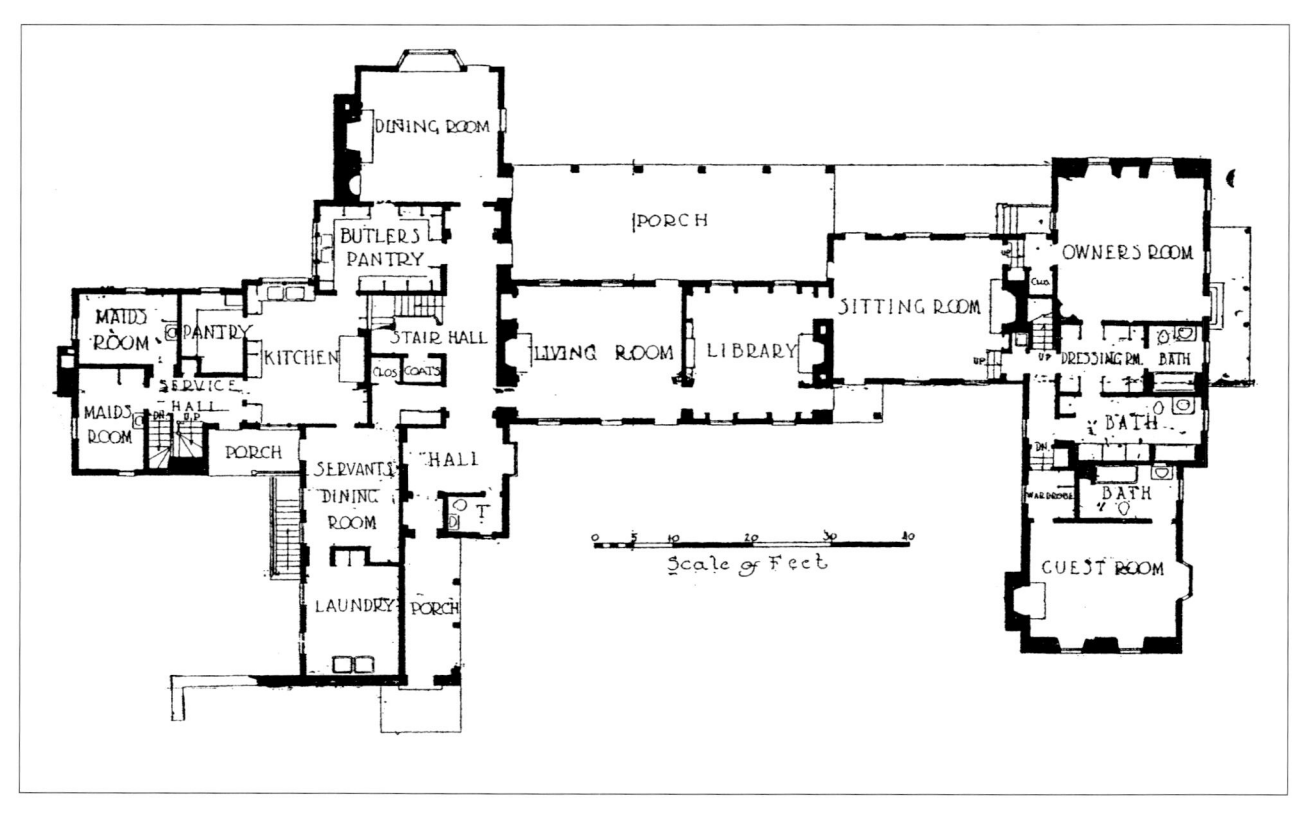

First floor plan, Blair house

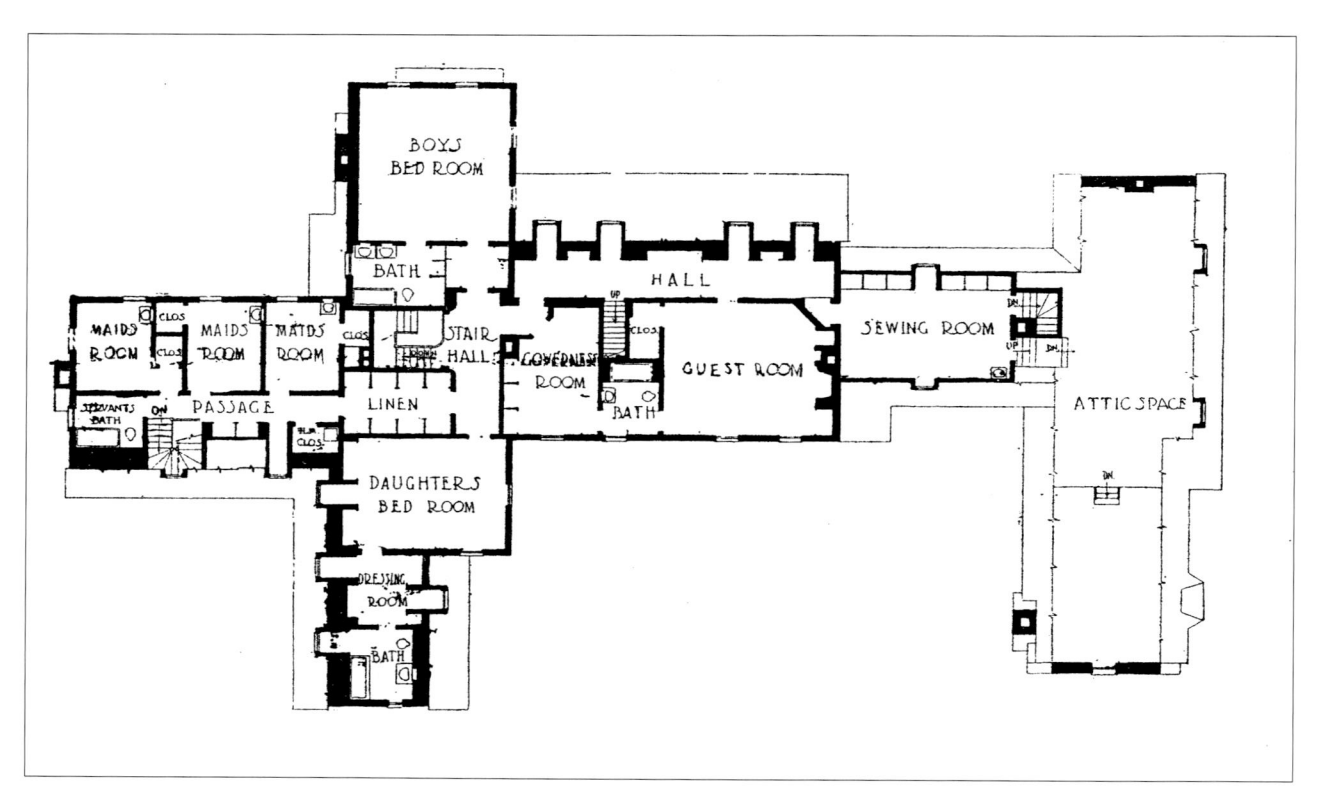

Second floor plan, Blair house

Robert Mandel House

Highland Park (1926–29)

Robert Mandel's 20-room French Norman chateau was built on eight beautiful lakefront acres between 1926 and 1929. David Adler's only estate house in Highland Park, it bears the architect's hallmarks of fine materials and elegant formality. On the exterior, the house walls are limestone, topped by a rich orange Ludovici tile roof. Where there is half-timbering, it is infilled with herringbone-patterned brickwork.

  Entered from a long drive off Sheridan Road, only the coach house is visible from the street. This small symmetrical structure was reached by a driveway lined with low boxwood hedges that were

Garden facade

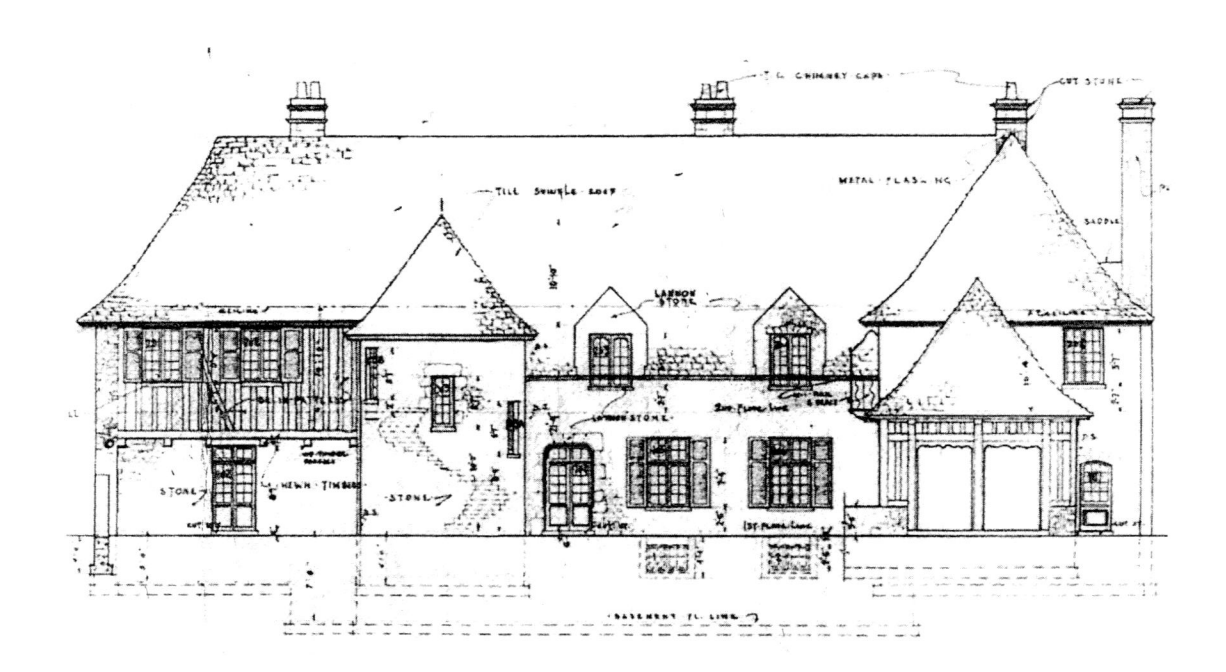

Garden elevation

Formal garden

Coach house

carefully pruned in a geometric pattern, reinforcing the tight formal relationship between Adler's architecture and the landscape. Beyond the coach house, the drive crosses a small bridge and enters a round gravel forecourt, where the deceptively simple entrance to the house is located.

Once inside, the visitor is treated to a sumptuous feast for the eyes. The spacious rectangular vestibule has marble floors in a diamond pattern, scenic wallpaper made by the French firm Zuber et Cie., a beamed ceiling, and originally had a crystal chandelier. A chandelier of similar brilliance, however, continues to grace the dining room, whose walls are covered with imported 18th-century Chinese wallpaper. Equally exquisite are the sconces, found even in the smallest bathrooms. These touches are the work of Frances Elkins, Adler's sister and the world-renowned interior decorator, who added her own sophisticated chic to many Adler-designed residences. The paneled library, reminiscent of a great hall, has an imported Louis XV fireplace mantel and *parquet de Versailles* floors. Paneled walls contain bookshelves set within openings behind finely scaled metal grillwork. There is a clear vista from the vestibule, through the library and a sun porch to Lake Michigan.

Robert Mandel, who lived in the house from its completion until 1946, was chairman of the board of Mandel Brothers, a prestigious department store on State Street—historically, Chicago's premier

Entry hall

Gallery

Sun porch

shopping street. This large company, run by three generations of Mandels until it was bought out by the Wieboldts' Department Store in 1960, can trace is origins back to the 1850s, when Robert Mandel's father and two uncles founded the business. The family was part of the North Shore's German Jewish elite, made up of successful businessmen and bankers who settled in Glencoe and Highland Park near Lake Shore Country Club. Like Mandel, who selected Adler, they typically hired the same prominent architects as the North Shore's Protestant establishment. As part of his education, Robert studied in France for a year, so like Adler he was attracted to French architecture in designing his own home. The house has had only two owners between 1926 and 2003. When Mandel became ill, it was sold to a couple who remained in the house over a half century. The house was then sold to a new owner who also prizes its significance.

HARLEY LYMAN CLARKE HOUSE

Evanston (1927)

IN 1926 HARLEY LYMAN CLARKE, president of the Utilities Power and Light Corporation, purchased lakefront property in Evanston from the Deering family of International Harvester. The property lay immediately north of the Evanston Lighthouse (1874) and near the northern edge of Northwestern University's campus. Harley Clarke was born in Richmond, Michigan, in 1881. His family moved to Chicago, where he attended Lakeview High School, and then the University of Michigan, where he studied law. Clarke was a successful utilities magnate, and at one time was president and treasurer of fifty different subsidiary light, power, and gas companies. In 1930, he became president of the Fox Film Corporation. Clarke was a member of Chicago's Union League Club and the Chicago Athletic Club, and he was a promoter of the Shakespeare repertory at the Civic Theater, a performance hall (now demolished) inside the Civic Opera House building.

House from Sheridan Road

Lake facade

The house built for Harley and Hildur Freeman Clarke and their two children was completed in 1927 and won a design award granted by the Evanston Art Commission. It was the last house of its size to be built in Evanston before the 1929 stock market crash. The Clarkes hired Richard Powers to design their 16-room mansion. Born in Boston, Powers worked in the Boston office of the supervising architect of the Treasury before relocating to Chicago. The Clarke house was constructed by Robert Black, a general contractor, who lived in Wilmette.

The house Powers designed was supposedly modeled after 16th-century English Tudor country houses. The roof suggests Norman influences, although it has a Cotswold look with its random-coursed ashlar masonry walls enriched with both carved limestone and red sandstone trim and a red Ludovici tile roof. The facade is pleasantly picturesque, with sloping eaves that carry the principal roof almost to the ground and with numerous chimney breasts. At the south end of the house is a large, glass-roofed conservatory with stone and glass walls and canopied east- and west-facing entrances. These are flanked by large, square, limestone piers with Ionic capitals supporting carved stone bouquets of flowers as with the one over the main entry porch. At the front of the house, decorative lead rainwater-collection boxes empty into semicircular decorative metal cisterns. Just west of the main house, at the southern edge of the property, is a substantial coach house built in the same style. Jens Jensen designed the landscaping, grounds, and bluff going down to a private sand beach, in an informal manner, as wooded areas with

Entrance to conservatory

Stair hall

Library

grassy clearings. The woods feature one of Jensen's signature Indian Council Rings. As with Olmsted, Jensen was famous for his naturalistic landscapes, which in Jensen's case were re-creations of the midwestern prairie.

The main block of the house is oriented north-south, with its principal length lying parallel to the lake. At the north end is a service wing laid out perpendicular to the house with a lower roof. The principal rooms are laid out *en suite* along the back of the house to afford lake views. The view through the house along its north-south axis culminates at one end in the dining room fireplace, and at the opposite end in the door to the conservatory, providing a view to greenery year round as an antidote to bleak Chicago winters. From the main entry hall, a wood-paneled oval

Master bath

space with a curving stair and fireplace, stunning views of Lake Michigan are revealed through the tall windows of the east-facing bay-windowed sun porch. A sitting room on the second-floor landing at the head of the stairs provides a second vista of the lake.

The Clarkes moved from Evanston in 1949 and sold the house to the Sigma Chi Fraternity, which used it as their national headquarters. Sigma Chi sold the house to the city of Evanston in 1963, and it now houses the Evanston Art Center, with the main-floor rooms converted to exhibition galleries and the second-floor bedrooms and third-floor ballroom used for classroom space. The main floor of the house comprising the wood-paneled entry hall and library, which is still intact, is open to the public.

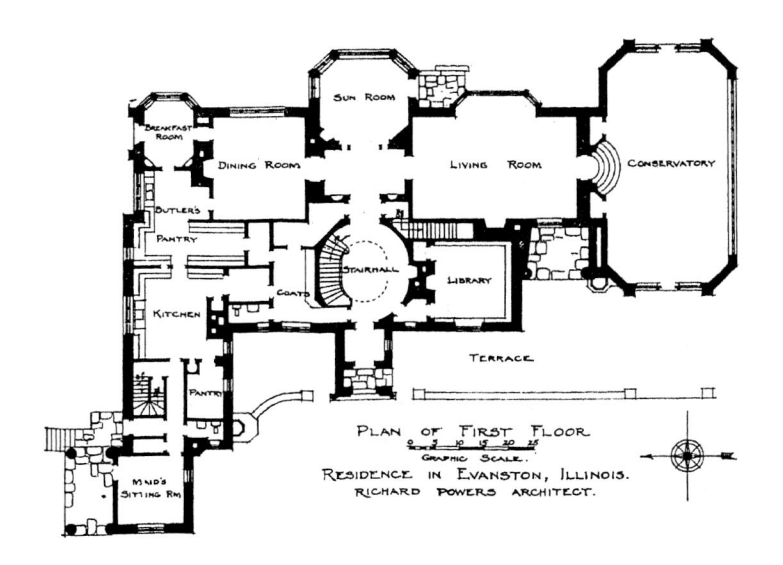

First floor plan

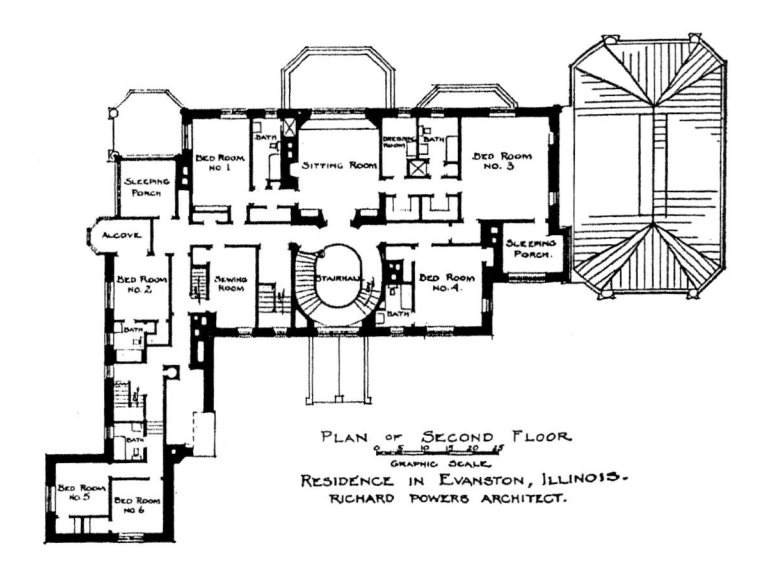

Second floor plan

MILL ROAD FARM

ALBERT D. LASKER ESTATE

Lake Forest (1928)

The house David Adler designed for advertising genius Albert D. Lasker is grand in size and imposing in stature, but superlatives are equally applied to the entire estate. Designed in the style of a French Norman chateau, the Lasker house took three years to build, between 1925 and 1928. The whitewashed brick structure contains 55 rooms, sited around a central forecourt with a flowing circular fountain. Wings with gracefully flaring mansards flank the center block of the house, capped by

Aerial view

Entrance court

a hipped red tile roof. The interior, designed by Adler's sister, prominent California decorator Frances Elkins, contains 13 bathrooms and 10 fireplaces. Its elegant detailing, associated with both Adler and Elkins, can be seen in the oval domed library, the dining room with its antique wallpaper, and the paneled living room with parquetry floors.

Approached by a long, tree-lined drive, the house rested on a parcel of almost 500 acres. There were 27 dependencies on the estate grounds, among them: a garage for 12 cars, a 100-by-40-foot swimming pool with symmetrical pool houses, a private theater that seated 50 people in large armchairs, a barbeque pit, a guest house, a sundial with 57 faces that told the time in 57 cities, a dovecote, and a large stable topped by a cupola. These and more were set in 250 landscaped acres—

Mill Road Farm

Terrace facade facing golf course

Garden facade

Living room

MILL ROAD FARM

Library

Hall

Dressing room

of which 97 acres were gardens—designed by Louise Hubbard and completed, after 1931, by New York landscape architect, James L. Greenleaf. The estate grounds also included a working farm complete with a herd of prize Guernsey dairy cattle and flocks of poultry, and Lasker's private 18-hole par-70 golf course with its own pro shop. The golf course was so challenging that no player succeeded in scoring par until 1927 when Tommy Arnold, playing in the U.S. Open held there, finished with a score of 69. Lasker's staff numbered over 50, including groundskeepers and golf course attendants. Albert Lasker, who reputedly built the estate at a cost of $3.5 million, was said to be the largest employer of labor in the Lake Forest area.

Albert Lasker was considered remarkable in the world of advertising. He was born in 1880, while his German Jewish parents were traveling in Germany. Albert's father launched him on his destined career at age 18 by arranging a job at the advertising firm of Lord and Thomas. By the age of 26, he was an owner of the firm. Only intending to stay with Lord and Thomas a short time and before embarking on a career in journalism, Lasker remained 44 years, becoming a millionaire many times over. Recognizing the need to woo the consumer, Lasker made a name for himself by creating advertising campaigns with catchy slogans. His clients included Quaker Oats ("Grains shot from guns"), Palmolive ("Keep that school girl complexion"), and Lucky Strike ("Reach for a Lucky"). Sunkist, Studebaker, Goodyear, and Kleenex for Kimberly Clark were also his accounts. He introduced *Amos and Andy* and Mary Martin on radio for Pepsodent toothpaste. Miraculously, the Depression did not affect Lasker's success. A man with a multitude of talents and interests, he was popular with political, entertainment, and sports figures—including President Theodore Roosevelt, boxer Gene Tunney, and cartoonist Rube Goldberg—many of whom he hosted at Mill Road Farm.

Lasker always considered Mill Road Farm home for his wife, Flora, and their three children. After Flora died in 1935, Lasker lost interest in this vast estate. In 1939, he donated the property to the University of Chicago, where he served on the board of trustees. Unable to maintain the property, the university sold the estate to residential developers. The 32,000-square-foot house sold for $110,000 to architect Jerome Cerny. As a young man, while working in the office of David Adler, Cerny had served as a draftsman on the design of the property. In 1940, Lasker married Mary Woodard Reinhardt, moved to New York, and shared her life of philanthropy in art and medicine. He sold his agency, Lord and Thomas, and the firm became known as Foote, Cone, and Belding. Albert Lasker died in 1952.

Today, the estate house, subdivided into three dwelling units by Cerny, is restored as a single-family home. The large outbuildings, surrounded by and scattered among newer homes, are converted into residences. Albert D. Lasker's estate house and remnants of the property evoke fascinating memories of his once-opulent lifestyle.

Mill Road Farm

Pool houses

Coach house

Mill Road Farm

Garden and dovecote

Shadow Pond

Arthur Stanley Jackson estate

Lake Forest (1928)

In 1928, Arthur Stanley Jackson built a Tuscan villa in west Lake Forest, where land was available and many of the largest country estates were located. Facing a tranquil pond that was part of a bucolic landscape designed by Jens Jensen, the house was called "Shadow Pond." It was reached from a curving forested drive that passed a coach house and culminated in a formal courtyard encircling a fountain in front of the imposing front entrance tower. Other grand country houses throughout

Aerial view

Shadow Pond

Main entrance

Garden facade from pond

the North Shore were inspired by Italian villa design, but several have been demolished or considerably altered. Shadow Pond and its surrounding property look very much as it did when the Jacksons lived there. Although constructed in the 1920s, its irregular massing and front "campanile" recall the earlier, more romantic designs of Italianate villas, such as the Edward King house by Richard Upjohn in Newport, Rhode Island, built on the East Coast in the mid-19th century.

The 23-room Italian Renaissance Jackson house is a two-story smooth-faced stucco estate house, dominated by a broad three-story tower that has a large, arched leaded window located over the classical entrance porch. Quoining defines the corners. Roofs are low-pitched, supported by beefy wood brackets and topped by barrel-vaulted tiles. There are many tall, arched French doors opening onto balconies and verandas. Some recall the tripartite motif of a central arch flanked by two side windows, commonly found in 16th-century Palladian villas. The interior is lavish, with imposing marble fireplaces and door surrounds, vaulted ceilings with classical fresco designs, Venetian glass chandeliers, and patterned tile floors.

Although the architect for the Jackson house is unknown, a cartouche on the original drawings states "John S. Van Bergen, Architect Associated." Art Miller, Archivist and Librarian for Special Collections at Lake Forest College, postulates a great likelihood that the house was designed by Arthur Heun, who built other houses with Italian references in Highland Park and Lake Forest. Heun was architect for J. Ogden Armour's opulent Mellody Farm. Miller also thinks that it is possible that Ferruccio Vitale, an Italian landscape architect who spent many summers during the 1920s in Lake Forest developing programs for the Foundation for Architecture and Landscape Architecture, might

Entrance hall

Living room

have had a hand in the formal aspects of the Jackson house gardens, or even the design of the house itself. The symmetrical elements that are typically associated with the Italian landscape tradition are located at the front and south side of the house.

A great deal is known about the landscape architect who laid out the property. Jens Jensen is recognized as a dean of American landscape architecture, often discussed in the same breath as Frederick Law Olmsted, Andrew Jackson Downing, Horace Cleveland, and fellow Chicago naturalist Ossian C. Simonds. Jensen's work is associated with the strong midwestern regionalism of Frank Lloyd Wright and other Prairie School architects. They all acknowledged the powerful aesthetic influence of the flatness

Dining room

and openness of the prairie—the Midwest's most striking natural feature. The elements of nature were the tools of an artist to Jensen. He commented that his materials were "the contours of the earth, the vegetation that covers it, the changing seasons, the rays of the setting sun, and the after glow and the light of the moon." He was a pioneer in the use of native plant material. For the Jackson house, Jensen created a landscape with beautiful vistas from the back of the house toward a broad lawn with curving edges, recalling the prairie, and the natural-looking pond.

Arthur Stanley Jackson was a wealthy lumber baron and a dealer in stocks, bonds, and grains. He was a member of the Chicago Board of Trade, the New York Stock Exchange, and the New York Produce Exchange. Born in Middletown, New York, in 1870, he was educated in Chicago public schools. Starting in the lumber business in Wisconsin in 1896, he set up a commission business, Jackson Brothers and Company, in 1905. Enormously successful and a member of several city and country clubs, he retained his home on Chicago's Gold Coast while owning this elegant country estate. Upon Jackson's death in 1933, the estate was willed to the Roman Catholic Archdiocese of Chicago, who no longer occupy it. Despite institutional ownership, the house has been altered little.

WALTER T. FISHER HOUSE

Winnetka (1929)

IN THE EARLY 1930S, the prominent architectural historian Henry Russell Hitchcock and a young Philip Johnson brought European modernism to the attention of the American public. They curated an exhibition at the Museum of Modern Art in 1932, and subsequently published their book *The International Style*. In a 1929 article about the Walter T. Fisher house in *Arts Magazine*, Hitchcock wrote: "It is very nearly the first (house) in America to which the most rigid international

Front facade

Entrance terrace

Roof terrace

standards of contemporary architectural criticism may profitably be applied." Designed by Howard Fisher for his older brother, a prominent Chicago attorney, the house was part of a family compound of houses Fisher designed. This included a flat-roofed prefabricated metal house for his sister, the well-known dancer Ruth Page, and a modest house Fisher built for himself. Fisher's parents first built on the property in 1896. The senior, Walter Lowrie Fisher, was also a lawyer and served as Secretary of the Interior under William Howard Taft. Appropriately, the family houses were on a curving Winnetka street named Fisher Lane.

In addition to its publication by Hitchcock, Fisher's house appeared in *Hound and Horn*, *House Beautiful*, and *Architectural Record*. What made all this attention remarkable was that it was the first house by a 26-year-old architect who had designed it as his thesis for Harvard University. The year 1929 was hardly a fortuitous time to open an architectural practice, and in 1932, at the height of the Depression, Fisher founded General Houses Inc. Patterned after General Motors, Fisher's company became an important designer and manufacturer of prefabricated, factory-built metal houses. General Houses had financial and technical support from corporate giants such as the Pullman Car Company, General Electric, Pittsburgh Plate Glass, and the A. O. Smith Company, the country's largest manufacturer of automobile frames. At its peak in the 1930s, General Houses, which was profiled in *Fortune Magazine*, employed the talents of Lawrence Perkins, his partner-to-be Philip Will, Jr., and Edward Larrabee Barnes, all of whom went on to become well-known architects.

Living room

In the design of the large brick house for his brother, Howard Fisher employed an almost Wrightian floor plan. It was cross-shaped in its organization, with the main stair and entry hall at its center. The open stair extends to the third floor, giving access to the many roof terraces that are open, covered, and screened. The stair allows light to flood through the center of the house. On the exterior, the walls, terraces, and patio walls are all of the same textured, red-brown brick. This provides the house with a tactility that Hitchcock felt distracted from its modern planar quality. Strictly speaking, the brickwork, third-floor roof terraces, and corner windows are more suggestive of modern Dutch architecture of the 1920s than the International Style. Perhaps the most inventive feature of the exterior is the horizontal wood handrails made from spaced boards—a domestication of the metal ship's railings used by Le Corbusier on his houses.

Hitchcock wrote about the interiors that "the living room, however is surely one of the finest modern rooms in America. . . . The major excellences of the room are so frequent and so great as to throw the majority of the modern decoration in New York into the scrapheap." This is clearly polemical, but the interiors of the Fisher house are indeed a surprise. Although devoid of moldings as one would expect, they are neither stark nor aggressively modern. The rooms are handsomely proportioned. A

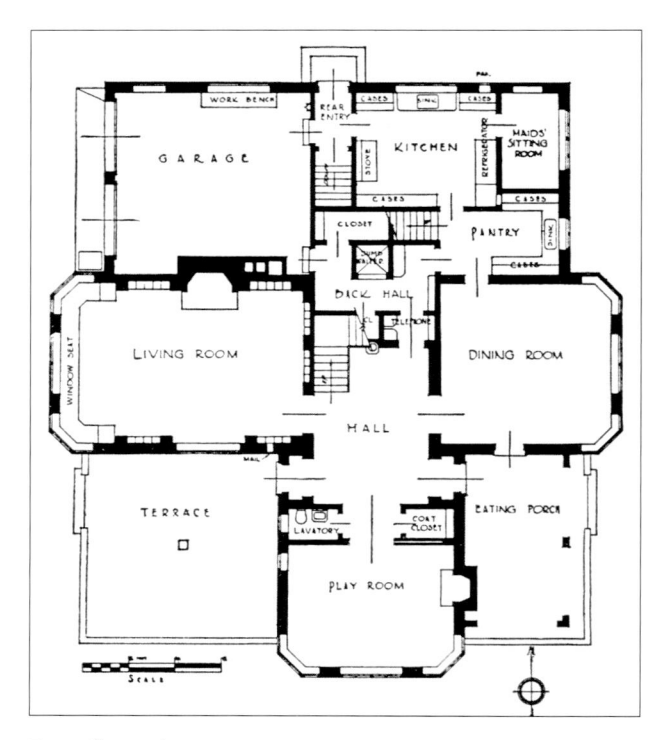

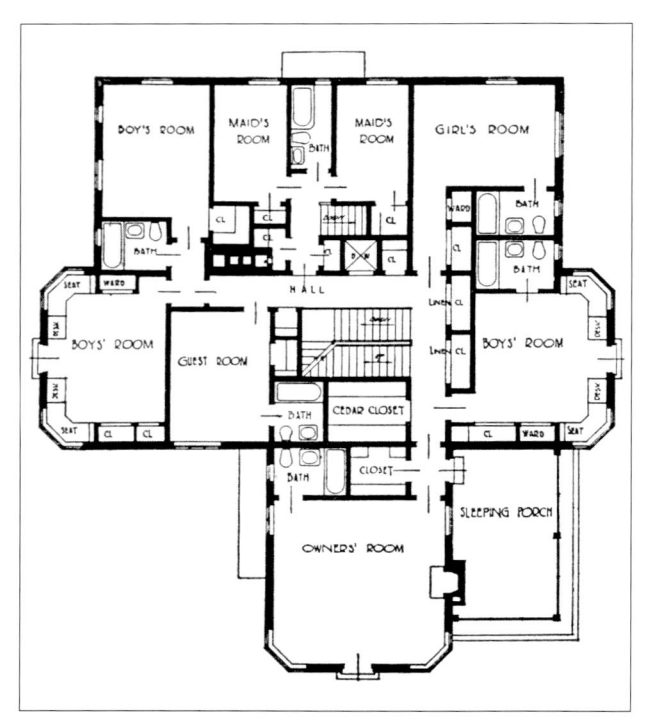

First floor plan

Second floor plan

cork tile floor running throughout has a rich patina and looks like stone. The openings to the major first-floor rooms have shallow arches, which Hitchcock hated, and the stair has a wrought-iron railing, which Hitchcock never mentions. Although photographs portray the house as International Style, more traditional elements such as the stair and railing are suggestive of Mediterranean influences and give the interiors a feeling of elegance and an unexpected warmth. Fisher worked with his sister-in-law Katherine on the planning of the house, which included a first-floor playroom for the children as a counterpart to the living room, a squash court with a viewing gallery in the basement, an eating porch, a second-floor sleeping porch, and a shuffleboard court on the roof. The uppermost roof terrace was served by a dumbwaiter used to bring up food. The dumbwaiter was removed, the shaft enlarged, and an elevator was installed when Katherine's elderly mother moved in with them. Certainly, the most unusual features of the house were its terraces, porches, and roof decks, the uppermost of which included an outside brick fireplace.

Walter Fisher, who died at the age of 99, lived in his house until 1962, when he moved to Highland Park. A graduate of Harvard Law School, he joined his father's law firm in 1918. A distinguished lawyer and labor arbitrator, Fisher also served as chairman of the Illinois Commerce Commission. Fisher's house still stands, unaltered and in its original condition, on Fisher Lane.

1930–1940

EDGECLIFF

Max Epstein Estate

Winnetka (1930)

The Max Epstein house, barely visible through a pair of matching gatehouses on Sheridan Road, is one of the North Shore's most stunning examples of French eclectic architecture. It was a style that appealed to clients who wanted large country houses that reflected French culture and fine taste, as well as the owner's financial success. French architecture suited the style of the Epsteins and the subsequent owners, some of whom made a mark as prominent art collectors.

Samuel Marx was the architect for this 1930 house. Although classically trained at the Ecole des Beaux-Arts, Marx was adroit at simplifying and integrating sophisticated modern detailing into his designs. The house is clearly French, derived stylistically from the 17th- and 18th-century French manor houses scattered throughout Normandy and the Loire valley. Formal symmetry dominates the approach down a long straight drive that culminates in a large forecourt. Standing two stories high, the center section of the whitewashed brick house is topped by a steeply pitched hip roof. The two one-story wings have Mansard roofs that are gracefully flared at the eaves, like the roofs on the front gatehouses. French doors

House from Sheridan Road

EDGECLIFF

Front facade

Pool

flood the interior with light. This said, the house is also very modern, composed of simple geometric shapes, flat surfaces, crisp edges, and sparse exterior ornamentation. The windows and doors have no moldings. Classical elements, including the keystone over the front door and the Greek key pattern on the rounded rear window bays, are highly abstracted. This somewhat Spartan approach to design became increasingly characteristic of historical revival houses during the 1930s. On the interior, there are several fashionable details including pewter inlaid terrazzo flooring and a silver leaf ceiling in the oval library. The living room has paneling imported from a 17th-century French manor house. Mrs. Walter Brewster was the landscape architect for the estate. She was a nationally significant garden figure, a founder of the Lake Forest Garden Club and author of *The Little Garden for Little Money*.

Stair hall

The ownership of Edgecliff is associated with the lives of three successful Chicago businessmen. Max Epstein, who was the original owner, was born in 1877, in Cincinnati, Ohio. He attended the College of the City of New York, married, and moved to Chicago, where he invested in a company called Atlantic Seaboard Dispatch that promoted the new idea of renting refrigerated railroad cars. In 1902, he incorporated the company, changing the name to the General American Tank Car Corporation, later known as GATX. Epstein was president until 1929, when he became chairman of the board and began construction of his Sheridan Road house. Epstein was a great lover of art and had in his collection Valesquez' portrait of Queen Isabella, as well as canvases by Rubens, Van Dyck, and Titian. He died in 1954.

Edgecliff

Living room

The second owner of the house was Nathan Cummings, born in Brunswick, Canada, in 1896. After marrying and moving to Chicago, he began purchasing grocery concerns. By 1947, he was chairman of the board of a company that became Consolidated Foods, then the Sara Lee Corporation. The 1970 *Who's Who in America* described Cummings as "one of the largest and most important names in the processing, distribution, and retailing of foods in the United States." Nathan Cummings purchased Edgecliff in 1955, and lived there with his daughter Beatrice and her husband Robert Mayer until he remarried, moved to New York, and transferred title to the Mayers in 1961. Mayer began his career with Maurice L. Rothschild, a State Street clothing store, and worked his way up from stock boy to president. In 1961, when he and his wife assumed ownership of the Epstein house, he retired. In 1970, Mayer listed his occupation as "art collector," and had one of the largest private collections of contemporary art in the United States. He and his wife had added wings to the house to accommodate the works in their collection. The present owner has undertaken restoration of the house and removed the wings added by the Mayers.

Library

Dining room

Women's powder room

Second floor bath

TANGLEY OAKS

PHILIP D. ARMOUR III ESTATE

―――

Lake Bluff (1917, 1932)

PHILIP D. ARMOUR III was the grandson of Philip Danforth Armour (1831–1901), founder of Armour and Company meatpackers. Along with his son Jonathan Ogden Armour, Philip's uncle, and the Swift family, P. D. Armour completely changed the distribution of American foodstuffs. The Armours, who distributed meat and grains to the East Coast and Europe, introduced the use of refrigerator cars and turned meatpacking into a modern manufacturing industry. According to Alfred Granger's *Welcome to Chicago*, the senior Armour claimed that "nothing of the pig was wasted but his squeal."

Entrance front

Tangley Oaks

South front

Tangley Oaks

South terrace

Stair hall

Coach house

TANGLEY OAKS

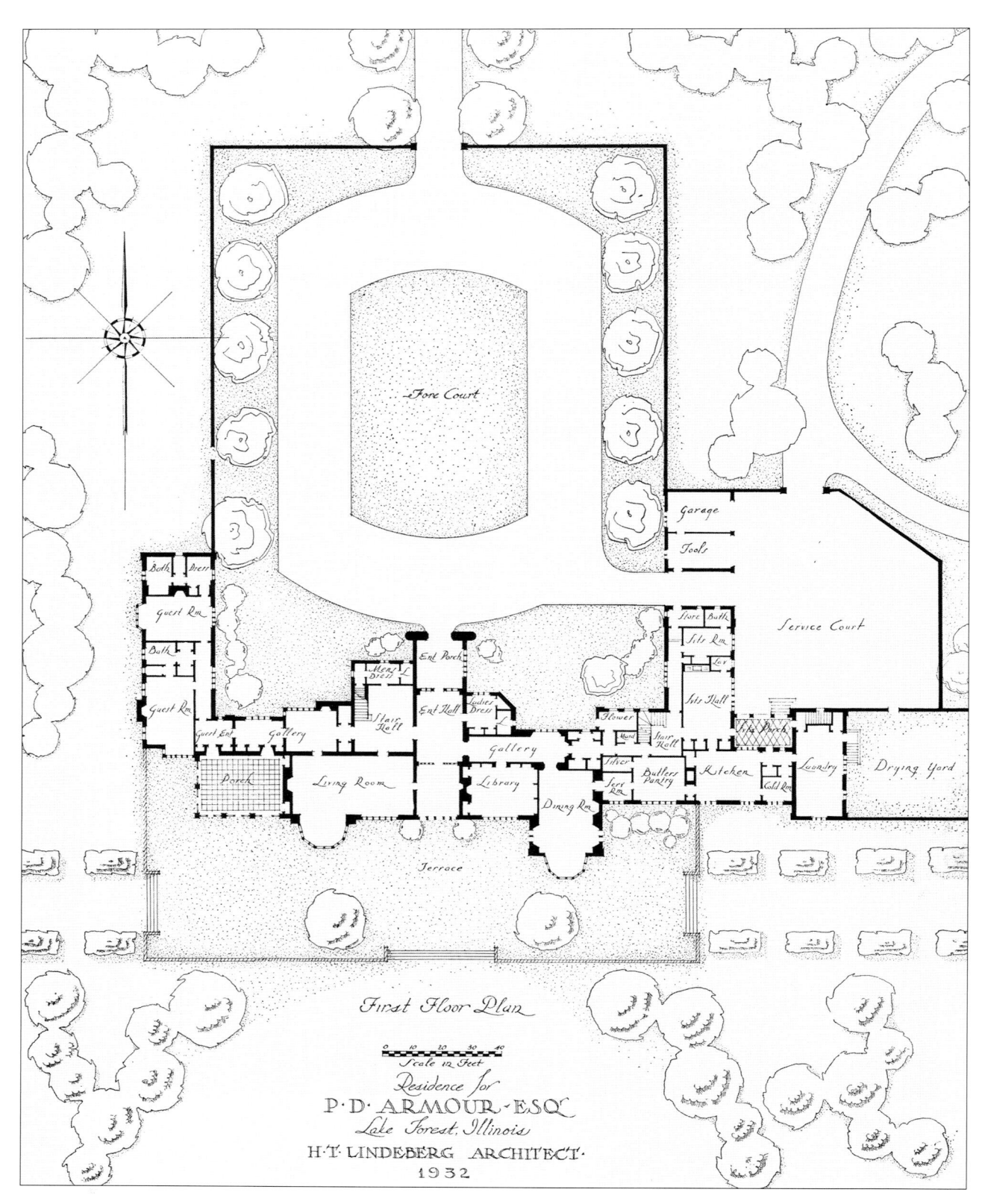

First floor and site plan

Tangley Oaks

In 1916, when Philip and his wife Gwendolyn bought over 200 acres of land in Lake Bluff, the Armour family fortune was the second largest in the country. Philip hired Harrie T. Lindeberg, a New York architect, to begin planning their estate. While Lindeberg had not yet been selected as the architect for the Onwentsia Club, he had built two houses in Lake Forest and made a national reputation building large country houses on Long Island. Work began on Philip Armour III's estate in 1917 with the construction of the entry courtyard and a gatehouse that was to serve as a temporary home for the Armours until the early 1930s when work began on the main house.

The hiatus in construction was in large part due to disastrous financial events that affected Armour and Company at the end of World War I. With the signing of the Armistice, the government, which had bought huge supplies of meat, dumped its surpluses on the market. Meat prices fell dramatically and coupled with other bad investments left Armour and Company $56 million in debt by the end of 1922. The Armour family lost control of the business, and Philip, who was a vice president, resigned. Happily the family fortune was restored through a fluke investment in oil refining.

Completed in 1932, Philip Armour's 26,000-square-foot Tudor Gothic–style manor house was named Tangley Oaks. The house is approached by a long winding drive that culminated in a formal walled entry courtyard. The house has broad expanses of windows and its planning shows a Renaissance Beaux-Arts influence, probably from Lindeberg's apprenticeship with McKim, Mead, and White, the architects who were responsible for the Classical Revival in America. While the plan of the house is picturesque in its resulting mass, with balanced asymmetries of its projecting bays, the main spaces of the house are ordered by a large central entry hall that runs through the house from front to back. This provides a dramatic view south through the house to an English-style meadow and pond. The main body of the house, which is sited east-west, has the main first-floor rooms—living, dining, and library—arranged along the back. These open onto a terrace that stretches nearly the full length of the house. The length of the terrace was emphasized through its extension into the landscape by a formal allée of trees that lead in both directions. Coventry, Meyer, and Miller have noted that a "dominant vista across informally arranged terrain with formal elements to the side was typical of the midwestern country place type." From the entry hall, the living room and stair hall are accessed directly and the library and dining room are entered from a gallery space. The stair hall has a sweeping stairway with a great window that looks back over the house's walled entry court. The east side of the house has a two-story wing that contains the kitchen, pantries, laundry, servants' hall, servants' bedrooms, and a garage that faces its own walled service court. The west wing is one story and contains guest suites that are reached from a gallery leading off from the stair hall.

Armour lived at his Lake Bluff estate until 1953, just after the death of his wife. The house and grounds were sold to United Educators, Inc., a reference book publisher. Most of the land was sold off in 1978, and was planned as a development of houses. Enough land was retained to provide for views and a reasonable approach to the manor house. Tangley Oaks is now used as the headquarters for Paterno Imports, wine importers. The main rooms of the ground floor were restored for Paterno Imports by architect Thomas Rajkovich.

MRS. KERSEY COATES REED HOUSE

Lake Forest (1932)

THE MRS. KERSEY COATES REED HOUSE, designed in 1931–32 by David Adler, is arguably his most important commission. In this Georgian Revival masterpiece, Adler combined the disciplined classicism he is known for with sophisticated elements of Art Deco to create a highly original synthesis. In collaboration with his sister, noted interior decorator Frances Elkins, he designed a 32,000-square-foot estate house that is neither pretentious nor overly lavish. Rather it is elegant and orderly, expressing Adler's sensitive and innovative use of materials and his keen eye for detail, proportion, and symmetry. Although it was completed during the early years of the Depression, there is no compromise in its level of finish.

Front facade

Lake facade drawing

Helen Shedd Reed and her husband lived in Chicago in a luxurious apartment at 1550 North State Parkway when they began planning for a house in Lake Forest many years before work began. Although Kersey Coates Reed died suddenly at age 49 in 1929, plans were not abandoned. Construction of a tennis house with living quarters was completed first. Located across the road, it served as a summer home for Mrs. Reed and her two children while their new country house was being built. When both structures were finished, the grounds were landscaped by East Coast landscape architect Ferruccio Vitale, who cleverly devised a formal design that spanned the road, axially connecting the two pieces of property.

Mr. Reed was a successful attorney. Mrs. Reed was the daughter of John G. Shedd, who rose through the ranks to become president and chairman of Marshall Field and Company, then Chicago's most exclusive department store. He was also the benefactor of Chicago's world-renowned Shedd Aquarium. When Helen and her husband planned their dream house, they went to David Adler, who designed a home for them comparable in size to Lake Forest's grandest estate houses, with 72 rooms—29 of them for family and guests, and 43 for the use of servants. The large number of servants' rooms includes six bedrooms for maids plus a suite for the houseman and butler, the kitchen and butler's pantry, laundry, wine cellar, linen room, flower-arranging room, and silver vault, but also a trunk room and a curtain room with a railing to store draperies. There are two elevators, one that was only for transporting firewood.

It is the elegance and classical design, not size, that distinguishes the Reed house. Reflecting Adler's Beaux-Arts training, the floor plan of the house is controlled by axes and cross axes. The entrance hall, with its marble floor that has black and white squares set on the diagonal, is flanked by two corridors opposite one another, one leading to the guest wing, one to the service area. Immediately ahead, through the spacious 16-by-40-foot gallery and the living room doorway, is a view to Lake Michigan. The north end of the gallery terminates in an elliptical staircase, framed by black Ionic Belgian marble columns. This stairway has a woven Moroccan runner and a balustrade with an ebony rail and glass balusters thought to be by Steuben. The guest bath, women's dressing room, and

Entrance hall

Stair and gallery

Gallery and main stair hall

Living room

Dining room

Library

Women's dressing room

Helen Reed's bath are all mirrored, with Adler's signature star executed in marble on the floor of Mrs. Reed's. The men's dressing room was given much simpler and more masculine—but equally impressive—decorative treatment, including a mother-of-pearl fireplace mantel, a bas-relief plaster overmantel, and sconces in the shape of a hand holding an urn-shaped light. The plaster pieces were designed by Alberto and Diego Giacometti. Furnishings were designed for the space by Jean-Michel Frank. The dining room is decorated with antique Chinese wallpaper and Chippendale wood trim. The most sophisticated room may be the library, with walls fitted out in Hermès leather that has hand-stitched welted seams suggesting paneling. The list of exquisite features, expressed in sumptuous materials, is practically endless.

Frances Elkins, who had a remarkable talent for combining traditional pieces with the latest styles, was responsible for acquiring many of the furnishings and coordinating with Adler on the interior. She selected such pieces as the white gessoed eagle console tables in the front hall that were custom-made in London for this space, and the leather chairs, desk, and table designed by Frank, and the ivory posted canopy beds in the first-floor guest room. Mark Hampton, the noted decorator, devoted considerable attention to the Reed house in his chapter on Elkins in *Legendary Decorators of the Twentieth Century* (1992). When he visited the house, his response was, "I was simply astonished by its perfection, by the impeccable finesse with which traditional Anglo-American decoration and up-to-the-minute thirties design had been combined." He was a great admirer of Frances Elkins, concluding his chapter on her by saying, "No other decorator did more to define the broad aspects of American taste."

The lineage of Adler's Georgian Revival design, with an imposing two-story center block connected by lower sections to taller dependencies, can be traced back to the 16th-century Italian villas of Palladio that inspired both English Georgian country houses and American Georgian mansions like the Hammond Harwood house in Annapolis, Maryland (1770). Adler very much admired Georgian architecture and had a library that contained numerous volumes on both Georgian and Georgian Revival buildings. But the exterior is not red brick like most Georgian Revivals. The walls were constructed of gray, mauve, and caramel-hued Pennsylvania stone containing bits of mica, causing the house to shimmer in the sun.

The Reed house and tennis house are each privately owned. Architectural historian Peter Reed, who is Mrs. Reed's grandson, is curator of the Department of Architecture and Design at the Museum of Modern Art in New York.

Herbert Bruning House

Wilmette (1936)

Over the years, the 1936 Herbert Bruning House has brought great praise to architect George Fred Keck. It was his first major modern residential commission. The architectural press recognized its significance, and it was published almost immediately after its completion, with articles appearing in both *Architectural Record* and *Architectural Forum*, illustrated with stunning Hedrich Blessing photographs.

Front facade

West facade

When Keck opened his office in 1926, his practice focused on getting business, and his early homes were designed in the popular styles of the period. Colonial, Tudor, and French-inspired residences dominated Keck's work. Many of these early commissions were built in the Indian Hill subdivision of Wilmette, where the Bruning house was to be located. During the late 1920s and early 1930s, Keck was able to convince only a small number of clients to build simple modern structures with planar surfaces, geometric massing, minimal trim, and flat roofs—that is, in what would be called the International Style. But these few examples of modern architecture put him at the forefront of the modern movement in America. Unfortunately, few of his important early buildings are extant. The simple and sophisticated Miralago Ballroom in Wilmette (1929) was destroyed by fire three years after it was constructed. The more radical House of Tomorrow, built for the Chicago Century of Progress Exposition (1933), was disassembled, moved to the dunes of Beverly Shores, Indiana, and altered so that it no longer resembles Keck's original design. His steel-truss and all-glass Crystal House, built for the fair in 1934, was taken down.

The Brunings gave Keck carte blanche to build a modern house. There were no compromises. He had total control of everything from the siting to the furniture. He designed the house and supervised its construction. His only assistance came from his draftsmen, Robert Bruce Tague and his brother

Stair

Living room

William Keck, who later became his partner. Despite the fact that the Brunings' neighbors circulated a petition in 1936 to halt construction, the client remained undeterred. In his book on the firm of Keck and Keck, Robert Boyce quoted the Brunings. They wanted the finished structure "to be of such a character that the children would not be ashamed of it when they reached the age of reason—i.e. that it be simple, permanent and economically maintained."

The steel-frame Bruning house has walls sheathed in white stucco topped by a flat roof. Its most dramatic feature is the half-cylindrical glass-block tower that dominates the front facade and backlights the spiral staircase it surrounds. The interior of the first floor combines an open plan, where the entrance vestibule, living room, and library spaces flow together, with a formal oval dining room. At the rear are the kitchen, back stairs, master bedroom, and three children's bedrooms, forming a U around a two-car garage that is integrated into the massing of the house. On the second floor are two guest rooms, a den, and two maid's rooms that open off a small hallway. The basement contains a recreation room, accessed by the spiral stair, with a playful Art Deco mural over the fireplace and movable leather and aluminum chairs, very likely designed by Keck.

Basement recreation room

Keck applied progressive technology to the design of the Bruning house. He was one of a relatively small number of architects who, at this time, were interested in solar heating. Keck claimed his interest stemmed from his observations of how warm his all-glass Crystal House at the 1934 fair remained on sunny winter days. The application of solar energy influenced the siting of the Bruning house. Having made careful studies of the sun's angles and path, he oriented the house north-south at the east end of the property, with the long side facing west. This was done to take advantage of passive solar heating and to provide the principal living spaces with access to the yard, terraces, and roof decks. The flat concrete-slab roof was designed to carry a thin film of water that would cool the house through evaporation. The interior temperature was further managed by custom double-glazed window units introduced by Libby Owens Corning in 1935, and featured external chain-activated Venetian blinds. These were all innovations Keck would refine and use throughout his career, when he no longer was obliged to compromise his integrity by designing traditional homes.

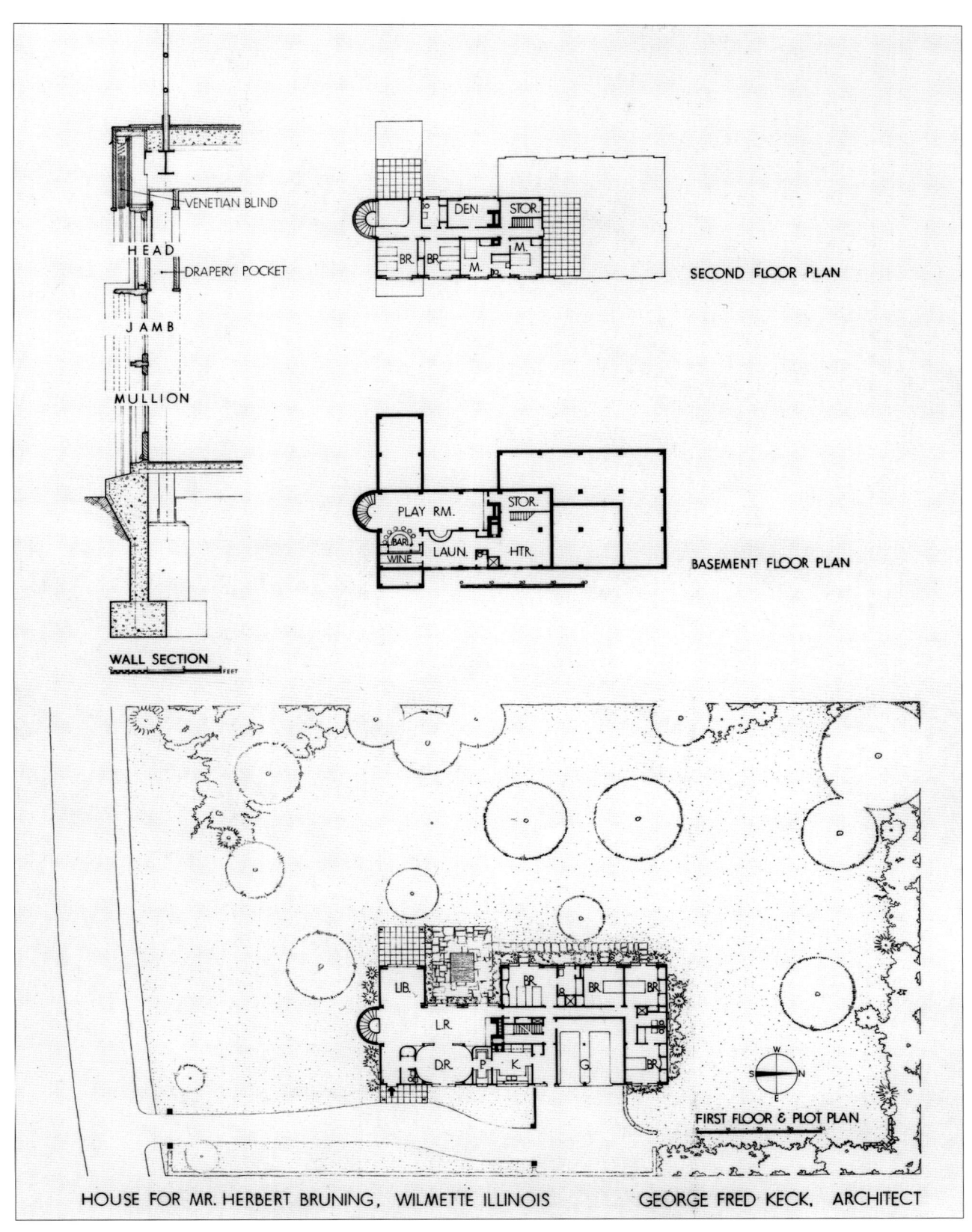

Plans

Bertram J. Cahn House

Lake Forest (1936)

When questioned by architect George Fred Keck about what kind of house his client would want to build, Irma (Mrs. Bertram) Cahn said she wanted the "house of the day after tomorrow." The Cahns had been to the 1933 World's Fair and had seen Keck's "House of Tomorrow." They knew they had found the architect who could perfectly satisfy their desire for a contemporary house that was comfortable, convenient to maintain, and suitable for simple entertaining. They wanted

Front facade

Pool

a house that "could be closed in a few minutes, with nothing that would deteriorate when it was unoccupied, and could be opened as quickly; a house to be practically servantless for present informal living." They also had some specific requirements. Mrs. Cahn had injured a hip as a young girl, and still walked with a limp, so she didn't want any floor rugs or lamp cords to trip over. She smoked heavily, and her husband wanted the house as fireproof as possible.

Keck met the needs of his clients perfectly by designing a curving one-story steel-frame building sheathed in stucco. It was located on a wooded, 30-acre parcel in Lake Forest on property where Irma Cahn's grandfather, Louis B. Kuppenheimer, had previously built a small summer house. Jens Jensen, who had designed the landscaping, approved the location of the house, and it was placed on the same site as the old wooden house.

The Cahn house, completed in 1936 at a cost of $125,000, had four bedrooms, six baths, and a screened porch that overlooked the swimming pool. The plan, which has a convex hallway adjacent to the entrance court, provided for complete privacy on the front, with light coming from glass block walls. At the rear, where the living and bedrooms were located, all of the walls had large glazed openings that faced south. The living-dining room with windows on three sides offered dramatic views of the park-like setting, as well as both the sunrise and the sunset. It was a large room, with a high

Living room

Living room fireplace

Bedroom

ceiling and hard surfaces, and thus provided good acoustics for listening to string quartets or recorded music. Loudspeakers on wheels were plugged into outlets that had remote controls in many of the rooms. None of the materials in the house required much care. The floors were without rugs, and the windows were without draperies. The colors in the living room were dramatic, with the acoustical tile ceiling painted dark blue, walls painted yellow, and floors of black rubber. Keck designed the furniture, which was yellow like the walls and upholstered with a fabric that combined jute and leather. Many of the pieces were built-in and had ashtrays in the arms. Those that were movable were aluminum. The Keck-designed dining room table was made up of square units that could be pulled apart for playing bridge. Lighting in the living room that accentuated the sparse interior and the room's vivid primary colors was provided by 18 recessed pinhole fixtures so that reading could take place anywhere. The bedrooms also had pinhole lights in the ceiling, designed so that they were tilted and masked to shine only on the top half of the bed.

George Fred Keck, whose brother William later joined him as partner, was at the forefront of residential design incorporating passive solar heating. He designed the south side of the house with broad overhangs that allowed the low winter sun to penetrate the interior, but prevented it from overheating the house in the summer. External, chain-driven blinds took the place of more traditional shutters.

Although the Cahns' contemporary taste was atypical for the North Shore, their background was like that of other wealthy clients who built homes in the area. When Bertram Cahn married Irma

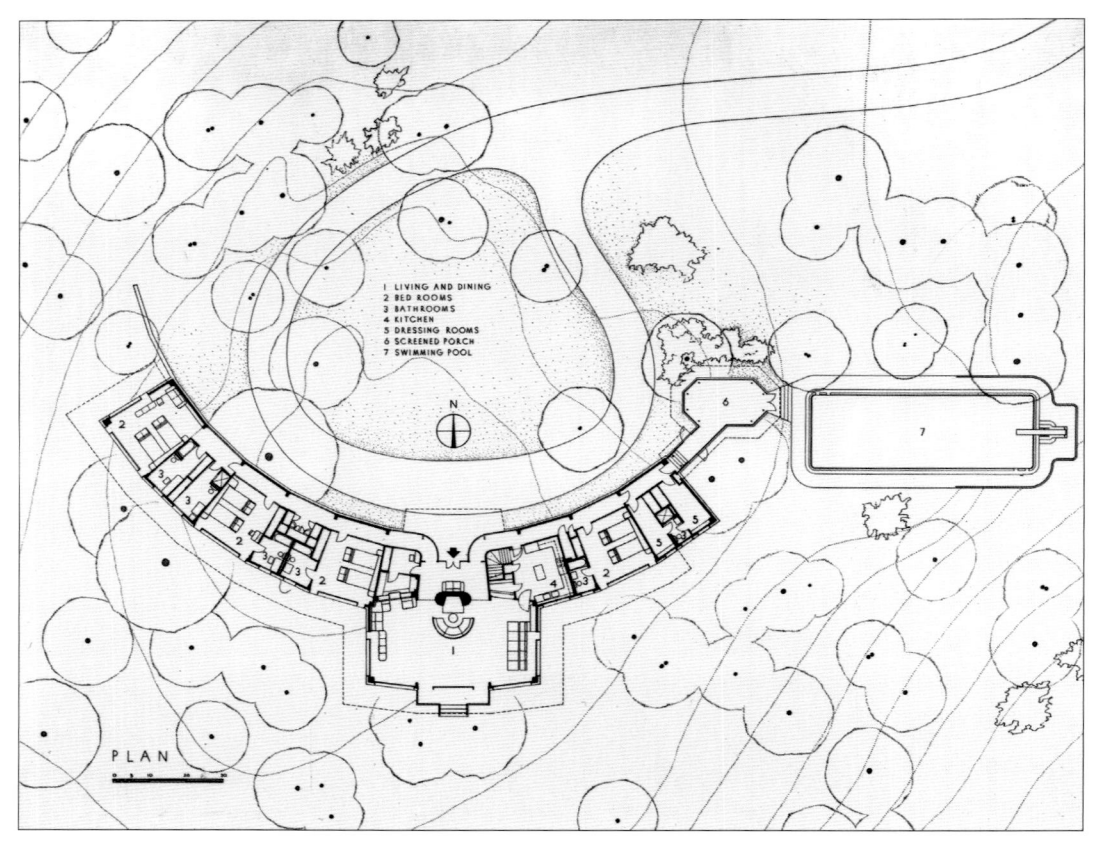

Plan

Kuppenheimer, he was brought into the family's men's clothing business, B. Kuppenheimer and Company. Born in Chicago in 1875, Bertram J. Cahn was the son of a pioneer clothing manufacturer. He graduated from Yale in 1896, attended Northwestern University Law School, and while practicing law, married his childhood friend Irma, the daughter of Jonas Kuppenheimer. Wanting to keep the business in the family, his father-in-law offered Cahn a position. He became chairman of B. Kuppenheimer in 1927, and president in 1932, retaining these titles until his death in 1959. His volunteer activities included presidency of the Chicago Crime Commission and chairman of the Research Council for Economic Security. Cahn raised hundreds of thousands of dollars for the American Cancer Society and was personally an ardent benefactor of Northwestern University.

Mrs. Cahn, who died in 1943, was quoted in July 1939 issue of *Architectural Forum* as saying that "we like the house because it is spacious, colorful, bright, restful and in harmony with the surrounding landscape." She and her husband complimented Keck with the ultimate accolade: "If we were to build again, we would repeat what we have done in every respect." The house still stands but with substantial alterations.

Appendices

1917. Evanston residence of industrialist George B. Dryden
George Maher, architect
Subdivided into condominiums

Portfolio of Houses
1880–1940

1881. Evanston residence of real estate developer
John Hume Kedzie
Cass Chapman, architect
Demolished

c. 1882. Evanston residence of architect
William Holabird
1909 addition by Holabird and Roche, architects
Demolished

1889. Evanston residence of
Dr. Edward Hutchins Webster
Holabird and Roche, architects
Demolished

1890. Evanston residence of dry goods wholesaler
Simeon and Ebenette Smith Farwell
John Mills Van Osdel, architect
Private residence

PORTFOLIO

1892. RAVINE LODGE. Highland Park residence of
attorney and real estate investor Sylvester Millard
William W. Boyington, architect
Private residence

1892. PRALLMERE. Highland Park residence of real
estate developer Colonel F. S. Prall
Architect unknown
Private residence

1893. Kenilworth residence of architect
George W. Maher
Private residence

1893. Lake Forest estate of architect
Henry Ives Cobb; later the Onwentsia Country Club
Frederick Law Olmsted, landscape architect
Demolished

c. 1895. Highland Park residence of insurance company
executive William. A. Alexander
Architect unknown
Demolished

1895. PEMBROKE HALL. Lake Forest residence of
mining and real estate entrepreneur David B. Jones
Henry Ives Cobb, architect
Private residence

[297]

PORTFOLIO

1894. Evanston residence of Superior Court Judge
Charles Elliot Anthony
Pond and Pond, architects
Private residence

c. 1897. Highland Park residence of E. E. Prussing
Architect unknown
Demolished

1896. WALDEN. Lake Forest estate of farm implement
manufacturer Cyrus H. McCormick, Jr.
Jarvis Hunt, architect; Warren Manning, landscape
architect
Demolished

1896. ARDLEIGH. Lake Forest residence of dry goods
merchant John V. Farwell, Jr.
Arthur Heun, architect
Private residence

1897. Evanston residence from 1904 to 1909 of Charles
G. Dawes, vice-president of the United States 1925–29
under Calvin Coolidge
Franklin. P. Burnham, architect
Private residence

1897. EASTOVER. Lake Forest residence of architect
Charles S. Frost
Private residence

[298]

PORTFOLIO

1897. Evanston residence of Allis-Chalmers Co. assistant manager Charles M. Howe
Pond and Pond, architects
Private residence

1897. WOODLEIGH. Lake Forest residence of architect Alfred Granger
Private residence

1897. Evanston duplex residence of Catherine White, widow of attorney Hugh A. White
Myron Hunt, architect
Private residences

1899. WESTLEIGH FARMS. Lake Forest estate of meatpacking magnate Louis F. Swift
William Carbys Zimmerman, architect
Private residence

c. 1900 MIRALAGO. Highland Park residence of baking company executive George Everhardt
Architect unknown
Offices

1904. Kenilworth residence of attorney Francis Lackner
George W. Maher, architect
Private residence

[299]

PORTFOLIO

1906. Lake Forest residence of attorney
Charles Garfield King
Howard Van Doren Shaw, architect
Private residence

1907. Evanston residence of patent attorney
Charles C. Linthicum
Tallmadge and Watson, architects
Private residence

1907. Winnetka residence of paper-box businessman
Henry W. Schultz
George W. Maher, architect
Private residence

1909. Wilmette residence of chemist and businessman
Frank J. Baker
Frank Lloyd Wright, architect
Private residence

1911. Evanston residence of corset stay manufacturer
Edward Kirk Warren
William Carbys Zimmerman, architect
Private residence

1910. Lake Forest estate of meatpacking magnate
Laurence Armour
Albro and Lindeberg, architects; later addition by
David Adler
Private residence

[300]

PORTFOLIO

1910. Evanston residence of real estate and insurance executive Frederick B. Carter
Walter Burley Griffin, architect
Private residence

1911. Glencoe residence of hat manufacturer Charles A. Stonehill
David Adler, architect
Demolished

1911. Glencoe residence of liquor wholesaler and distiller Charles H. Hermann
Howard Van Doren Shaw, architect
Private residence

1912. Lake Forest residence of steel manufacturer Clayton Mark
Howard Van Doren Shaw, architect
Remodeled (wing removed)
Private residence

1913 Highland Park residence of merchant tailor Alexander H. Stewart
Robert Seyfarth, architect
Private residence

1915. Wilmette residence of engraver Alfred Bersbach
John Van Bergen, architect
Private residence

PORTFOLIO

1916. Winnetka residence of attorney and politician
Harold L. Ickes
Perkins, Fellows and Hamilton, architects
Private residence

1916. BAGATELLE. Lake Forest estate of city planner
Edward H. Bennett
Edward H. Bennett, architect
Private residence

1918. Highland Park residence of automobile repair
business owner Arthur G. McPherson
Robert Seyfarth, architect
Private residence

1921. Glencoe residence of wholesale milliner
Jesse Strauss
David Adler, architect
Private residence

1922 Winnetka residence of architect
Spencer S. Beman
Private residence

1922. Winnetka residence of real estate executive
Buckingham Chandler
Spencer S. Beman, architect
Private residence

[302]

PORTFOLIO

1924. Lake Forest estate of steel manufacturer
Robert P. Lamont
Howard Van Doren Shaw, architect
Private residence

1928. Evanston residence of lingerie manufacturer
Harold N. Selling
Mayo and Mayo, architects
Private residence

1928. Lake Forest residence of investment broker
Robert A. Gardner
Harrie T. Lindeberg, architect
Private residence

1928 (remodeling). Evanston residence of grain broker
Robert W. McKinnon
Mayo and Mayo, architects; Remodeling of c. 1870
Luther Greenleaf house
Private residence

1928. Lake Forest residence of bank president
James R. Leavell
Anderson and Ticknor, architects
Private residence

1929. Winnetka residence of real estate broker
Walter O. Wilson
Edwin H. Clark, architect
Private residence

Portfolio

1929. Winnetka residence of dancer Ruth Page
Howard Fisher, General Houses, Inc., architect
Demolished

1930. Highland Park residence of architect Henry Dubin
Private residence

1930. Lake Forest residence of architect
Ralph Milman
Private residence

1932. Lake Forest residence of scale manufacturer
Robert Hosmer Morse
Zimmerman, Saxe and Zimmerman, architects
Private residence

1935. Lake Forest residence of
William B. McIlvaine, Jr.
Stanley Anderson, architect
Private residence

1938. Lake Bluff residence of architect Philip Maher
Demolished

Architects' Biographies

David Adler
(1882–1949)

David Adler devoted his practice almost exclusively to the design of houses for elite members of Chicago society. Among his clients, Adler counted Mr. and Mrs. Joseph Ryerson (steel), Mr. and Mrs. Albert Lasker (advertising), Mr. and Mrs. William McCormick Blair (finance), and Mr. and Mrs. Lester Armour (meatpacking). The society editor of the *Chicago Daily News* wrote in 1971 that, "as status symbols go, a David Adler house makes a Rolls Royce look like a dime-store purchase." Most of Adler's residences were located along Chicago's North Shore, especially in Lake Forest, but he also built at least a dozen houses elsewhere in the country. His non-Chicago commissions included: an apartment for Mr. and Mrs. Marshall Field III in Manhattan (demolished); a home for Mrs. Diego Suarez (Evelyn Field), the former Mrs. Marshall Field III, on Long Island, New York; homes for Richard T. Crane in Ipswich, Massachusetts, and on Jekyll Island in Georgia; a house for Stanley Field in Sarasota, Florida; and one for Walter Dillingham in Honolulu.

Adler was born in 1882 in Milwaukee, the son of a wealthy German-Jewish clothing manufacturer. After graduating from Princeton University in 1904, Adler studied architecture at both the Polytechnic University in Munich and the Ecole des Beaux-Arts in Paris. From Paris, Adler toured Europe, collecting hundreds of postcards, which along with his collection of photographs, newspaper and magazine clippings, and books served as important sources of inspiration. Returning to Chicago in 1911, Adler went to work in the office of Howard Van Doren Shaw, a leading architect of country houses for the wealthy. A year later, Adler formed a partnership with Henry C. Dangler, a friend from the Ecole des Beaux-Arts who was also working for Shaw. After Dangler's sudden death in 1917, Adler took Robert Work, another colleague from Shaw's office, as a partner. Work had been Shaw's first employee in his Hyde Park office in Chicago. Adler never passed the Illinois state architectural licensing exam, and both Dangler and Work, in addition to being licensed and able to sign drawings, brought their technical expertise to his projects. After Dangler's death, Adler again failed the state exam in 1917, receiving one of the lowest scores ever recorded. Asked to size the diagonal web members in a steel truss, Adler is said to have answered, "I have people in my office that attend to such matters." In 1928, with an impressive array of recommendations from clients as well as fellow architects, the examining board granted him a license. Once licensed, he never again had a partner.

Like New York architect Stanford White, Adler traveled to Europe regularly, collecting architectural details, wood paneling, parquet floors, and occasionally, entire rooms for his clients. He often collaborated with his sister Frances Elkins, who became a leading interior decorator. Drawing upon her relationships with Europe's most avant-garde designers—Jean Michel Frank, Alberto and Diego Giacometti, and others—Elkins introduced her own sophisticated brand of chic into Adler's later houses. After his death, the *Chicago Tribune* described Adler as "a residential architect of great distinction whose taste in the decorative arts was unequalled in his time."

STANLEY D. ANDERSON
(1895–1960)

Stanley D. Anderson was born in Lake Forest, and earned a bachelor's degree from Lake Forest College in 1916. He studied architecture and engineering at the University of Illinois and the Atelier Laloux at the Sorbonne. Serving in the armed forces during World War I, he was stationed in France. Following the war, Anderson traveled through France and England, and having gained considerable exposure to historical European architecture, he returned to Chicago in 1920. He spent six years in the office of Howard Van Doren Shaw, Chicago's foremost architect of country houses. In 1921, Anderson and James Ticknor, who was to be his partner for 20 years, spent a summer studying under renowned Beaux-Arts architect Paul Cret at the University of Pennsylvania. Between 1919 and 1925, Anderson was given a considerable amount of responsibility in Shaw's office. Paul Bergmann, curator of the Stanley D. Anderson Archives, points out that Anderson served as chief draftsman, supervised all of Shaw's construction in Lake Forest, and finished much of Shaw's work after his death in 1926.

When Anderson and Ticknor opened their practice after Shaw's death, several of Shaw's draftsmen went to work for them. During the years that Anderson and Ticknor practiced together, the firm designed many country houses and gentlemen's farms, as well as some 30 public and commercial buildings in Lake Forest and Lake Bluff, including Lake Forest High School, Lake Forest Hospital, and the old First National Bank Building. They also designed many residences in other North Shore suburbs.

After Anderson and Ticknor parted company in 1945, the firm became Stanley D. Anderson and Associates, with William Bergmann serving as his partner until Anderson's death in 1960. Although he worked in a variety of architectural styles throughout his career, he was known for his English Georgian–style architecture.

SOLON SPENCER BEMAN
(1853–1914)

Solon Spencer Beman was born in Brooklyn, New York, in 1853. His father was a roofer with an interest in architecture. In 1870, after completing elementary and secondary school, Beman went to work for the well-known New York architect Richard Upjohn. He remained in Upjohn's office until 1877, when he opened his own practice in New York City. In 1879, Beman moved from New York to Chicago with the commission to remodel George Pullman's mansion on Prairie Avenue, then Chicago's most fashionable residential street. Pullman, who had a house in Long Beach, New Jersey, met Beman through Nathan Barrett, who had landscaped Pullman's New Jersey property. At the same time, Pullman asked Beman to expand his manufacturing facilities and to design a company town. This was his first major commission, and remains his most significant work. The town of Pullman, built over a number of years, contained factories, an administration building, commercial and residential buildings, a hotel, a market hall, an arcade building, a steam power plant, and a water tower. By 1879, the town of Pullman was nearly complete and brought national recognition to Beman. This led to the commission in Cincinnati to rebuild the Procter and Gamble factory, which had burned down. Beman also designed Ivorydale, a company town named after the soap, for Procter and Gamble. Ivorydale was only partially completed when, in 1889, plans for housing were set aside. In 1890, Beman built the Grand Central Station for the Chicago and Northern Pacific Railway. Three years later, in 1893, when the World's Columbian Exposition opened in Chicago, Beman's Mines and Mining Building and his smaller Merchants' Tailors Building, were among the few designed by Chicago architects. Henry Ives Cobb, Louis Sullivan, and Daniel H. Burnham also designed major buildings for the fair. After 1899, Beman's architectural practice consisted primarily of luxury residences, apartment buildings, commercial and industrial projects, including commissions for the Studebaker automobile company and the Pabst Breweries. Beman's Fine Arts Building, originally the Studebaker Building, is a skyscraper with a theater on the ground floor. Built in 1885, it remains standing on South Michigan Avenue.

SPENCER SOLON BEMAN
(1887–1952)

Spencer Solon Beman was the son of Solon Spencer Beman, the architect responsible for the design of Pullman, a planned company town for railroad car manufacturer, George Pullman. The younger Beman was born in Chicago and educated at Oxford University in England and the University of Michigan. Beman opened his own architectural practice in 1914, building primarily houses and churches. He was a Christian Scientist, like his father, and took over his father's ecclesiastical work, designing and building 80 Christian Science churches in his lifetime. A resident of Winnetka, Beman built houses there, as well as elsewhere on the North Shore. His best-known houses were picturesque interpretations of the Tudor and the Jacobean styles popular on the North Shore during the 1920s, with steeply pitched roofs, dormers, towers, and garden walls that extended the footprint of the house.

EDWARD H. BENNETT
(1874–1954)

Edward H. Bennett is best known for his collaboration with Daniel H. Burnham and his co-authorship with Burnham of the 1909 Plan of Chicago. Born in Bristol, England, the young Bennett moved with his family to San Francisco after his father decided to become a rancher in California. He worked for Robert White, a residential architect, and became friendly with the famous architect Bernard Maybeck, who encouraged him to study at the Ecole des Beaux-Arts in Paris. After the Ecole, he worked for George B. Post, a prominent New York architect. Post had worked with Daniel Burnham on the 1893 Chicago World's Columbian Exposition and "loaned" Bennett to Burnham to work on the planning of the United States Military Academy at West Point. Pierce Anderson, Burnham's chief designer and Bennett's best friend at the Ecole, had recommended Bennett for the job. In 1903, Bennett was invited by Burnham to move to Chicago to work with him on the plan for San Francisco, then the plan of Chicago.

After Burnham's death in 1912, Bennett remained in Chicago and practiced architecture and planning in partnership with William E. Parsons and Harry T. Frost. Bennett was a consultant to the Chicago Plan Commission until 1930. He developed plans for a number of American cities, and was the planning architect for the 1933–34 Century of Progress Exposition in Chicago. He also designed a plan for the North Shore suburb of Winnetka. Bennett was a resident of Lake Forest where he built his home known as Bagatelle — a French name, he said, that Americans would not mispronounce. Bagatelle was built as an interpretation of the Chateau Bagatelle in the Bois de Boulogne in Paris.

WILLIAM W. BOYINGTON
(1839–1898)

W. W. Boyington, as he was known, was born in Springfield, Massachusetts, and studied architecture in New York. He came to Chicago as a young man and established an active practice in the city prior to the fire of 1871 that destroyed 18,000 buildings and most of Chicago's business district. Today he is best known in Chicago as the architect of The Chicago Water Tower and Pumping Station, two of only a few remaining pre-fire buildings. Boyington built the old Central Union Depot, a number of churches, hotels, and other buildings, including the observatory at the University of Chicago. After the fire, Boyington took an active role in the reconstruction of the city, including the rebuilding of many of his early buildings that had been destroyed. According to Michael Ebner in *Creating Chicago's North Shore: A Suburban History* (1988), Boyington was regarded by his contemporaries as Chicago's answer to London's Sir Christopher Wren—a comparison most likely based on Wren's role in the rebuilding of London after the fire of 1666. Boyington was the architect of the original 1848 Chicago Board of Trade Building, whose tower rose at the foot of LaSalle Street. The tower began sinking shortly after completion and was removed, with the rest of the building being demolished in the 1920s to make way for the much larger and more imposing Board of Trade Building, Holabird and Roche's Art Deco masterpiece, which stands on the site today. Boyington built a house for himself in the suburb of Highland Park. Active in local politics he was elected mayor of that suburb in 1874.

DANIEL HUDSON BURNHAM
(1846–1912)

Daniel H. Burnham is best remembered as the planner of the 1893 World's Columbian Exposition in Chicago, his work as a city planner who prepared plans for Chicago, Washington, D.C., Cleveland, San Francisco, and Manila, and for his famous adage: "Make no little plans, they have no magic to stir men's blood." Burnham was the first corporate architect to practice architecture on the scale of big business. According to Chicago architect Louis Sullivan, Burnham said he was "not going to stay satisfied with houses; my idea is to work up a big business, to handle big things, deal with big businessmen, and to build up a big organization."

Burnham was born in Henderson, New York, and moved with his family to Chicago in 1854. He showed artistic talent early on, but failed to pass the entry exams at both Harvard and Yale universities. Because of his son's interest in architecture, Burnham's father arranged an apprenticeship for him in the office of William Le Baron Jenney, the designer of Chicago's first metal-frame skyscraper. Burnham later worked for Carter Drake and Wight, under Peter B. Wight, who Burnham regarded as a mentor. Wight, who moved to Chicago from New York the year of the Chicago fire, was the architect of the National Academy of Design and of Street Hall at Yale University. He also authored numerous writings on Chicago architecture.

In Wight's office, Burnham met John Wellborn Root, with whom he formed a partnership that lasted until Root's premature death in 1891. Burnham and Root received their first commission from John B. Sherman, whose wealth came from the Chicago Stockyards. Burnham married Sherman's daughter, which led to important social connections and numerous residential, small commercial, and train station commissions throughout the Midwest. In the 1890s and 1900s, the firm built iron- and steel-frame office buildings that were among the world's first skyscrapers. Most important of these tall buildings were the Monadnock Building in Chicago, the Rookery and Reliance buildings, also in Chicago, and the Flat Iron Building in New York. The Reliance Building, which Root had begun work on, was finished by Charles Atwood after Root's death. After the 1893 world's fair, Daniel H. Burnham and Company embraced Beaux-Arts classicism in important commissions such as Union Station in Washington, D.C. The White City of Burnham's World's Columbian Exposition was the impetus for and chief influence on the City Beautiful movement of American urban design from the turn of the century through the 1920s. Burnham lived in Evanston, a town he described as the "most beautiful suburb in the world."

FRANKLIN PIERCE BURNHAM
(1853–1909)

Franklin Pierce Burnham—no relation to Daniel H. Burnham—was born at Rockford, Illinois, son of a builder. He moved to Chicago with his parents in 1860, and was trained in various Chicago architecture offices, including the firm of J. H. Barrows, for whom he went to work at the age of 14. Burnham is remembered as having been the chief architect for the Kenilworth Company. Hired by Joseph Sears, who developed the suburb of Kenilworth in 1890, Burnham designed the Kenilworth train station, Kenilworth Union Church, and a number of private residences there and elsewhere along the North Shore. He was in partnership with Willoughby J. Edbrooke (1843–1896) from 1879 until 1892, when Edbrooke was appointed supervising architect of the U.S. Treasury. Burnham had acted as the firm's principal designer. During this period, Edbrooke and Burnham won the national competition to design the Georgia State Capitol in Atlanta. They were also responsible for several opera houses, churches, and buildings at Notre Dame University. In *Joseph Sears and his Kenilworth* (1969), Colleen Browne Kilner suggests that Franklin Burnham was a young assistant working for Daniel H. Burnham, and that Burnham recommended him to his friend Sears to design his house. This story seems unlikely, as the dates of Franklin Burnham's partnership with Edbrooke are well documented, and he would have been working with Edbrooke at the time he designed the Sears house. In 1899, he left Kenilworth, where he had built a wonderful stone-and-wood Shingle Style house overlooking Lake Michigan, to establish an architectural practice in Los Angeles.

Edwin Hill Clark
(1878–1967)

Edwin H. Clark was born and educated in Chicago, where his father was a successful businessman. He was an early member of the Chicago Board of Trade, then owner of a paint manufacturing company. Clark graduated from Yale in 1900 and worked with his father's business from 1900 to 1906, when he took a job with Chicago architect William Otis as a beginning draftsman. A year later, the two formed a partnership, and the firm became Otis and Clark. They worked together until 1920, when Clark opened an office with Chester Walcott, establishing the firm of Clark and Walcott. This practice was to last until 1924. Except for a few brief stints with other partners, Clark worked alone for the balance of his career.

Clark designed many handsome North Shore residences, including two homes for himself in Winnetka, where he lived 35 years. However, he is best remembered for larger commercial and municipal commissions, including the Winnetka Village Hall (1926) and the Municipal Building (1925) in Hinsdale, Illinois. On the North Shore he also designed the prestigious Indian Hill Country Club in Winnetka, several buildings on the campus of North Shore Country Day School, also in Winnetka, and in 1926, Wilmette's Plaza del Lago, a very early shopping center designed to accommodate the automobile. His prestigious Chicago commissions included the Municipal Tuberculosis Sanitarium (1915), the Brookfield Zoo (1934) and several structures for the Chicago Park District.

Henry Ives Cobb
(1859–1931)

Born in Brookline, Massachusetts, Henry Ives Cobb graduated from the Lawrence Scientific School at Harvard and then studied architecture at the Massachusetts Institute of Technology. After a year spent traveling in Europe, Cobb worked in Boston for Peabody and Stearns, whose residential work was influenced by the Shingle Style made popular by H. H. Richardson and McKim, Mead, and White. While working in the office of Peabody and Stearns, Cobb won a competition to design the Union Club in Chicago. In 1882, he moved to Chicago to complete the commission, forming a partnership with Charles Sumner Frost (1856–1931), an MIT graduate who had also worked for Peabody and Stearns and had moved to Chicago the year before. Cobb and Frost designed such important Chicago buildings as the Newberry Library, the old Chicago Historical Society building (a Richardsonian stone structure that still stands at the corner of Dearborn and Ontario Streets), the Chicago Athletic Club, and the old Post Office building. In 1887, Cobb, working with Frost, designed the shingle and stone First Presbyterian Church in the suburb of Lake Forest, where he also designed Ferry Hall for Lake Forest University. In 1893, the same year Cobb built the fisheries and horticulture buildings for the World's Columbian Exposition, his new house in Lake Forest was completed. Frederick Law Olmsted, who was in Chicago working on the fair grounds, designed its landscaping and grounds. Cobb's farm and farmhouse became the grounds and clubhouse for the Onwentsia Club. Among Cobb's significant Chicago commissions were his buildings for the University of Chicago and his mansion for Potter Palmer. In 1898 Cobb ended his partnership with Charles Frost, who later formed the firm of Frost and Granger. Elected a Fellow of the American Institute of Architects in 1889, Cobb moved to New York, where he practiced until his death in 1931.

William Adams Delano
(1874–1960)
•
Chester Holmes Aldrich
(1871–1940)

William Adams Delano and Chester Holmes Aldrich were noted society architects whose Long Island country houses for wealthy clients such as John D. Rockefeller, and the Astor, Vanderbilt, and the Whitney families brought national recognition to their firm. Delano had a degree from Yale University, and then studied architecture at Columbia University and the Ecole des Beaux-Arts in Paris. Aldrich followed the same path, studying architecture at Columbia and then at the Ecole. The two met while working at the firm of Carrère and Hastings in New York, and started their own practice in 1903. Delano taught architecture at Columbia University between 1903 and 1910, and was elected a Fellow of the American Institute of Architects in 1912. From 1924 to 1928 he served on the Fine Arts Commission's oversight committee for the architecture and planning of Washington D. C., and on the advisory committee for the design of the Federal Triangle. Delano and Aldrich received the commission to design the new post office building. Delano's work in Washington also included remodeling projects at the White House under presidents Coolidge and Truman. In 1953 he received the American Institute of Architects' Gold Medal, the highest recognition the AIA confers. Aldrich also taught architecture at Columbia University and in 1935 he was made director of the American Academy in Rome, where he died in 1940. By 1935, the firm had built 111 country houses, 32 of which were on Long Island. Delano and Aldrich also designed public, commercial, and religious buildings, including buildings at Yale University and Smith College. Both partners were very social and were members of many of New York's elite city clubs. They designed buildings for the Knickerbocker, Colony, and Union clubs of New York. The firm designed only two residences in the Chicago area, one in Lake Bluff and Fairlawn in Lake Forest.

Henry Dubin
(1892–1963)

Henry Dubin was born in Chicago. He studied architecture at the University of Illinois, which had one of the first schools of architecture in the country. Graduating in 1915, Dubin received the Plym Fellowship, which allowed him to travel extensively throughout Europe. Returning to Chicago, Dubin went to work in his brother's architectural firm, Dubin and Eisenberg. He built an award-winning International Style modern house for himself and his family in Highland Park. Known as the "battledeck" house, it was built with a floor structure of steel beams and welded-steel plates like a ship. In 1932 the firm became Dubin and Dubin, and continued to build houses on the North Shore. Later renamed Dubin, Dubin, Black, and Moutoussamy, the firm expanded to build apartment buildings, college dormitories, industrial buildings, and train stations. Today, architects from the third generation of the family run the firm of Dubin, Dubin, and Moutoussamy.

Henry Edwards-Ficken
(c.1844–1929)

Henry Edwards-Ficken was born in London, educated in Scotland, and studied art in Europe before coming to New York in 1869. He first received recognition as an architectural renderer, and worked for the firms of Potter and Robinson, McKim, Mead, and Bigelow, and Charles Gambrill (who was briefly in partnership with H. H. Richardson), before opening his own office in 1883. Edwards-Ficken had been a champion athlete, winning the high jump in the U.S. Men's Outdoor Track and Field Championships of 1876, 1877, and 1878, and 120-yard hurdle races in 1877 and 1878. Selected as the architect for the New York Athletic Club's new building, he won a well-publicized legal suit over his fees when he was fired from the job. He married into New York society, which would be the source of many of his commissions. He designed residential, commercial, and institutional buildings, including the Ferguson Memorial Building in Stamford, Connecticut, the town hall in Birmingham, Connecticut, and the Stone Trust Association in New Haven, Connecticut. In 1913, Edwards-Ficken became the supervising architect for Woodlawn Cemetery in New York.

Howard Taylor Fisher
(1903–1979)

Howard T. Fisher was an important pioneer in the field of prefabricated housing in America. He was born and educated in Winnetka, Illinois, and attended Harvard University, where he studied architecture. Fisher came from a prominent Chicago family. His father Walter Lowrie Fisher, a lawyer, was secretary of the interior under President William Howard Taft. His brother Walter was a well-known attorney and president of the Amalgamated Trust and Savings Bank. The modern brick house Fisher designed for his brother Walter while he was still a student at Harvard gained national attention. In 1932, Fisher founded General Houses, Inc., a company that designed metal prefabricated houses. He believed that, rather than producing a standardized house like Ford's Model T automobile, custom designs could be assembled in great variety from standardized parts. He successfully enlisted the support of industry and big business in manufacturing house components.

Fisher's first prefabricated house was for another family member, his sister-in-law, the dancer Ruth Page. His company also built a model prefabricated house for the 1933–34 Century of Progress International Exposition in Chicago. In 1935, Fisher designed prefabricated houses for Sears, Roebuck, and Co., which had historically sold pre-cut houses. Fisher's company successfully designed and built houses during the Great Depression when other architects were without work. When World War II created a steel shortage, General Houses developed designs for prefabricated wood houses. In 1940, Fisher left his company to go to Washington to work for the National Housing Agency. In the late 1940s, he returned to Chicago to practice architecture. Fisher taught urban and regional planning at Northwestern University between 1957 and 1964, developing SYMAP, a computer program for statistical mapping. In 1965, Fisher was appointed professor of city and regional planning at Harvard University, and later became founding director of Harvard's Laboratory for Computer Graphics. He retired from teaching in 1974.

CHARLES SUMNER FROST
(1856–1931)

Charles Sumner Frost was born in Lewistown, Maine, and worked for his father, who was a builder, lumber merchant, and owner of a lumber mill. He apprenticed for an architect in Lewistown briefly before attending the Massachusetts Institute of Technology, from which he graduated in 1876. He worked in Boston for Peabody and Stearns until 1881, and then moved to Chicago. He entered into practice with Henry Ives Cobb, with whom he had worked at Peabody and Stearns. Cobb and Frost practiced successfully together until 1898, when Cobb moved to New York. Frost then formed a partnership with Alfred Granger. Known primarily for their design of railroad stations, their commissions included the passenger terminal of the Chicago and North Western Railway as well as stations in St. Paul, Minnesota, and Omaha, Nebraska. Frost and Granger also built the office building for the Chicago and North Western. The president of the railway had three daughters—one was married to Charles Frost and another married Alfred Granger. Along with the third sister and her husband, Frost and Granger and their families lived in three adjacent houses in Lake Forest. Frost designed his own house, a brick Georgian, and next to it, Granger designed two houses in Tudor and Georgian styles, one for himself and one for his sister-in-law. As prominent Lake Forest residents, Frost and Granger built the local Church of the Holy Spirit. They also built St. Luke's Hospital and the Memorial Hospital for Infectious Diseases, both in Chicago. Frost designed Chicago's Navy Pier in 1916. Originally a member of the Western Association of Architects that merged with the American Institute of Architects, Frost was elected a Fellow of the AIA in 1889.

PHILIP LIPPINCOTT GOODWIN
(1885–1958)

Philip L. Goodwin is listed as the co-designer, along with Edward Durell Stone, of the original building for the Museum of Modern Art in New York (1939). Born in New York, Goodwin graduated from Yale University and studied architecture at Columbia University before spending a year studying in Paris (1914–15). On his return to the United States, he worked for New York country house architects, Delano and Aldrich, before forming the partnership Goodwin, Bullard, and Woolsey. After 1921, and until his retirement in 1953, he practiced independently. In addition to country houses and the Museum of Modern Art in New York, Goodwin designed the Christ Church Parish House in Hartford, Connecticut. He was a collector of modern art and served on the board of directors of the Museum of Modern Art. Goodwin was a Fellow of the American Institute of Architects and author of several books including one on French provincial architecture, a style that influenced designs for some of his early houses.

ALFRED HOYT GRANGER
(1867–1939)

Alfred H. Granger was born in Zanesville, Ohio, and attended Kenyon College. He studied architecture at the Massachusetts Institute of Technology, graduating in 1887, and then at the Ecole des Beaux-Arts. Returning from Paris, Granger went to work in the Boston office of Shepley, Rutan, and Coolidge, the successors to H. H. Richardson. While he was working on the firm's commissions for the Chicago Public Library and the Art Institute of Chicago, Granger was sent to Chicago to supervise construction. Remaining there, he formed a partnership with Frank B. Meade for four years before going into partnership with Charles S. Frost. Granger's partnership with Frost ended in 1910, when he moved to Philadelphia, where he practiced briefly. Returning to Chicago in 1924, he established the firm of Granger, Lowe, and Bollenbacher that later became

Granger and Bollenbacher. The firm designed the medical and dental building for the University of Illinois at Chicago, Pierce Hall at Kenyon College, and the administration and student union building at the University of Indiana. In 1922, Granger chaired the jury for the international competition for a new administration building for the *Chicago Tribune*. In 1933, Granger wrote *Chicago Welcomes You*, a guidebook to the city written for visitors to the Century of Progess world's fair. Like his former partner Frost, Granger was active in the American Institute of Architects, serving as president of the Chicago chapter. He was elected a Fellow of the AIA in 1926.

ARTHUR HEUN
(1866–1946)

Born in Saginaw, Michigan, Arthur Heun began his career in architecture as an apprentice to his uncle, Volusin Bude, who practiced architecture in Grand Rapids. Heun moved to Chicago at the age of 21, and went to work for Francis Whitehouse, a residential architect who counted among his clients such prominent Chicagoans as General A. C. McClurg. When Whitehouse retired in 1893, Heun took over his practice. He could have known Barbara Armour, one of Whitehouse's clients, and this may have been his introduction to J. Ogden Armour, for whom he later designed Mellody Farm in Lake Forest (1908). Heun had an office in Dwight Perkins' Steinway Hall (1905) on the floor below the studio shared by Walter Burley Griffin, Robert Spencer, Horace Powers, Henry Tomlinson, William Drummond, and Allen and Irving Pond. Heun was included in the "18," a dining club of Chicago's "young Turks" who met monthly to discuss architecture. In addition to residences, Heun designed the Casino Club in Chicago.

WILLIAM HOLABIRD
(1854–1923)
•
MARTIN ROCHE
(1855–1927)

William Holabird was born in Dutchess County, New York, the son of Samuel Beckley Holabird, an Army general. In 1873, young Holabird entered West Point and studied engineering, but resigned from the academy in 1875. Moving to Chicago, Holabird worked part-time in the office of the Army quartermaster general before taking a job with the Chicago architect William Le Baron Jenney. In Jenney's office he met Ossian Cole Simonds, with whom he would form a partnership in 1880. Also working for Jenney at the time was Martin Roche, who joined Holabird and Simonds in their practice in 1881. Roche became the firm's designer, since both Holabird and Simonds had engineering backgrounds. In 1883, Simonds left the partnership to pursue a career as a landscape architect, and the firm became Holabird and Roche.

Martin Roche was born in Cleveland, Ohio, in 1855. His family moved to Chicago in 1857. After elementary and high school, Roche attended the School of the Chicago Art Institute, and in 1867 took an apprenticeship with a cabinetmaker. In 1872 he began his architectural career, working for Jenney until he left to form a partnership with William Holabird. During their early years, the firm had so few commissions that Roche took assignments designing furniture for local manufacturers to help keep their business afloat. In 1885, Holabird and Roche built a two-story apartment building with ground-floor shops. Shortly thereafter, in the late 1880s when his father was quartermaster general, William and his partner received the commission for Fort Sheridan, the job that was to launch their career. At roughly the same time, they received the commission for the Tacoma Building (1889), the firm's first office building in the Loop. By the 1890s, Holabird and Roche had almost 40 employees and by 1910, over 100, becoming famous for their skyscraper designs and for inventing the "Chicago Window," the grouping of a large fixed pane with two side windows for ventilation. By the 1950s, their design became known as the "picture window" and was found in ranch houses everywhere.

William Holabird moved to Evanston in the 1880s, where he built a house for himself. The firm designed a number of houses in that suburb along with the Evanston City Hall (demolished) and Fayerweather Hall at Northwestern University (demolished).

JARVIS HUNT
(1859–1941)

Jarvis Hunt was the nephew of Richard Morris Hunt, the New York architect who was instrumental in instituting the Beaux-Arts method of studio education for architects in the United States. Hunt was born in Wethersfield,

Vermont, and attended Harvard University before studying architecture at the Massachusetts Institute of Technology. In 1893 he was sent to Chicago to supervise the construction of the Vermont State Building at the World's Columbian Exposition. He remained there, practicing successfully for the next 35 years before retiring to St. Petersburg, Florida. In addition to a number of distinguished residences, Hunt was the architect of the original buildings at the Great Lakes Naval Training Station, railroad stations in Kansas City, Dallas, and Joliet, Illinois, the Newark Museum in Newark, New Jersey, the 900 North Michigan Avenue building (demolished), and the Lake Shore Athletic Club.

JENS JENSEN
(1860–1951)

Jens Jensen was born outside the village of Dybbol in the Danish province of Slesvig, Denmark, and attended Tune Agricultural School near Copenhagen. He came to the United States in 1884 and worked initially as a gardener for Chicago's West Park System. Rising through the ranks, he became Superintendent and Landscape Architect in 1905. In that capacity he was responsible for the redesign of Humboldt, Garfield, and Douglas Parks. Jensen's work in 1901-2 surveying lands surrounding Chicago led to the founding of the Cook County Forest Preserve. During those years he acquired his first private clients, Harry Rubens and Hermann Paepcke in Glencoe. Like Frederick Law Olmsted, Jensen used native plants, grasses, weeds and wildflowers to produce natural-looking landscapes. But, unlike Olmsted, Jensen's inspiration was the flat Midwestern prairie, and in his park designs for Chicago and in his landscapes for private clients, he created prairie meadows and planted simulated prairie rivers with native wetland plants. A unique feature of Jensen's landscapes was the council ring, comprised of low, circular stone seating intended to accommodate outdoor social gatherings, musical and dramatic performances. From the early 1900s until 1935, when he left his Highland Park studio for the Clearing in Door County, Wisconsin, Jensen created landscaped settings for many important estate houses on the North Shore. His natural looking landscapes, as opposed to formal gardens, worked well with Prairie Style architecture, but also with popular English revival styles. In prestige, Jens Jensen is the Midwest's counterpart to Frederick Law Olmsted in the history of American landscape architecture.

GEORGE FRED KECK
(1895–1980)

George Fred Keck was famous for his modern houses, innovative construction, and interest in solar heating and evaporative cooling. Keck was born in Watertown, Wisconsin, and educated at the University of Illinois, where he studied architectural engineering. After graduating, he worked for D. H. Burnham and Company, and for Schmidt, Garden, and Martin. Keck taught at the University of Illinois from 1923 to 1924, and opened his own architectural practice in 1926. His Miralago Ballroom, built in Wilmette in 1929 and razed after a fire three years later, was one of the first International Style buildings in the Chicago area.

In 1931, Keck's younger brother William joined the practice and the firm became Keck and Keck. Keck built two extraordinary exhibition houses at the 1933–34 Century of Progress International Exposition in Chicago. The first, an octagonal house, known as the House of Tomorrow, had a central core and floor-to-ceiling plate-glass windows influenced by the Dymaxion House designed by Keck's friend Buckminster Fuller, who lived in Chicago at the time. It featured a garage for a car and a small airplane. In 1934, Keck built the Crystal House, a unique house for its time and location, and largely ignored because it does not fit into the conventional histories of the development of 20th-century modern architecture. Keck's all-glass house had an external skeleton of truss columns and truss roof beams, like Mies van der Rohe's designs of the 1950s. The roof and floors were hung from the external structure. All the parts were pre-fabricated and the house was erected in three days.

In the mid-1930s, Keck built significant International Style houses in Wilmette and Lake Forest. that explored solar heating and sun screening. In the late 1930s, 1940s and 1950s his work was concerned with solar heating, sun screening, evaporative cooling, and energy efficiency. Keck designed numerous flat-roofed, wood, stone, and glass houses that were very much like the work Marcel Breuer was doing at the time. These were published regularly in shelter magazines and architectural journals.

Keck was a friend of Laszlo Moholy-Nagy, who had come to Chicago to open the new Bauhaus. Moholy-Nagy asked Keck to teach courses in architecture at the school that later became the Institute of Design at Illinois Institute of Technology (IIT) after Mies van der Rohe became head of the school of architecture. Keck also knew the critic Sigfried Giedion, who wrote in *Space, Time, and Architecture* (1941) that "nothing happened in Chicago between the deplorable 1893 World's Fair and the arrival of Mies van der Rohe in 1938." Giedion totally ignored Keck's contribution, and presented modernism as an exclusively European development.

HARRIE T. LINDEBERG
(1880–1959)

Harrie T. Lindeberg and his partner Lewis Colt Albro (1876–1924) were known nationally for their Long Island country houses. Lindeberg built over 100 houses during his long career, seven of them in Lake Forest where he received the locally prestigious commission to design the Onwentsia Club, completed in 1927. Lindeberg was born at Bergen Point, New Jersey. His parents had emigrated from Sweden and lived in Hoboken, where his father sold neckties. There is no indication that Lindeberg attended college. He did, however, apprentice with McKim Mead, and White from 1901 to 1906. He worked directly with Stanford White on the James L. Breese estate at Southampton, Long Island, a colonial revival house that was one of the firm's most influential residential designs. Lindeberg and Albro, who also worked for McKim, Mead, and White, left the firm in 1906 after Stanford White's murder, to open their own architectural practice in New York City. Lindeberg had few social connections. It was Lindeberg's wealthy partner Albro who supplied them with work. Very different in their design sensibilities, Albro was a classicist, while Lindeberg preferred to design in a picturesque English manner.

In 1914, Lindeberg, already established as one of the country's leading residential architects, parted from Albro. Lindeberg's first wife had died in 1906, and in 1914 he married Lucia Hull, who was related to one of his clients and had the social connections to help sustain his new practice. The critic Russell Whitehead observed in *Architectural Record* (April 1924) that Lindeberg invented or adapted, "more house motives which have become a general part of our architectural vocabulary than any other country house architect." Lindeberg designed houses in Massachusetts, Missouri, Ohio, Rhode Island, Tennessee and Texas as well as in Illinois and the New York area. His only public projects date from the 1930s, when he was commissioned by the United States government to design consulate buildings for Shanghai, Moscow, and Helsinki. These projects were interrupted by World War II and never completed.

GEORGE WASHINGTON MAHER
(1846–1926)

George Maher was born in Mill Creek, West Virginia. His family moved to New Albany, Indiana, and then to Chicago, but Maher's father could not find work. The young Maher had to support himself, and in 1878, at the age of 13, he went to work for the architectural firm of Bauer and Hill. He then worked for Joseph Lyman Silsbee, a fashionable residential architect who also employed Frank Lloyd Wright and George Grant Elmslie as draftsmen at the same time that Maher worked in the office. In 1889, Maher opened his own practice and was briefly in partnership with Charles Corwin. In 1893, Maher met J. L. Cochran, who was developing the northern suburb of Edgewater, later annexed to Chicago. Cochran hired him to design homes for Edgewater, which launched Maher's successful career as a residential architect. The following year, he built a house for himself in Kenilworth. There he was to build a number of houses as well as the Kenilworth Club—known originally as the Kenilworth Assembly Hall—and the Joseph Sears School (demolished). Maher also built the stone entrance pylons at the south end of Kenilworth that mark the entrance to Kenilworth along Sheridan Road and the fountain that defines the west end of the Kenilworth's central boulevard.

Maher received commissions for three particularly significant houses from Chicago businessmen— John Farson in Oak Park, James Patten in Evanston, and Harry Rubens in Glencoe. Because he designed not only the buildings themselves, but also the interior furnishings, art glass, and lighting fixtures, these three commissions were instrumental in securing larger projects for Maher. His client, James Patten, as head of the board of trustees of Evanston's Northwestern University, donated the money for a new gymnasium. The project went to Maher, along with a commission to design a new science building funded by the Swift meatpacking family. The last of Maher's large commercial commissions was the Winona Savings Bank (1915), the result of work he had done for the J. R. Watkins Medical Company of Winona, Minnesota.

Maher was active in the American Institute of Architects and elected a Fellow in 1916. He was instrumental in the civic group that was responsible for rebuilding Charles Atwood's (Daniel H. Burnham and Co.) Fine Arts Building from the 1893 World's Columbian Exposition, although the actual restoration was not planned until 1929, after Maher's death. The building was restored in 1934, and now houses Chicago's Museum of Science and Industry. Maher's son, Philip Brooks Maher, became an architect and joined his father's architectural practice in 1914.

Maher was concerned with the development of an indigenous American architectural expression. In "Originality in American Architecture," an article he published in *Inland Architect* (1887), Maher wrote: "No building has genuine style, which does not speak of the thought which first brought it into existence. Thus the true path toward an original style is to follow the dictation of necessity and then to improve upon detail." In the same essay, he admired the work of H. H. Richardson and praised shingled houses, perhaps reflecting the influence of his early work with Silsbee.

Philip Brooks Maher
(1894–1981)

Philip Maher practiced with his father, George Washington Maher, first in 1914. He then attended college, served in the army, and returned home, practicing with his father from 1921 to 1924 in the firm of George W. Maher & Son. In 1924 he established his own firm. The younger Maher, unlike his father, was not primarily a residential architect. Whereas most of his father's commissions were suburban, Philip Maher's reputation rested primarily on his urban projects, although he built the Glencoe Women's Club and a number of houses along the North Shore. Born in Kenilworth in 1894, Maher studied architecture at the University of Michigan and then traveled extensively in England, France, and Italy. Trained in the Beaux-Arts tradition, Philip may have been the designer of the Georgian houses done during the time he worked for his father.

Philip Maher's work in the late 1920s was influenced by the Art Deco movement, which can be seen in the stripped-down classicism of many of his designs for buildings along Chicago's North Michigan Avenue. These included the Farwell Building at 644 North Michigan. Other projects, now demolished, included the Decorative Arts Building at 620 North Michigan, the Jacques Shop at 900 North Michigan, the buildings at 545 and 669 North Michigan, as well as, the Blackstone Shop. Maher also designed the Woman's Athletic Club at 626 North Michigan Avenue, and 1260 and 1301 North Astor, the street's most sophisticated high-rise Art Deco style apartment houses. Maher was made a Fellow of the American Institute of Architects in 1940. Although he built a modern International-Style house for himself in Lake Bluff, at the time of his death Maher was living in his father's Kenilworth house where he grew up.

Benjamin Marshall
(1874–1944)

Handsome and charismatic, Benjamin Marshall was a self-made man. With no formal training or college education, he entered the architectural office of Marble and Wilson as a clerk at the age of 19. When Marble died two years later, Wilson made Marshall his partner. In 1902, Marshall established his own practice, and in 1905 formed a partnership with Charles E. Fox, who handled the firm's construction work. This partnership lasted until Fox died in 1926. Marshall built a studio residence in 1921, facing the Wilmette yacht harbor on Lake Michigan. Known as a bon vivant, Marshall became famous for his parties and important guests. He built hundreds of buildings in Chicago and across the country, including the South Shore Country Club in Chicago (1906), Chicago's Blackstone Theater (1910), the *Popular Mechanics* building and printing plant (1922) in Chicago, and from 1915 to 1937, fast food restaurants for Horn and Hardart in Chicago and for Thompson Restaurants of Houston. He designed both the Lake Shore Bank building (1921) and the Uptown Bank in Chicago. Marshall's most important commissions were for hotels and apartment buildings along Chicago Gold Coast. For many of these projects, Marshall was also an investor. Today, apartments in buildings he designed are prized as among the most luxurious and elegant in the city. Marshall's hotel commissions in Chicago included the Blackstone and the Drake, and the now demolished Edgewater Beach Hotel, a tropical fantasy in peach-colored stucco built on its own beach before the construction of Lake Shore Drive on landfill. In addition, he built mansions and country houses for many wealthy clients, among them, Samuel Insull of Chicago's Commonwealth Edison Company, which in the early 1900s supplied all of Chicago's electricity, and coal magnate Francis Stuyvesant Peabody.

SAMUEL ABRAHAM MARX
(1885–1964)

Although he was a talented architect, Samuel Marx was best known for his elegant interiors. The ultra-chic Pump Room (1938) at Chicago's Ambassador East Hotel and the Cotillion Room (1941) at the Pierre Hotel in New York City brought Marx national recognition. Educated at the Massachusetts Institute of Technology, he studied at the Ecole des Beaux-Arts in Paris until 1909. That same year he won a national competition to design the Delgado Museum of Art in New Orleans. In addition to many residences, Marx was the architect for the May Department Stores (1939) in Los Angeles, St. Louis, and Denver. He also designed stunning contemporary furniture for many of his interiors, examples of which are found in the collection of the Art Institute of Chicago. For the Pullman Company, Marx designed the first aluminum train car, which was exhibited at Chicago's 1933–34 Century of Progress International Exposition. Considered to be an accomplished artist, an entire room was devoted to his work for the 1945 international watercolor exhibition held at the Art Institute of Chicago. Marx later served as trustee and member of their board of directors and was a member of the advisory council of the Museum of Modern Art in New York.

ERNEST ALFRED MAYO
(1868–1946)
•
PETER B. MAYO
(1895–1976)

Ernest Mayo was born and educated in Birmingham, England, where he worked in the office of architect H. M. Townsend. He opened his own practice in South Africa, and became a member of the Royal Institute of British Architects. From South Africa he came to Chicago and worked as an architectural advisor for the construction division of the 1893 World's Columbian Exposition. Mayo subsequently opened an office in Chicago and built a thriving practice designing large houses. An Evanston resident, Mayo built 38 houses in that suburb alone. Peter B. Mayo graduated from Yale University in 1917, and the following year attended the Ecole d'Artillerie at Fontainebleau, France. He joined his father's architectural practice in 1918, and was later made a partner. Mayo and Mayo operated a highly successful firm designing many distinguished Tudor Revival, French Renaissance, and Arts and Crafts houses for wealthy North Shore professionals and businessmen.

DWIGHT H. PERKINS
(1867–1941)

Famous as a designer of schools, Perkins was architect for the Chicago Board of Education between 1905 and 1911, and was responsible for the design of 40 public schools. Many of these—including Carl Schurz High School (1908–10), Lyman Trumbull Elementary School (1909–10), and Grover Cleveland Elementary School (1911)—are important as the earliest institutional buildings reflecting the design principles of the Prairie School. Born in Memphis, Tennessee, Perkins studied architecture at the Massachusetts Institute of Technology. He taught at MIT, worked briefly for H. H. Richardson, and then moved to Chicago to apprentice first with Wheelock and Clay and then with Burnham and Root. Perkins managed Burnham's office while Burnham was busy with the 1893 World's Columbian Exposition. He opened his own office in 1894 in Chicago's Steinway Hall, which had been one of his first commissions. There he shared office space with a group of progressive young architects that included his friend Frank Lloyd Wright. Perkins first practiced in partnership with William Fellows and John Hamilton. After 1925, he practiced with Melvin Chatten and C. Herrick Hammond until he retired in 1933. A close friend of landscape architect Jens Jensen, Perkins was instrumental in establishing the West Park System for Chicago, and later the Commission of the Cook County Forest Preserve System. He served as chairman of the City Planning Commission of Chicago, the Municipal Art

Commission, and was honorary president of Chicago's Regional Planning Commission. Perkins also served on the Planning Commission of the Cook County Forest Preserves, and was president of the Northwest Park District of Evanston. In 1904, Perkins moved into a house he designed for himself in Evanston, with landscaping by Jens Jensen.

Frederick Wainwright Perkins
(1866–1928)

Frederick Perkins was born at Burlington, Wisconsin, and educated at the Massachusetts Institute of Technology and the Ecole des Beaux-Arts in Paris. He moved to Chicago in the 1880s, where he worked until he moved to Boston in 1920. Although a Boston resident, Perkins maintained an office in Chicago. Perhaps his most significant residential project was the mansion he built for Marshall Field & Company president John G. Shedd on Chicago's South Side in 1896. His North Shore residential designs included the Schweppe house for Shedd's daughter Laura (1915) and the second Finley Barrell house (1916), both in Lake Forest.

Charles Adams Platt
(1861–1933)

Recognized as one of America's foremost country house designers, Platt began his architectural career after achieving recognition first as an etcher and painter, and then as a landscape architect. He was born in Manhattan, where his father was a successful corporate lawyer. Showing little interest in an academic education, Platt decided as a boy that he would become an artist. He took classes at the National Academy of Design and at the Art Students League of New York. The artist Stephen Parrish introduced Platt to the art of etching, and his work soon received national attention. Interested in landscape painting, Platt left for Paris in 1882 to study at the Academie Julian. Returning to New York in 1887, he planned a trip to Italy with his younger brother William who was studying landscape architecture in the office of Frederick Law Olmsted. Believing William's training under Olmsted to be lacking in design principles, Platt decided that they should devote their trip to measuring, drawing, and photographing the formal gardens of the Italian Renaissance. In 1893, Platt wrote two articles about Italian gardens for Harper's Magazine reissued as a book the following year. This was the first book in English on Italian gardens, and the first to be illustrated with photographs rather than drawings. The book was a great success and led to commissions for Platt as a garden designer. He spent his summers in the artists' colony at Cornish, New Hampshire, where friends began asking him to design not only their gardens but also their houses. This led to his decision to practice architecture.

In addition to recommendations from his artist friends, including Augustus Saint-Gaudens, Platt's rapid rise to success as an architect was promoted by his friendship with two of the most important architectural critics of the time. Royal Cortissoz, art critic for the *New York Tribune* (later renamed *New York Herald-Tribune*), and Herbert Croly, editor of *Architectural Record* (who later became the first editor of *New Republic*) both reviewed his work in highly favorable terms. Platt had designed a house in Cornish for Croly. His designs set the standard for contemporary classical country houses. A monograph on his work published in 1913 became a standard reference in architectural offices, and young architects referred to it as "the bible." In addition to his houses and gardens, Platt was the architect of the Freer Art Gallery in Washington, D.C., and prepared a campus plan for the University of Illinois at Champaign-Urbana, where he designed nine buildings constructed between 1922 and 1930. Platt also developed a comprehensive plan and designed a number of buildings for the Phillips Exeter Academy at Andover, Massachusetts. Elected a Fellow of the American Institute of Architects, Platt retired from practice in 1928. That same year, he succeeded William R. Mead, of the architectural firm of McKim, Mead, and White, as head of the American Academy in Rome, a position he held until his death in 1933.

Irving Kane Pond
(1857–1939)

•

Allen Bartlit Pond
(1858–1929)

Although Irving and Allen Pond did many fashionable residences, they were best known for their association with Jane Addams' Hull House in Chicago and their interest in social reform. They designed 10 buildings over an 18-year period as additions to the original Hull House structure of

1856. Allen Pond served as secretary of Hull House from 1895 until his death. Born in Ann Arbor, Michigan, both brothers attended the University of Michigan. On graduating, Allen taught at Ann Arbor High School and Michigan State University. He also worked as an assistant to his father, who was warden at the Michigan State Prison at Jackson. Irving graduated with a degree in civil engineering, and worked in Chicago for William Le Baron Jenney. Irving then joined the office of Solon Spencer Beman, working on the design for the town of Pullman. The brothers formed a partnership in 1886 and practiced together until Allen's death in 1929. In Chicago, they built the Baptist Training School for Nurses, the City Club, and Presbyterian churches in Ravenswood and Hyde Park. They also designed buildings for several Midwestern universities including the student union buildings at the University of Michigan and Purdue University, as well as the campus buildings for Lake Forest University (1892-1894) later Lake Forest College. Both brothers were Fellows of the American Institute of Architects. Irving, who was active in the AIA, was elected national president in 1908, succeeding New York architect Cass Gilbert. He also wrote extensively about architecture for various journals, and in 1918, published *Meaning in Architecture*, a book on architectural theory.

RICHARD POWERS
(B. 1886)

Born in Cambridge, Massachusetts, Richard Powers attended George Washington University in Washington, D.C. With no formal architectural education, he trained in various architectural offices in Boston. When he became a member of the American Institute of Architects in 1927, he was living in Chicago and had been in practice for 12 years, including serving as a supervising architect of the Treasury.

JAMES GAMBLE ROGERS
(1867–1947)

James G. Rogers was born in 1867 at Bryant's Station, Kentucky, but grew up on the north side of Chicago. He earned a scholarship to Yale University, and after graduation, traveled through Europe as part of an American exhibition baseball team that introduced the sport to the continent. Returning to Chicago in 1889, he worked for William Le Baron Jenney, and then for Burnham and Root. This was his only architectural training before opening his own firm. He practiced briefly, and then went to Paris in 1892 to study at the Ecole des Beaux-Arts. Returning to Chicago, he reopened his architectural practice. Early commissions included modest-sized half-timbered Tudor style residences. Rogers married Anne Day, the daughter of Albert Morgan Day, president of the Chicago Stock Exchange. Albert Day was related to the McCormick family through his wife, and Anne's sister married Francis C. Farwell, of one of Chicago's oldest families. John V. Farwell had been Marshall Field's partner in the dry-goods business and was one of the largest property owners in Chicago. These family connections were the source of Rogers' commissions for Lake Forest mansions and some of his later academic buildings.

In 1905, Rogers moved his office from Chicago to New York, lured by the prospect of larger commissions that he secured through East Coast friends from his college days at Yale. The building that launched his New York career was the lavish mansion he designed for Edward Harkness, whose family fortune came from early investments in, and 15 percent ownership of, John D. Rockefeller's Standard Oil Company. His relationship with the Harkness family led to important public and institutional commissions throughout his career. He is best known for his designs for university buildings, particularly at Yale, where he was responsible for the Harkness Memorial Quadrangle, Harkness Tower, and the Sterling Memorial Library, a commission he received after the original architect, Bertram Goodhue, died. Rogers also designed Yale's Sterling Law buildings, the Hall of Graduate Studies, and eight residential colleges. At Northwestern University in Evanston, he designed the Deering Library and Sorority Quadrangle. Rogers designed buildings at the University of Chicago as well as Princeton and Columbia universities, and more than any other American architect, was responsible for the development of what became known as the Collegiate Gothic style.

ROBERT SEYFARTH
(1878–1950)

Robert Seyfarth was one of the North Shore's most prolific architects of quality residential designs. He built over 50 houses just in Highland Park, where he lived from 1911 until his death. Seyfarth built small and medium sized houses for Chicago merchants and businessmen. These elegantly proportioned houses were characterized by simple roof lines, inset dormers, classical stone or wood entrances, and large, floor-to-ceiling double-hung windows. Seyfarth was born in the South Side Chicago suburb of Blue Island. He attended the Chicago Manual Training School, which offered courses in architecture and construction. Seyfarth worked for George W. Maher from 1898 to 1909. While employed by Maher, Seyfarth supervised the construction of the James A. Patton house in Evanston. In 1909, he opened his own architectural practice. Two years later, Seyfarth established his reputation designing houses on the North Shore when he built his own house on Sheridan Road in Highland Park. During the 1920 and early 1930s, he had an office in the Tribune Tower in Chicago. From 1934 on, he worked from his house in Highland Park, preparing all his own drawings.

HOWARD VAN DOREN SHAW
(1869–1926)

Howard Van Doren Shaw was the leading country house architect of his generation in the Chicago area. In 1926, he was awarded the Gold Metal of the American Institute of Architects. At the time, he was one of only nine American architects to have been granted the highest award bestowed by the AIA, and the only country house architect so unanimously respected by his peers. Shaw was born in Chicago in 1869. He attended Yale University, graduating in 1890, and then studied architecture at the Massachusetts Institute of Technology. After graduating in 1892, he worked in Chicago for Jenney and Mundie, the firm where many Chicago School architects including Louis Sullivan had trained. In 1893, he married Frances Wells, his childhood sweetheart, and opened his own architectural practice. His first independent commission was a house built in Connecticut for Frances' father. Shaw set up an office on the top floor of his father's house in Hyde Park near the University of Chicago. There, he employed as his first draftsman, Robert Work, who would later be David Adler's partner. Shaw began by designing adjoining townhouses in Hyde Park for his family and for Frances' sister and her husband. He built a number of houses in Hyde Park, but it was with the construction of his summer house, Ragdale, in Lake Forest that his career as a significant residential architect and designer of country houses began. Shaw's family ties, Yale friends, and club memberships, brought him commissions for houses for many of Chicago's most prominent families, such as the Ryersons (steel) and the Donnelleys (printing). For Yale classmate, Thomas Donnelley, he built a Lake Forest house and for his father Rueben R. Donnelley, he built the Lakeside Press building in Chicago. Shaw built Market Square in Lake Forest, probably the country's first shopping center; and, Marktown, Indiana, a model worker's town like Pullman, for his residential client Clayton Mark. He also built the Lake Shore Country Club, the Quadrangle Club at the University of Chicago, and commissions for the Art Institute of Chicago where he was a trustee. For the Art Institute he designed the Burnham Library, McKinlock Court, and the Goodman Theater. Shaw renovated James Renwick's Second Presbyterian Church on North Michigan Avenue in Chicago. He designed the apartment building at 1130 Lake Shore Drive where he lived on the top floor, until 1923 when he moved to the apartment building at 2450 Lake View Avenue, another of his designs.

Shaw's office served as a training ground for other important Chicago architects: Hugh Garden, David Adler, Henry Dangler, Robert Work, Edward Bennett, Ralph Milman, Stanley Anderson, and Horace Powers. Shaw's early work in Chicago was in the English Tudor style. Most of Shaw's later houses were free compositions of traditional residential elements reminiscent largely of English and occasionally of Italian architecture. The English Arts and Crafts movement had an important influence on him, as it did on the Prairie School architects, and shows up particularly in Shaw's interiors. Shaw was friendly with Frank Lloyd Wright and the other Prairie School architects, with whom he regularly dined. It would be interesting to speculate on possible reciprocal influences between Shaw and Wright, such as spatial planning, covered porches as extensions of interior spaces, and the use of materials such as stucco that Shaw employed at Ragdale.

Joseph Lyman Silsbee
(1845–1913)

Today, Joseph Lyman Silsbee is perhaps best known as Frank Lloyd Wright's first employer. Silsbee had done work for Wright's uncle, Jenkin Lloyd Jones, and gave the young Wright, who had no architectural education, his first job. George W. Maher and George Grant Elmslie also worked for Silsbee as draftsmen. Although he did commercial work, Silsbee was primarily a residential architect. He designed fashionable Shingle Style houses in Chicago, and his influence may be seen in Frank Lloyd Wright's own 1889, shingled house in Oak Park. Born at Salem, Massachusetts, he attended Phillips Exeter Academy before entering Harvard University. He then studied architecture for three years at the Massachusetts Institute of Technology. Silsbee practiced architecture for 10 years in Syracuse, New York, before moving to Chicago in 1882, where he formed a partnership with Edward Kent, a colleague from Syracuse. He practiced with Kent until 1890, when Kent returned to the East. In 1884, Silsbee and Kent were hired to design the interiors of the Potter Palmer mansion on Lake Shore Drive in Chicago. The mansion had been designed by Cobb and Frost, and was then under construction. Silsbee was also the architect for the Illinois Bell Telephone Exchange building and the glass and iron conservatory in Chicago's Lincoln Park.

Robert Closson Spencer, Jr.
(1864–1953)

Robert Spencer was born in Milwaukee and received a degree in mechanical engineering from the University of Wisconsin in 1886. He then studied architecture at the Massachusetts Institute of Technology where he met Dwight Perkins, also a student there. After graduation he worked in Boston for the architectural firm of Wheelwright and Haven and then for Shepley, Rutan, and Coolidge, H. H. Richardson's successors. Spencer traveled through Europe on a Rotch traveling fellowship. He returned briefly to Boston where he rejoined Shepley, Rutan, and Coolidge, before moving to Chicago in 1893 to work in that firm's Chicago office. In 1895, he opened his own practice renting space in the Schiller Building designed by Adler and Sullivan, where Frank Lloyd Wright and his partner Cecil Corwin had their office. When Dwight Perkins moved into Steinway Hall, which he had designed, he occupied a loft on the top floor and went looking for office mates to share the space and the rent. The first to move in was Robert Spencer, next were Wright and Corwin. After Corwin left for the East, Spencer and Wright became best friends. H. Allen Brooks speculates in *The Prairie School* (1972) that Spencer had a big impact on the development of Wright's important early ideas and designs. In 1905, Spencer took Horace Swett Powers (1872–1928), a graduate of the Armour Institute of Technology, as a partner. Powers had worked for Nimmons and Fellows, Howard Van Doren Shaw, and Daniel Burnham. Spencer, like Wright, Irving Pond, and Tallmadge, wrote about architecture. He published articles in the *Architectural Review* and *The Brickbuilder*, and after 1905 was a regular contributor to *House Beautiful*, then published in Chicago. Spencer and Powers practiced together until 1923, when Spencer took a position as professor at Oklahoma A. and M. College. He taught at the University of Florida from 1930 to 1934. While teaching, he started a company that manufactured and sold casement window hardware.

Thomas Eddy Tallmadge
(1876–1940)

•

Vernon Spencer Watson
(1879–1950)

Thomas Tallmadge was born and educated in Washington, D. C. He studied architecture at the Massachusetts Institute of Technology and then moved to Chicago. Vernon Watson was born in Chicago and studied at the Armour Institute of Technology, which later became the Illinois Institute of Technology. The two architects met while both were working in Daniel H. Burnham's office. In 1904 Tallmadge won the Chicago Architectural Club Traveling Scholarship, and upon his return from Europe in 1905, he and Watson opened a firm. Tallmadge and Watson were best known for their early Prairie-style houses and their later ecclesiastical work. They designed simplified Gothic- or Federal-style churches including the First Methodist, Baptist, and First Congregational churches in Evanston, where Tallmadge resided. Although Tallmadge was better known, Vernon Watson was probably the firm's designer, according to H. Allen Brooks' *The Prairie School* (1972). Tallmadge and Watson were also the architects of the Colonial Village at the 1933–34 Century of Progress Exposition in Chicago, which led to Tallmadge serving as a member of the architectural commission for the restoration of Colonial Williamsburg. Thomas Tallmadge taught architectural history at the Armour Institute from 1906 to 1926, and also lectured on architectural history at the Art Institute of Chicago. Tallmadge is credited with coining "Chicago School" (1908) to describe Chicago's progressive architecture. He gained national recognition as an author as well as an architect. He wrote extensively about architecture, and authored several books, including *The Story of Architecture in America* (1927), *The Story of England's Architecture* (1934), *The Origin of the Skyscraper* (1939), and the posthumously-published *Architecture in Old Chicago* (1941). Tallmadge and Watson practiced together 31 years until Watson's retirement in 1936. Tallmadge was elected a Fellow of the American Institute of Architects in 1923.

JOHN SHELLETTE VAN BERGEN
(1885–1969)

Primarily a residential architect, John Van Bergen was an important member of the Prairie School. Born in Chicago, Van Bergen grew up in the western suburb of Oak Park. His architectural education was gained through apprenticeship and courses he took at the Chicago Technical College. Van Bergen worked for Walter Burley Griffin in his office in Steinway Hall, and later for Frank Lloyd Wright in his Oak Park studio. He remained in Wright's employ until 1909, when Wright left for Europe and the Oak Park studio closed. Van Bergen then joined the office of another prominent Prairie School architect, William Drummond. He was licensed in 1911, and opened his own office in Evanston, later moving to Highland Park. There, he designed a number of Prairie-style houses into the 1930s, long after the style peaked in popularity. Among his important non-residential commissions was the Braeside School in Highland Park. In 1955, Van Bergen moved to Santa Barbara, California, where he continued to practice architecture until the year before he died.

FRANK LLOYD WRIGHT
(1867–1959)

Frank Lloyd Wright is arguably America's most famous architect of the 20th century. His professional career covered 70 years, during which he built over 300 buildings. Like other great 20th-century architects with long careers, Wright's architecture developed and changed, and his work is best discussed by periods. In his early and most innovative period working in Chicago and its suburbs, he produced a body of work that had an important impact on the development of 20th-century European modern architecture. Throughout his career, Wright built important religious, civic, and commercial structures, such as Unity Temple in Oak Park, Illinois (1906), the Larkin Building in Buffalo, New York (1904), the Johnson Wax Building in Racine, Wisconsin (1936–46), and the Guggenheim Museum in New York City (completed after his death).

It was as a residential architect that Wright made his greatest impact and did his most important work. Wright worked in the Chicago area from 1887 to 1909, and it was during this period that he developed a language of highly original residential architecture by reinventing, transforming, and abstracting the elements of the traditional house. He understood interior space and its visual relationship to the exterior in a new way that stressed the spatial connections between rooms and also between inside spaces and outdoor porches and terraces. Wright's work, and the work of Chicago architects that he influenced, came to be known as the Prairie School of architecture. Wright believed that his low, horizontally extended houses reflected the topography of the Midwestern prairie landscape and constituted a new American architecture.

Wright was born 1867 in Richland Center, Wisconsin. His father William, a New England clergyman, settled the family in Madison, Wisconsin, when Wright was 11. They lived near the family of Wright's mother, the Lloyd Joneses, who were Welsh Unitarian farmers. His early education at home was based on the Froebel Kindergarten method and especially on Froebel "gifts," materials given to children that involved stringing beads, folding paper, cutting out shapes, and arranging building blocks on a gridded tabletop. Wright later acknowledged the Froebel gifts as an important influence on his architecture. His father abandoned his family and Wright never finished high school, though he spent one semester as a special student at the University of Wisconsin in the engineering department. It was through a recommendation from his uncle, Jenkin Lloyd Jones, that he went to work in the Chicago office of Joseph Lyman Silsbee.

Silsbee had designed a small Unitarian chapel for Wright's uncle, and took the young man on as an apprentice. From Silsbee's office, Wright went to work for Louis Sullivan. Wright is said to have gotten the job by showing Sullivan freehand drawings he had made of plates from Owen Jones' *The Grammar of Ornament* (1856). Sullivan assigned Wright the task of drawing the ornament for the Auditorium Theater, a major project of Sullivan's. He was employed by Adler and Sullivan from 1888 to 1893, during which time he was put in charge of the residential commissions in the office.

In 1889, Wright married and, with Sullivan's help, bought property in Oak Park, where he designed and built a fashionable Shingle Style house like those he had worked on in Silsbee's office. Wright also designed residences for friends in Oak Park, but since this was in violation of his contract with Sullivan, he was fired. Wright set up his own practice in Chicago, working with his friend Cecil Corwin and sharing space with Dwight Perkins in Steinway Hall. In 1895, he added an office and studio to his home in Oak Park and moved his practice there, hiring Walter Burley Griffin and Marion Mahony Griffin, John Van Bergen, William Drummond, and Barry Byrne to work with him. Important residential commissions from this period included the Frederick Robie house in Chicago (1909), the Ward Willits house in Highland Park (1902), the Darwin Martin house in Buffalo, New York (1904), and the Avery Coonley house in River Forest, Illinois (1908).

In 1909, Wright left his family in Chicago to go to Berlin with the wife of his client Edwin Cheney. Wright and Mrs. Cheney were having an affair and their departure together caused a great scandal. The purpose of the trip was to arrange for the publication of a portfolio of drawings of his work to be issued by the Berlin publisher Ernst Wasmuth with an introduction by the English Arts and Crafts designer Charles Ashbee, who had spent time in Chicago. The Wasmuth portfolio greatly enhanced Wright's growing international reputation at a time when his life was in shambles. His wife refused to give him a divorce, and the growing scandal caused by his departure for Europe with Mrs. Cheney effectively ended his career in Chicago. Wright moved on, building a new home and studio in 1911, which he called Taliesin, meaning "shining brow," on farm property his mother owned near Spring Green, Wisconsin. While most of Wright's work was in Oak Park or Chicago, he designed a number of important commissions on the North Shore, including the Ward Willits House and the Ravine Bluffs Development.

WILLIAM CARBYS ZIMMERMAN
(1856–1932)

Carbys Zimmerman was born in Thiensville, Wisconsin, and studied architecture at the Massachusetts Institute of Technology. After graduating from MIT in 1880, Zimmerman worked for the firm of Burnham and Root for several years and for S. V. Shipman for a year, before opening the firm of Flanders and Zimmerman.

He married into the socially prominent Hamill family of Lake Forest. Best known for public commissions, the firm's work included the Supreme Court building in Springfield, Illinois, the physics building at the University of Illinois, the Pulaski Field House and the Seventh Regiment Armory in Chicago, and the Illinois State Penitentiary at Joliet. Flanders and Zimmerman also produced residential architecture such as the Edward Kirk Warren house in Evanston. In 1893, the firm became Zimmerman, Saxe, and Zimmerman, when Carbys made his son and Albert Moore Saxe partners. Saxe was probably the designer of the Robert Morse house, one of the North Shore's Art Deco masterpieces. From 1905 to 1913, Zimmerman was the architect for the state of Illinois. He retired from practice in the mid-1920s and continued to live in Chicago.

BIBLIOGRAPHY

GENERAL REFERENCES

American Institute of Architects. *American Architects Directory*. 2nd ed. New York: R. R. Bowker Co., 1962.

The Book of Chicagoans. Chicago: A. N. Marquis Company, 1905, 1911, 1917, and 1926.

Handbook for Architects and Builders. Chicago: Illinois Society of Architects, 1898-

Who's Who in Chicago. Chicago: A. N. Marquis Company, 1931.

Who's Who in Chicago and Vicinity. Chicago: A. N. Marquis Company, 1936 and 1941

Withey, Henry F., and Elsie Rathburn. *Biographical Dictionary of American Architects (Deceased)*. Los Angeles: Hennessey and Ingalls, Inc., 1970.

PERIODICALS AND NEWSPAPERS

American Architect and Building News. Boston & New York, 1876–1938.

The Architect. New York, 1910 – 1932.

The Architectural Forum; Brickbuilder. New York, 1896–1924.

The Architectural Record. New York, 1891–1932.

The Architectural Review. Boston, 1891–1921.

Architecture. New York, 1900–1930.

Chicago Daily News.

Chicago Architectural Journal/Chicago Architectural Club, 1981-

Chicago Tribune.

Country Life in America. New York and Garden City, 1900–1942.

Geo. W. Maher Quarterly. Sauk City, Wisconsin

House and Garden. Chicago and New York. 1901-1993; 1996-

House Beautiful. New York, 1896– .

Inland Architect and News Record. Chicago, 1889–1908.

Prairie School Review. Chicago, 1964–1981

Town and Country. New York, 1846–.

Western Architect. Minneapolis, 1902-1931

BOOKS, PRINTED MATERIAL, AND ARTICLES

Arpee, Edward. *Lake Forest Illinois: History and Reminiscences, 1861–1961*. Lake Forest: Lake Forest - Lake Bluff Historical Society, 1979.

Art Institute of Chicago. *The David Adler Archive at the Art Institute of Chicago: Finding Aid*. Chicago: Art Institute of Chicago, 1998.

Benjamin, Susan S., ed. *An Architectural Album: Chicago's North Shore*. Evanston: Junior League of Evanston, 1988.

———, ed. *Winnetka Architecture: Where Past Is Present*. Winnetka: Winnetka Historical Museum, 1990.

Berger, Philip, ed. *Highland Park: American Suburb at Its Best, an Architectural and Historical Survey*. Highland Park, Illinois: Landmark Preservation Committee, 1982.

Bernardi, Adria. *Houses with Names: The Italian Immigrants of Highwood, Illinois*. Chicago: University of Illinois Press, 1990.

Birnbaum, Charles A. and Robin Karson, eds. *Pioneers of American Landscape Design*. New York: McGraw Hill, 2000.

Boutin, S. and Shirley M. Paddock. *Lake Forest Cemetery Burial Book*. Lake Forest: Lake Forest - Lake Bluff Historical Society, 1995.

Bibliography

Boyce, Robert. *Keck and Keck*. New York: Princeton Architectural Press, 1993.

Brooks, H. Allen. *The Prairie School: Frank Lloyd Wright and His Midwest Contemporaries*. Toronto: University of Toronto Press, 1972.

Bushnell, George D. *Wilmette: A History*. Wilmette, Illinois: The Wilmette Bicentennial Commission, 1976.

Cairns, Malcolm. *The Landscape Architecture Heritage of Illinois*. Muncie, Indiana: Ball State University Press, 1993.

Chamberlin, Everett. *Chicago and Its Suburbs*. Chicago: T. A. Hungerford and Company, 1874.

Cohen, Stuart E. *Chicago Architects*. Chicago: Swallow Press, 1976.

———. "Robert E. Seyfarth, Architect." *Positions in Architecture: Chicago Architectural Journal* 9, (2000).

Coventry, Kim, Daniel Meyer, and Arthur H. Miller. *Classic Country Estates of Lake Forest: Architecture and Landscape Design, 1856–1940*. New York: W. W. Norton, 2003.

Cummings, Kathleen Roy. *Architecture at Northwestern: A Guide to the Evanston Campus*. Northwestern University: Mary and Leigh Block Gallery, 1986.

Dart, Susan. *Market Square*. Lake Forest: Lake Forest - Lake Bluff Historical Society, 1984

———. *Supplement to Lake Forest, Illinois: History and Reminiscences, 1861–1961*. Lake Forest: Lake Forest - Lake Bluff Historical Society, 1991.

David, Arthur C. "The Architecture of Ideas." *Architectural Record* 15 (April 1904).

Domestic Architecture of H. T. Lindeberg. Introduction by Royal Cortissoz. New York: William Helburn, 1940. Reprint, with a new introduction by Mark Alan Hewitt, New York: Acanthus Press, 1996.

Downing, Andrew Jackson. *The Architecture of Country Houses*. New York: D. Appleton, 1850.

Downing, Antoinette F. and Scully, Vincent J., Jr. *The Architectural Heritage of Newport, Rhode Island, 1640–1915*. 2nd rev. ed. New York: American Legacy Press, 1967.

Eaton, Leonard K. *Landscape Artist in America: The Life and Work of Jens Jensen*. Chicago: University of Chicago Press, 1964.

———. *Two Chicago Architects and Their Clients: Frank Lloyd Wright and Howard Van Doren Shaw*. Cambridge, Mass.: M.I.T. Press, 1969.

Ebner, Michael. H. *Creating Chicago's North Shore: A Suburban History*. Chicago: University of Chicago Press, 1988.

"A Farm Group in Libertyville, Illinois, David Adler, Architect and Owner." *House Beautiful* (May 1924).

Foley, Mary Mix. *The American House*. New York: Harper and Row, 1980.

"Garage for Noble Judah, Esq., Lake Forest, Illinois." *Architectural Record* 58 (November 1925).

Glencoe Lights 100 Candles, 1869–1969. Glencoe, Illinois, 1969.

Goodwin, Philip Lippincott and Henry Oothout Milliken. *French Provincial Architecture as Shown in Various Examples of Town and Country Houses, Shops and Public Places Adaptable to American Conditions*. New York: Charles Scribner's Sons, 1924.

Granger, Alfred. *Chicago Welcomes You*. Chicago: A. Kroch, 1933.

Greene, Virginia. *The Architecture of Howard Van Doren Shaw*. Chicago: Chicago Review Press, 1998.

Grese, Robert E. *Jens Jensen: Maker of Natural Parks and Gardens*. Baltimore: Johns Hopkins University Press, 1992.

Hampton, Mark. *Legendary Decorators of the Twentieth Century*. New York: Doubleday, 1992.

Harnsberger, Caroline Thomas. *Winnetka: The Biography of a Village*. Evanston: Schori Press, 1977.

Hayes, Alice and Susan Moon. *Ragdale: A History and Guide*. Lake Forest: The Ragdale Foundation; Berkeley, California: Open Books, 1990.

Hewitt, Mark Alan. *The Architect and the American Country House, 1890–1940*. New Haven: Yale University Press, 1990.

"Historical Data and Maps of Gage's Tract Tell Many Interesting Things about Early Village." *Wilmette Life* (13 August 1953).

Hitchcock, Henry-Russell. *In the Nature of Materials, 1887 - 1941, The Buildings of Frank Lloyd Wright*. 1942. Reprint, New York: Da Capo Press, 1973.

Illinois: A Descriptive and Historical Guide. Chicago: Henry Horner, Governor, State of Illinois and A. C. McClurg 1939.

Jellicoe, Geoffrey and Susan. *The Landscape of Man: Shaping the Environment from Prehistory to the Present Day.* New York: Viking Press, 1975.

Jensen, Jens. "Landscape Art: An Inspiration from the Western Plains." *The Sketchbook* (September 1906).

Kilner, Colleen Browne. *Joseph Sears and His Kenilworth.* Kenilworth: Kenilworth Historical Society, 1990.

Kimball, Fiske. *Domestic Architecture of the American Colonies and of the Early Republic.* New York: Charles Scribner's Sons, 1922. New York: Dover Press, 1966.

Lake Bluff, Illinois: A Pictorial History. Lake Bluff: Village of Lake Bluff Centennial Committee, 1995.

Lake Forest, Illinois: A Preservation Guide to National Register Properties. Lake Forest: Lake Forest Preservation Foundation, 1994.

Lowe, David. *Lost Chicago.* New York: American Legacy Press, 1985.

Mackay, Robert B., Anthony Baker, and Carol A. Traynor. *Long Island Country Houses and Their Architects, 1860–1940.* New York: W. W. Norton in association with the Society for the Preservation of Long Island Antiquities, 1997.

Manson, Grant Carpenter. *Frank Lloyd Wright to 1910: The First Golden Age.* New York: Van Nostrand Reinhold, 1958.

McAlester, Virginia and Lee. *A Field Guide to American Houses.* New York: Alfred A. Knopf, 1985.

Meeker, Arthur. *Prairie Avenue.* New York: Alfred A. Knopf, 1949.

Meites, Hyman L., ed. *History of the Jews of Chicago.* 1924. Reprint, with new introduction by James R. Grossman, Chicago: Chicago Jewish Historical Society and Wellington Publishing, 1990.

"Melody Farm, The Country Home of J. Ogden Armour, Esq., Lake Forest, Ill. Arthur Heun, Architect." *Architectural Record* 39 (February 1916).

Miller, Arthur H. and Shirley M. Paddock. *Lake Forest: Estates, People, and Culture.* Chicago: Arcadia Publishing, 2000.

Miller, Donald L. *City of the Century: The Epic of Chicago and the Making of America.* New York: Simon and Schuster, Touchstone Books, 1996.

Moore, Patricia. "Status: An Adler Home." *Chicago Daily News,* 1 June 1971.

Morgan, Keith N. *Charles A. Platt: the Artist as Architect.* Cambridge: M.I.T. Press, 1985.

Pardridge, A. J. and Bradley, Harold. *Directory to Apartments of the Better Class along the North Side of Chicago.* Chicago: Pardridge & Bradley, 1917.

Paseltiner, Ellen Kettler and Ellen Shubart. *Glencoe, Illinois.* Chicago: Arcadia Press, 2002.

Pennoyer, Peter and Anne Walker. *The Architecture of Delano and Aldrich.* Foreword by Robert M. Stern. New York: W. W. Norton, 2003.

Perkins, Margery Blair. *Evanstoniana: An Informal History of Evanston and its Architecture,* comp. and ed. Barbara J. Buchbinder-Green. Evanston: Evanston Historical Society; Chicago: Chicago Review Press, 1984.

Pratt, Richard. *David Adler.* New York: M. Evans 1970.

Price, Matlack. "House of William McCormick Blair, Esq., Lake Forest, Ill." *Architectural Forum* 50 (January 1929).

Randall, Frank A. *History of the Development of Building Construction in Chicago.* Urbana, Illinois: University of Illinois Press, 1949.

"Residence of David Adler, Esquire, Libertyville, Illinois, David Adler Architect." *Architectural Record* 32 (November 1923).

Rudd, J. William. "George W. Maher: Architect of the Prairie School." *The Prairie School Review* I, 1st Quarter (1964).

Salny, Stephen M. *The Country Houses of David Adler.* New York: W. W. Norton, 2001.

———. "Historic Interiors; Frances Elkins." *Architectural Digest* 43 (1986).

"The Salvaging of the Armour Fortune." *Fortune* (April 1931).

Samors, Neal. "Annexation and Chicago's Northern Border Communities." *Chicago History* 30 (Fall 2001).

Schulze, Franz, Rosemary Cowler and Arthur Miller. *30 Miles North: A History of Lake Forest College, Its Town and Its City of Chicago.* Lake Forest, Illinois: University of Chicago Press, 2000.

Scully, Vincent, Jr. *Frank Lloyd Wright.* New York:

George Braziller, 1960.

———. *The Shingle Style and the Stick Style: Architectural Theory and Design from Richardson in the Origins of Wright*. Rev. ed. New Haven, Connecticut.: Yale University Press, 1971.

Sinkevitch, Alice. ed. *AIA Guide to Chicago*. San Diego, California: Harcourt Brace, 1993.

Smith, Carl. *Urban Disorder and the Shape of Belief; The Great Chicago Fire, the Haymarket Bomb, and the Model Town of Pullman*. Chicago and London: University of Chicago Press, 1995.

Solway, Susan. "Frank Lloyd Wright and Glencoe." *Wright Angles: The Newsletter of the Frank Lloyd Wright Studio Foundation* (1993).

Stamper, John W. *Chicago's North Michigan Avenue: Planning and Development, 1900–1930*. Chicago: University of Chicago Press, 1991.

Storrer, William Allin. *The Frank Lloyd Wright Companion*. University of Chicago Press, 1993.

Thorne, Martha, ed. *David Adler, Architect: The Elements of Style*. New Haven: Art Institute of Chicago in association with Yale University Press, 2002.

United States Department of the Interior, National Park Service. "Adler, David, Estate." *National Register of Historic Places Registration Form*. Susan Benjamin, Preparer. Washington, D. C., 22 November 1999.

———. "Ely, Mrs. Carolyn Morse Ely, House." *National Register of Historic Places Registration Form*. Susan Benjamin, Preparer. Washington, D. C., 4 October 2000.

———. "Green Bay Road Historic District, Lake Forest Illinois." National Register of Historic Places Registration Form. Barbara Buchbinder-Green, Barbara, preparer. Washington, D.C. 7 July 1995.

———. "Reed, Mrs. Kersey Coates House." *National Register of Historic Places Registration Form*. Susan Benjamin, preparer. Washington, D.C. 17 January 2001.

Vliet, Elmer B. *Lake Bluff, The First 100 Years*. Lake Bluff: Elmer Vliet Historical Center in association with School District 65 of Lake Bluff, 1985.

White, Marian A. *A Book of the North Shore Homes, Gardens, Landscapes, Highways and Byways, Past and Present*. Chicago: J. Harrison White, 1910.

———. *Second Book of the North Shore Homes, Gardens, Landscapes, Highways and Byways, Past and Present*. Chicago: J. Harrison White, 1911.

Wight, Peter B. "Mellody Farm, the Country Home of J. Ogden Armour, Esq. Lake Forest, Ill." *Architectural Record* 34 (February 1926).

———. "The Residence of Harold L. Ickes, Esq., Hubbard Woods, Ill., and the Residence of Mrs. Cyrus H. McCormick, Lake Forest, Ill. Perkins, Fellows and Hamilton, Architects." *Architectural Record* 43 (March 1918).

Wright, Frank Lloyd. "A Fireproof House for $5,000." *Ladies Home Journal* 24 (April 1907).

———. *Ausgeführte Bauten und Entwürfe*. Berlin: Ernst Wasmuth, 1910. Translation, *Drawings and Plans of Frank Lloyd Wright: The Early Period, 1893–1909*. New York: Dover, 1983.

Unpublished and Privately Published Material

Benjamin, Susan and Victoria Granacki."Cultural Resource Management Plan for National Historic Landmark District, Fort Sheridan, Illinois." Paper prepared for the Local Redevelopment Authority comprised of the Municipalities of Highland Park and Highwood, Illinois, December 1997.

Benjamin, Susan and Susan Solway. "Historic American Engineering Record, Ravine Bluffs Development Bridge." HAER No. IL-14. [c. 1995]

"Gertrude Carolyn Morse Ely. Family Record for the Archives of the Chicago Historical Society," 25 August 1954.

Hackl, Martin. "The Work of John S. Van Bergen, Architect." Oak Park: Martin Hackl, 1999.

Hinchliff, William. "The J. Ogden Armour House: A Brief History." Lake Forest Academy-Ferry Hall Antiques Show Catalogue, 1983.

Notz, John K., Jr. "To Cathect or Not to Cathect." Paper delivered to the Chicago Literary Club, 11 March 1996.

"Preservation Foundation House Tour," c. 1982. Lake Forest Foundation for Historic Preservation, Lake Forest, Illinois.

Reed, Peter. The Home of Mrs. Kersey Coates Reed,

Bibliography

Lake Forest, Illinois: David Adler, Architect." Photographs by Luis Medina. Privately Published, 1982. Copies at the Lake Forest Public Library, Burnham Library of the Art Institute of Chicago

Salny, Stephen. "David Adler: The Epitome of an Era." Independent Study, Lake Forest College, 1977.

Solway, Susan, John Thorpe, and Peg Zak. "Wright Plus North in Glencoe: A Housewalk in Glencoe, Illinois." The Frank Lloyd Wright Home and Studio Foundation, the Glencoe Historic Preservation Commission, and the Glencoe Historical Society, Glencoe, Illinois, 2 October 1993. [is this a brochure? If so delete]

Real Estate Atlases and Aerial Photographs

Lake County Map Department, Waukegan, Illinois

Lake County Estate District of Country Homes, 1930. Anderson Co., Lake Forest, Illinois.

Subdivisions, Title records, Plats of Survey, Lake County Recorder of Deeds, Waukegan, Illinois

Title records, Cook County Recorder of Deeds, Chicago, Illinois

Archives

Art Institute of Chicago, Department of Architecture, Ryerson and Burnham Archives, Chicago

Chicago Historical Society, Chicago

David Adler Cultural Center, Libertyville

Elmer Vliet Historical Center, Lake Bluff

Evanston Historical Society, Evanston

Frances Willard Library, Evanston

Glencoe Historical Society, Glencoe

Highland Park Historical Society, Highland Park

Highland Park Public Library, Highland Park

Kenilworth Historical Society, Kenilworth

Lake Forest College Library, Special Collections and Archives, Lake Forest

Lake Forest - Lake Bluff Historical Society, Lake Forest

Lake Forest Preservation Foundation, Lake Forest

Wilmette Historical Society, Wilmette

Winnetka Historical Society, Winnetka

Index

A

Adams and Westlake Company, 79
Addams, Jane, 25, 40, 70, 227, 317
Adler, Dankmar, 40
Adler, David, 11, 27, 30, 34, 36, 37, 43, 44, 45, 69, 89, 176, 181–182, 184, 186, 188–189, 199, 200, 214, 220, 223, 227, 231, 233, 235, 237, 244, 276, 277, 282–283, 300, 301, 302, 305, 319, 320, 322
Adler, David, Cultural Center, 189, 227
Adler, David, estate, 184–190
Albro, Lewis Colt, 300, 314
Aldis, Arthur T., 31, 43
Aldrich, Chester Holmes, 309–310
Alexander, William A., house, 297
All Souls Center, 39
All Souls Unitarian Church, 39–40
Amalgamated Trust and Savings Bank, 310
American Academy in Rome, 41, 310, 317
American Architect, 91
American Cancer Society, 294
American Steel Foundries, 162–163
American System Ready-Cut structure, 33
The American Vitruvius: An Architect's Handbook of Civic Arts (Hegemann and Peets), 31
Anderson, Pierce, 307
Anderson, Stanley D., 30, 303, 304, 306
Anderson, Stanley D., and Associates, 306
Anderson, Stanley D., Archives, 306
Anglo-American decoration, 283
Angyllshire (Cyrus McCormick III), 30
Annapolis, Maryland, 283
Anthony, Charles Elliot, house, 298
Architectural Forum, 36, 227, 284, 294
Architectural League of America, 42
Architectural Record, 35, 36, 91, 109, 113, 128, 220, 260, 284, 314, 317
Architectural Review, 320
Architecture françoise (Blondel), 89
Ardleigh (Farwell, John V., Jr., house), 30, 298
Armour, Barbara, 312
Armour, Gwendolyn, 275
Armour, J. Ogden, 12, 36, 112–115, 254, 271, 312
Armour, J. Ogden, estate, 12, 110–116, 254, 312
Armour, Laurence, house, 300
Armour, Lester, estate, 34
Armour, Lolita Sheridan, 12, 112–113, 115
Armour, Mrs. Lester, 305
Armour, Philip D., III, 34, 271, 275
Armour, Philip Danforth, 114, 271
Armour and Company, 114–115, 163, 271, 275
Armour and Swift, 30
Armour Institute, 321
Arnold, Tommy, 249
Art Deco style, 24, 276, 287, 307, 315, 322
Art Institute of Chicago, 22, 28, 40, 227, 311, 316, 319, 321
  Architecture Department of, 186
  Burnham Library, 319
  Goodman Theater, 319
  McKinlock Court, 319
Arts and Crafts Society, 13, 28, 32, 40
Arts and Crafts style, 35, 40, 69–70, 71, 72, 94, 96, 117, 118, 174, 223, 316. *See also* English Arts and Crafts style
Arts Magazine, 258, 260
Ashbee, Charles Robert, 40, 70, 322
Asheville, North Carolina, 53
Aspen, Colorado, 12, 28
Aspen Institute of Humanistic Studies, 12, 101
Aspen Skiing Corporation, 101
Astor family, 309
Atlanta, Georgia, 308
Atlantic Seaboard Dispatch, 267
Atwood, Charles, 315
Ausgeführte Bauten und Entwürfe von Frank Lloyd Wright, 139
autographic stencils, 86, 89

B

Bach, Oscar, 166–167
Badger, Alpheus Shreve, 58
Bagatelle (Bennett, Edward H., house), 302, 307
Baker, Frank J., house, 300
Bank architecture, 35
Bankers Tudor style, 208
Barnes, Edward Larrabee, 260
Barrell, Finley, 131, 133
Barrell, Finley, and Company, 133
Barrell, Finley, house, 131–136, 317
Barrell, Grace, 133
Barrell, John Witbeck, 133
Barrett, Nathan, 306
Barrow, J. H., 308
Barrymore, Ethel, 197
Battledeck house, 310
Bauer and Hill, 314
Bauhaus, 314
Becker, A. G., 27, 96
Beman, Solon Spencer, 34, 43, 223, 226, 306, 307, 318
Beman, Spencer Solon, 43, 307
Beman, Spencer Solon, house, 302
Bennett, Edward H., 41, 43, 302, 307, 319
Bennett, Edward H., house, 302
Bergmann, Paul, 306
Bergmann, William, 306
Berkshire Mountains, 28
Bernstein, Leonard, 29
Bersbach, Alfred, house, 301
Bichl, Gerald, 205
Bichl, Gerald and Helen, house, 203–207
Biltmore estate, 53
Birmingham, Connecticut, 310
Black, Robert, 239
Blaine, Anita McCormick, 171, 174
Blair, Helen Bowen, 227
Blair, William, and Company, 227
Blair, William, I, 227
Blair, William McCormick, 188, 227, 305
Blair, William McCormick and Helen Bowen, estate, 34, 186, 223–232
Blessing, Hedrich, 284
Block, Maloney and Company, 133
Blomfield, Reginald, 41
Blondel, J. F., 89
Blue Island, 319
Book of the North Shore (White), 95
Booth, Elizabeth, 137
Booth, Sherman Miller, 28, 137–139
Boyce, Robert, 287
Boylington, William W., 29, 43, 297, 307
Braeside, 27
Breakers Beach Club, 24
Breuer, Marcel, 313
Brewster, Mrs. Walter, 266
The Brickbuilder, 42, 320
Brookfield Zoo, 157, 309
Brooks, H. Allen, 40, 102, 320, 321
Browne, Charles E., 26
Bruning, Herbert, house, 284–289
Bude, Volusin, 312
Buffalo, New York, 321
Burghley house, 160
Burnham, D. H., and Company, 313, 315
Burnham, Daniel Hudson, 11, 13, 22, 34, 38, 41, 43, 48, 51, 61, 62, 188, 196, 307, 308, 320
Burnham, Franklin Pierce, 11, 24, 42, 51, 298

Index

Burnham and Root, 316, 318
Burnham Plan for Chicago, 61, 124, 307
Byrne, Barry, 322

C

Cahn, Bertram J., 293–294
Cahn, Bertram J., house, 290–294
Cahn, Irma (Mrs. Bertram), 290–291, 293–294
Calumet Harbor, 15
Calvary Cemetery, 20
Carpenter Gothic architecture, 28
Carr, Clyde, 165
Carrère and Hastings, 309
Carson Pirie Scott, 195
Carter, Frederick B., house, 301
Casino, The, 110
Castle, The, 26
Centennial Exposition, 36, 97
Central Trust Company, 57
Central Union Depot, 307
Century of Progress Exposition, 15, 43, 285, 307, 310, 312, 313, 316
  Colonial Village, 321
Cerny, Jerome, 249
Chamberlin, William Everett, 18
Chandler, Buckingham, house, 302
Chapman, Kedzie Cass, 295
Charlton house, 160
Charney, George, 182
Chatfield-Taylor, Hobart, 30
Chatfield-Taylor, Rose, 30
Chatten, Melvin, 316
Cheney, Edwin, 322
Cheney, Mamah Borthwick, 139
Chicago, 17–18, 20
  Ambassador East Hotel, 316
  Auditorium Building, 84
  Auditorium Theater, 322
  Baptist Training School for Nurses, 318
  Blackstone Hotel, 195, 316
  Blackstone Shop, 315
  Blackstone Theater, 315
  Casino Club, 312
  Civic Opera House building, 238
  Cleveland, Grover, Elementary School, 316
  Decorative Arts Building, 315
  Douglas Park, 313
  Drake Hotel, 195, 316
  Farwell Building, 315
  Fine Arts Building, 306
  Garfield Park, 313
  Harris Trust and Savings Bank, 79
  Humboldt Park, 313
  Jacques Shop, 315
  Lake Shore Athletic Club, 313
  Lake Shore Trust and Savings Bank, 163
  Lakeside Press Building, 319
  Lincoln Park, 320
  Magerstadt, Ernest J., house, 93
  Memorial Hospital for Infectious Diseases, 311
  Merchants' Tailors Building, 306
  Mines and Mining Building, 306
  Municipal Art Commission, 317
  Newberry Library, 143, 309
  900 North Michigan Ave building, 313
  Orchestra Hall, 188
  Popular Mechanics building, 315
  Post Office building, 309
  Prairie Avenue, 306
  Pump Room, 316
  Regional Planning Commission, 317
  Robie, Frederick, house, 322
  Rush Street, 17
  St. Luke's Hospital, 311
  Schiller Building, 320
  Schurz, Carl, High School, 316
  Second Presbyterian Church, 319
  Seventh Regiment Armory, 322
  Tacoma Building, 312
  Tribune Tower, 319
  Trumbull, Lynn, Elementary School, 316
  Uptown Bank, 315
  Water Tower, 43
  West Park System, 101, 313, 316
  Woman's Athletic Club, 315
Chicago, North Shore and Milwaukee electric railroad, 28
Chicago and Its Suburbs (Chamberlin), 18
Chicago and Milwaukee Railroad, 17
Chicago and Northern Pacific Railway, 306
Chicago and North Western Railway, 17, 24, 51, 138, 311
Chicago Architectural Club, 13, 40, 42
Chicago Arts and Crafts Society, 40, 70, 94
Chicago Arts Club, 201
Chicago Athletic Club, 124, 238, 309
Chicago Board of Education, 316
Chicago Board of Trade, 64, 157, 257, 307, 309
Chicago Casement Hardware Company, 103
Chicago City Club, 318
Chicago Civic Opera Company, 124
Chicago Crime Commission, 294
Chicago Daily News, 182
Chicago Fire (1871), 18, 19, 307
Chicago Gold Coast, 257, 315
Chicago Historical Society, 143, 157, 227, 309
Chicago Orchestral Association, 124
Chicago Packing Box Company, 98
Chicago Park District, 309
Chicago Plan, 61, 124
Chicago Plan Commission, 307
Chicago Public Library, 22, 311
Chicago River, 17
Chicago Society of the New Jerusalem, 51
Chicago Stock Exchange, 89, 133, 318
Chicago Symphony Orchestra, 28
Chicago Tribune, 109, 312
Chicago Welcomes You (Granger), 312
Chicago West Tower and Pumping Station, 307
Chicago Window, 312
Chicago Zoological Garden, 124
Christ Church Parish House (Hartford, CT), 311
church architecture, 35–36
Cincinnati, 306
City Beautiful movement, 61
City Planning Commission of Chicago, 316–317
Civic Theater, 238
Clark, Edwin Hill, 24, 30, 303, 309
Clarke, Harley F., 28
Clarke, Harley Lyman, 238
Clarke, Harley Lyman, house, 238–243
Classical Revival architecture, 24–25, 231, 275
Classic Country Estates of Lake Forest (Coventry, Meyer, and Miller), 30, 41
Clearing (Door County, Wisconsin), 313
Cleveland, Horace W. S., 27–28, 256
Cleveland and French, 27–28
Cobb, Henry Ives, 13, 29, 30, 43, 297, 306, 309, 311
Cobb, Henry Ives, estate, 297
Cobb and Frost, 320
Cochran, J. I., 314
Coe, Matthew, 18
Coe's Glen, 18
Colgate-Palmolive-Peet Company, 208
Collegiate Gothic architecture, 124, 318
Colombia University, 310
Colonial architecture, 106, 285. *See also* Dutch Colonial architecture; Georgian Colonial architecture
Colonial Revival architecture, 25, 33, 36, 184, 186
Colonial Williamsburg, 321
Colony Club, 310
Columbia University, 318
Commercial Club of Chicago, 19, 124, 227
Commonwealth Edison, 195, 316
Comstock, Charles, 63–64, 66
Comstock, Hurd, house, 151
Consolidated Foods, 268
Container Corporation of America, 11–12, 98
Continental Bank and Trust Company, 109
Continental Illinois Bank and Trust Company, 163
Cook County Forest Preserve, 313, 316
Coolidge, Calvin, 52, 57, 298, 310
Coonley, Avery, 40
Coonley, Avery, house, 322
Coonley, Mrs., 40
Coonley, Prentiss, 40
Corning, Libby Owens, 288
Cornish, New Hampshire, 317
Cortissoz, Royal, 317
Corwin, Charles, 314, 320, 322
Country Life in America, 36
Country Life magazine, 89
Coventry, Meyer, and Miller, 275
Coward, Noel, 197
Crab Tree Farm (Durand, Scott S., and Grace, estate and Blair, William McCormick and Helen Bowen, estate), 34, 223–232
Crane, Richard T., 305
Crane, Walter, 40, 70
Creating Chicago's North Shore: A Suburban History (Ebner), 307
Cret, Paul, 306
Croly, Herbert, 317
Crow Island School, 25
Crystal House, 285, 288, 313
Cummings, Nathan, 268

D

Dallas, Texas, 313
Dana House, 151
Dance, George, 146
Dangler, Henry C., 305, 319
Das Englische Haus (Muthesius), 136
Daughters of the American Revolution, 36
Dawes, Charles Gates, 52, 57
Dawes, Charles Gates, house, 52–57, 298
Day, Albert Morgan, 89, 318
Dean, George, 40, 42

[329]

Index

Debs, Eugene, 25
Deering, J. V., 33
Delano, William Adams, 309–310
Delano and Aldrich, 30, 199, 201, 311
Delgado Museum of Art, 316
Denver, CO, 316
The Devil in the White City (Larson), 18
Dick, A. B., and Company, 86
Dick, A. B., house, 86–89
Dick, A. B., Mimeograph machine, 86
Dick, Albert Blake, 86, 89
Dick, Edison, 89
Dick, Mrs. A. B., Sr., 89
Dillingham, Walter, 305
Donnelley, Rueben R., 319
Donnelley, Thomas, 319
Donnelley, Thomas, house, 42, 109
Downing, Andrew Jackson, 28, 29, 33, 63, 256
Drover's National Bank, 109
Drummond, William, 153, 312, 321, 322
Dryden, George B., house, 295
Dubin, Dubin, and Moutoussamy, 310
Dubin, Dubin, Black, and Moutoussamy, 310
Dubin, Henry, 28, 43, 310
Dubin, Henry, house, 304
Dubin and Dubin, 310
Dubin and Eisenerg, 310
Durand, Grace Garrett, 223, 226
Durand, Scott S., 226
Durand, Scott S., and Grace, estate, 34, 223–232
Dutch architecture, 261
Dutch Colonial architecture, 227
Dymaxion House, 313

E
Eastbank, 63–66
Eastover (Frost, Charles S., house), 298
Eaton, Leonard, 37, 79, 143
Ebner, Michael, 226, 307
Eckstein, Mrs. Louis, 29
Eclectic Club, 64, 66
Ecole des Beaux-Arts tradition, 12, 36–37, 53, 64, 69, 78, 89, 161, 176, 226, 231, 264, 275, 277, 305, 306, 307, 309, 311, 312, 316, 317, 318
Edbrooke, Willoughby J., 51, 308
Edgecliff (Epstein, Max, estate), 264–270
Edgewater, 20, 314
Edgewater Beach Hotel, 195, 197, 316
Edison, Thomas Alva, 86, 89
Edwards-Ficken, Henry, 53, 310
Edward VIII, King of England, 197
"18," 40, 312
Elkins, Frances, 235, 245, 276, 282, 283, 305
Elmslie, George Grant, 41, 314, 320
Ely, Carolyn Morse, estate, 176–183, 186
Empire State Building, 62
English architecture, 36
English Arts and Crafts style, 40, 41, 89, 131, 146, 322. *See also* Arts and Crafts style
English Georgian architecture, 283, 306
English Renaissance architecture, 146
English Tudor architecture, 151, 160, 161, 239
Epstein, Max, 26, 267
Epstein, Max, estate, 264–270
Eucharistic Congress (1926), 205

Evans, John, 20
Evanston, 15, 20–22, 29, 43, 44–45, 208, 312, 316
  Anthony, Charles Elliot, house, 298
  Baptist Church in, 320
  Carter, Frederick B., house, 301
  Clarke, Harley Lyman, house, 238–243
  Comstock, Hurd, house, 151
  Dawes, Charles Gates, house, 52–57, 298
  Dryden, George B., house, 295
  Eastbank, 63–66
  Farwell, Simeon and Ebenette Smith, house, 296
  First Congregational Church, 320
  First Methodist Church, 320
  Greenleaf, Luther, house, 303
  Holabird, William, house, 296
  Howe, C. M., house, 42, 299
  Kedzie, John Hume, house, 296
  Linthicum, Charles C., house, 300
  McKinnon, Robert W., house, 303
  Northwest Park District, 317
  Patten, James, house, 43, 80–85, 93, 314, 319
  Ridge Avenue, 23, 80
  Selling, Harold N., house, 303
  Warren, Edward Kirk, house, 300
  Webster, Edward Hutchins, house, 295
  White, Catherine M., house, 40, 117, 299
  Williams, Nathan Wilbur, house, 12, 42, 148–152
  Y.M.C.A., 85
Evanston Art Center, 243
Evanston Art Commission, 239
Evanston City Hall, 312
Evanston High School, 21
Evanston Historical Society, 57
Evanston Hospital, 85
Evanston Lighthouse, 238
Everhardt, George, house, 299
Everts, William W., 29
Exmoor Country Club, 79, 152

F
Fairbanks Morse Scale Company, 26
Fairlawn (McGann, Robert Farwell, estate), 30, 199–202, 310
Farson, John, 314
Farwell, Anne, 89
Farwell, Charles B., 18, 30, 33, 201
Farwell, Francis C., 89, 318
Farwell, John V., 89, 201, 318
Farwell, John V., Jr., house, 298
Farwell, Simeon and Ebenette Smith, house, 296
The Favored Circle (Stevens), 41
Federal style, 320
Federal Triangle, 310
Fellows, William, 316
Ferguson Memorial Building, 310
Fernald, Bessie Swift, 109
Fernald, Charles, 106, 109
Fernald, Charles, house, 42, 106–109
Field, Evelyn, 305
Field, Marshall, 18, 89, 181, 317, 318
Field, Marshall, III, 305
Field, Stanley, 181, 305
Fine Arts Commission, 309–310
Fisher, Howard Taylor, 43, 260, 261, 304, 310–311
Fisher, Katherine, 262

Fisher, Walter Lowrie, 260, 310
Fisher, Walter T., 43, 262
Fisher, Walter T., house, 258–262
Flanders and Zimmerman, 322
Flatiron Building, 62
Florsheim, Harold, 96
Foote, Cone, and Belding, 249
Ford, Henry, 172
Forest Lawn, 30
The Formal Gardens of England (Blomfield), 41
Fort Dearborn National Bank, 109
Fort Sheridan, 13, 17, 18, 19, 20, 22, 29, 31, 44–45, 312
Fortune Magazine, 260
Foster, George, 63
Foundation for Architecture and Landscape Architecture, 254, 256
Fox, Charles E., 315
Fox Film Corporation, 238
Frank, Jean Michel, 282, 305
Frank Lloyd Wright to 1910: The First Golden Age (Manson), 125
Freeland Corners, 84
Freer Art Gallery (Washington), 317
French, William M. R., 28
French architecture, 176, 179, 285
French Baroque architecture, 221
French eclectic architecture, 264, 266
French Gothic architecture, 109, 160
French Norman architecture, 233, 239, 244–245
French provincial architecture, 311
French Provincial Architecture as Shown in Various Examples of Town and Country Houses, Shops and Public Spaces Adaptable to American Conditions (Milliken and Goodwin), 179
French Renaissance architecture, 53, 214, 316
Frommann and Jebsen, 11, 101
Frost, A. C., 28
Frost, Charles Summer, 29, 43, 309, 311, 312
Frost, Charles Summer, house, 298
Frost, Harry T., 307
Frost and Granger, 309
Fuller, Buckminster, 313
Furness, Frank, 42

G
Gambrill, Charles, 310
Garden, Hugh, 40, 319
Garden Club of America, 181
Gardner, Robert A., house, 303
GATX, 267
General American Tank Car Corporation, 267
General Electric, 260
General Houses, Inc., 260, 310–311
General Motors, 260
Georgian Colonial architecture, 36, 42, 89, 200, 231, 283, 311. *See also* Colonial architecture
Georgian Revival architecture, 176, 200, 276, 283
Georgia State Capital, 308
Germania Club, 95
Giacometti, Alberto, 282, 305
Giacometti, Diego, 282, 305
Giedion, Sigfried, 314
Gilbert, Cass, 318

[330]

Index

Glaser, Edward, 26, 157
Glaser, Etta Rosenbaum, 157
Glencoe, 17, 18, 24, 25–27, 44–45, 48, 237, 313
    Brigham, E. E., house, 138
    Hermann, Charles H., house, 301
    Indianola (Paepcke, Hermann, estate), 11–12, 97–101
    Ravine Bluffs Development, 28, 137–140, 322
    Rosemor Lodge (Glaser, Edward L., house), 156–157
    Rubens, Harry, estate, 91–93, 314
    Stonehill, Charles A., house, 301
    Strauss, Jesse, house, 302
Glencoe Company, 26
Glencoe School Board, 157
Glessner, John J., 84
Goldberg, Rube, 249
Goldblatt Brothers Department Store, 197
Goldblatt, Nathan, 197
Goodhue, Bertram, 318
Goodwin, Bullard, and Woolsey, 311
Goodwin, Philip Lippincott, 30, 37, 179, 214, 221–222, 311
Gothic architecture, 320. *See also* Carpenter Gothic; Collegiate Gothic; French Gothic architecture; Tudor Gothic architecture
The Grammar of Ornament (Jones), 322
Grand Central Station, 306
Grand Rapids, MI, 312
Granger, Alfred Hoyt, 15, 29, 40, 41, 43, 271, 311–312
Granger, Alfred Hoyt, house, 299
Granger, Lowe, and Bollenbacher, 311–312
Granger and Bollenbacher, 312
Great Depression, 115, 197, 249, 276, 311
Great Lakes Naval Training Station, 313
Green Bay, Wisconsin, 17
Green Bay Road, 29, 31, 34, 42, 69, 160, 220
Green Bay Trail, 17
Greenleaf, James L., 249
Greenleaf, Luther, 26
Greenleaf, Luther, house, 303
Grese, Robert, 94
Grey Towers, 53
Grey Walls, 89
Griffin, Marion Mahony, 322
Griffin, Walter Burley, 13, 39, 151, 153, 301, 312, 321, 322
Gross Point, 22–23
Gross Point Village Hall, 23
Guggenheim Museum, 321
Gurnee, Walter S., 17, 18, 25, 26, 27, 33
Gurnee's Castle, 26

H

Haddon Hall (Derbyshire), 211
Hamilton, John, 316
Hammond, Alexander, 26
Hammond, C. Herrick, 316
Hampton, Mark, 282–283
Harding, Warren G., 57
Harkness, Edward, 318
Harper's Magazine, 317
Harrison Conference Services, Inc., 163
Hartford, CT, 311
Harvard University, 260, 311

Laboratory for Computer Graphics, 311
Harwood, Hammond, house, 283
Hasbrouck, Wilbert, 42
Havenwood (Ryerson, Edward, house), 30, 142–147
Hawkins, Frank, 27
Haymarket Riots (1886), 18, 172
Heifetz, Jascha, 29
Hermann, Charles H., house, 301
Heun, Arthur, 12, 13, 30, 37, 39, 40, 102, 110, 113, 114, 254, 312
Hickox, Warren, house, 151
Higginbotham, H. N., 33
High Court (house), 128
Highland Park, 17, 18, 20, 27–29, 43, 44–45, 237, 262, 307, 313, 319, 321
    Alexander, William A., house, 297
    Braeside School, 43, 321
    Dubin, Henry, house, 304
    Mandel, Robert, house, 186, 233–237
    McPherson, Arthur G., house, 302
    Miralago (Everhardt, George, house), 299
    Prallmere (Prall, F. S., house), 297
    Prussing, E. E., house, 298
    Ravine Lodge (Millard, Sylvester, house), 297
    Rudolph, Emil, house, 93
    Seyfarth, Robert, house, 319
    Stewart, Alexander H., house, 301
    Willits, Ward W., house, 35, 42, 74–79, 153, 155, 322
Highland Park Building Company, 27, 28
Highwood, 18, 20, 22, 29, 44–45
Hinsdale, 309
Hitchcock, Henry Russell, 258, 260, 261–262
Holabird, Samuel Beckley, 19, 45, 312
Holabird, William, 41, 312
Holabird, William, house, 296
Holabird and Roche, 13, 19–20, 295, 307, 312
Honolulu, 305
Hotchkiss, Almerin, 30
Hound and Horn, 260
House and Garden, 179
House Beautiful, 36, 40, 70, 260, 320
House in the Woods (McCormick, Mrs. Cyrus [Nettie] estate), 30, 171–175
House of the Four Winds (McBirney, Hugh J., house), 41, 117–122, 136
House of Tomorrow, 285, 290, 313
Howe, C. M., house, 42, 299
Hubbard, Louise, 249
Hull House, 40, 70, 94, 227, 317
Humboldt Park, 101
Hunt, Jarvis, 64, 298, 312–313
Hunt, Myron, 39, 40, 43, 102, 117, 148, 299
Hunt, Richard Morris, 36–37, 53, 64, 66, 312
Hurlburd, Mr. and Mrs. DeForest, 182
Hyde Park, 69, 118, 318, 319

I

Iberian-Moorish influences, 117
Ickes, Harold L., house, 302
Illinois Bell Telephone Exchange building, 320
Illinois Commerce Commission, 262
Illinois Institute of Technology, Institute of Design, 314
Illinois Merchants Trust, 143
Illinois State Grain Inspection Department, 85
Imperial Hotel (Tokyo), 139
Indian Council Rings, 242
Indian Hill Country Club, 24, 103, 309
Indianola (Paepcke, Hermann, estate), 11–12, 97–101
Indigenous architecture, 91
Insull, Samuel, 115, 316
International Harvester Company, 124, 172, 238
International Style, 28, 35, 261, 285, 310, 313
The International Style (Hitchcock, and Johnson), 258
Ipswich, Massachusetts, 305
Italianate style, 28, 29, 63, 113, 124, 142
Italian Gardens (Platt), 128, 130
Italian palazzi, 203
Italian Renaissance architecture, 106, 114, 136, 207, 254
Italian villas, 36, 160, 254
Ivorydale, 306

J

Jackson, Arthur Stanley, 252, 257
Jackson, Arthur Stanley, estate, 252–257
Jackson Brothers and Company, 257
Jacobean style, 307
Japanese architecture, 78
Jekyll, Gertrude, 72
Jekyll Island, Georgia, 305
Jenney, William Le Baron, 41, 89, 312, 318, 319
Jenney and Mundie, 319
Jensen, Jens, 11, 28, 33–34, 72, 91, 94–95, 101, 103, 143, 158, 172, 181, 242, 252, 256–257, 291, 313, 316
Johnson Wax Building, 321
Joliet, 313
Jones, David B., house, 297
Jones, Jenkin Lloyd, 39–40, 320
Jones, Owen, 322
Joseph Sears and His Kenilworth (Kilner), 51, 308
Judah, Dorothy Patterson, 222
Judah, Noble Brandon, 13, 222
Judah, Noble Brandon, estate, 214–222
The Jungle (Sinclair), 114

K

Kankakee, 151
Kansas City, 313
Keck, George Fred, 24, 28, 284–285, 290, 293, 313–314
Keck, William, 28, 287–288, 293, 313
Kedzie, John Hume, house, 296
Kelley, Lillian, 163
Kelley, William V., 28, 33–34, 42, 158, 162–163
Kelley, William V., house, 33, 42, 158–164
Kenilworth, 15, 20, 24–25, 27, 44–45, 84, 308, 314, 315
    Kenilworth Club in, 42
    Kenilworth Union Church in, 42, 51
    Lackner, Francis, house, 299
    Maher, George W., house, 297
    North Shore Golf Club, 42
    Root-Badger house, 58–62
    Sears, Joseph, School, 42, 314
    train station, 308
    Wavery (Sears, Joseph, house), 48–51
Kenilworth (Scott), 24

Index

Kenilworth Assembly Hall, 314
Kenilworth Club, 314
Kenilworth Company, 24, 51, 308
Kenilworth Union Church, 308
Kent, Edward, 320
Kenyon College Pierce Hall, 312
Kilner, Colleen Browne, 51, 308
King, Charles Garfield, house, 300
King, Edward, house, 254
Knickerbocker Club, 310
Kuppenheimer, B., and Company, 294
Kuppenheimer, Jonas, 294
Kuppenheimer, Louis B., 291

L

Lackner, Francis, house, 299
Ladies' Home Journal, 40, 138
Lake, David J., 30
Lake Bluff, 17, 18, 20, 32–34, 44–45, 188, 306, 310, 315
    Crab Tree Farm (Durand, Scott S., and Grace, estate and Blair, William McCormick and Helen Bowen, estate), 34, 223–232
    Ely, Carolyn Morse, estate, 176–183
    Maher, Philip, house, 304
    Shore Acres Country Club, 89, 145
    Stonebridge (Kelley, William V., house), 33, 42, 158–164
    Tangley Oaks, 271–275
Lake Bluff Camp Meeting Association, 32, 33
Lake Cook Road, 27
Lake Forest, 11, 18, 21, 29–34, 43, 44–45, 188, 305, 306, 311, 313, 314, 318, 322
    Ardleigh (Farwell, John V., Jr., house), 30, 298
    Armour, Laurence, house, 300
    Bagatelle (Bennett, Edward H., house), 302, 307
    Barrell, Finley, house, 131–136, 317
    Cahn, Bertram J., house, 290–294
    Church of the Holy Spirit, 311
    Cobb, Henry Ives, estate, 297
    Donnelley, Thomas, house, 109
    Eastover (Frost, Charles S., house), 298
    Fairlawn (McGann, Robert Farwell, estate), 30, 199–202, 310
    Fernald, Charles, house, 42, 106–109
    First National Bank Building, 306
    First Presbyterian Church, 43, 309
    Gardner, Robert A., house, 303
    Havenwood (Ryerson, Edward, house), 30, 142–147
    House in the Woods (McCormick, Mrs. Cyrus (Nettie) estate), 30, 171–175
    House of the Four Winds (McBirney, Hugh J., house), 41, 117–122, 136
    Judah, Noble B., estate, 214–222
    King, Charles Garfield, house, 300
    Lamont, Robert P., house, 303
    Leavell, James R., house, 303
    Mark, Clayton, house, 301
    Market Square, 31–32, 43, 69, 161, 319
    McIlvaine, William B., Jr., house, 304
    Mellody Farm (Armour, J. Ogden, estate), 12, 110–116, 254, 312
    Mill Road Farm (Lasker, Albert D., estate), 244–251
    Milman, Ralph, house, 304
    Morse, Robert Hosmer, house, 304, 322
    Onwentsia Country Club, 30–31, 43, 67, 89, 124, 145, 152, 165, 275, 297, 309, 314
    Pembroke Hall (Jones, David B., house), 297
    Ragdale (Shaw, Howard Van Doren, house), 13, 41, 67–72, 319
    Reed, Mrs. Coates, house, 276–283
    Schweppe house, 317
    Shadow Pond (Jackson, Arthur Stanley, estate), 252–257
    Villa Turicum (McCormick, Harold and Edith Rockefeller, house), 12, 123–130, 145
    Walden (McCormick, Cyrus H., Jr., house), 298
    Westleigh Farms (Swift, Louis F., estate), 299
    Westmoreland (Dick, A. B., house), 86–89
    Westwood Farm, 109
    Woodleigh (Granger, Alfred, house), 299
    Wyldwood (Carr, Clyde, house), 165–170
Lake Forest Academy, 12, 165
Lake Forest Association, 30
Lake Forest Cemetery, 133
Lake Forest College, 29, 43, 89, 226, 254, 318
    Lily Reid Holt Chapel, 29
Lake Forest Garden Club, 266
Lake Forest High School, 306
Lake Forest Hospital, 89, 306
Lake Forest Improvement Trust, 31
Lake Forest Open Lands, 115
Lake Forest University, 29, 318
    Ferry Hall, 309
Lake Michigan, 11, 15, 17, 18, 20, 24, 25, 69, 130, 192, 197, 227, 231, 277, 308, 315
Lake Shore Country Club, 26–27, 157, 237, 319
Lake Shore Drive, 19, 20, 195, 316
Lamont, Robert P., house, 303
Larkin Building, 321
Larson, Erik, 18
Lasker, Albert D., 36, 244, 249, 305
Lasker, Albert D., estate, 244–251
Lasker, Flora, 249
Lasker, Mary Woodard Reinhardt, 249
Lazarus, Annie, 128
Leavell, James R., house, 303
Le Corbusier, 35, 153, 261
Legendary Decorators of the Twentieth Century (Hampton), 282–283
Le Notre, Andre, 221
Libertyville, 43, 45
    Adler, David, estate, 184–190
Lilly, Beatrice, 197
Lincoln, Abraham, Center, 39
Lincoln Park Conservatory, 40–41
Lindeberg, Harrie T., 13, 30, 34, 43, 89, 165, 166–167, 181, 275, 300, 303, 314
Lindeberg, Lucia Hall, 314
Linden Lodge (Henry Calvin Durand), 30
Lindsey, Vachel, 72
Lind University, 29
Linthicum, Charles C., house, 300
The Little Garden for Little Money (Brewster), 266
Lloyd, Henry Demarest, 25
Long Island, 113, 199, 305, 310
Lord and Thomas advertising firm, 249
Los Angeles, 308, 316
Louis XIV, King of France, 221
Lowy, Felix, 208
Lowy, Felix, house, 208–213
Loyola University, 20
Lunt, Orrington, 33
Lutyens, Edwin, 89, 136
Lyon, Potter and Company, 39
Lyttelton, Lord, 89

M

Magerstadt, Ernest J., house, 93
Magnus, Augustus, estate, 102–105, 151
Maher, George, and Son, 205
Maher, George Washington, 13, 24, 25, 40, 41, 43, 44, 80, 82, 84–85, 91, 93–94, 95, 151, 295, 299, 300, 314–315, 319, 320
Maher, George Washington, house, 297
Maher, Philip Brooks, 42, 205, 207, 315
Maher, Philip Brooks, house, 304
Mahony, Marion, 13, 39
Mallory, W. S., and Company, 165
Mallows, C. E., 136
Mandel, Robert, 26, 235, 237
Mandel, Robert, house, 186, 233–237
Mandel Brothers, 235, 237
Manning, Warren, 136, 167, 298, 3030
Manson, Grant, 125
Marble and Wilson, 315
Mark, Clayton, 319
Mark, Clayton, house, 301
Marktown, IN, 319
Marshall, Benjamin, 23, 34, 43, 156, 195–197, 315–316
Marshall, Benjamin, house and studio, 192–198
Marshall and Fox, 156
Marshall Field and Company, 32, 277
Martha's Vineyard, 32
Marx, Samuel Abraham, 26, 264, 316
Maybeck, Bernard, 307
May Department Store, 316
Mayer, Beatrice, 268
Mayer, Robert, 268
Mayo, Ernest Alfredo, 44, 208, 211, 213, 303, 316
Mayo, Peter B., 44, 208, 211, 213, 303, 316
McBirney, Hugh J., 41, 118
McBirney, Hugh J., house, 117–122, 136
McBirney, Mary Campbell, 118
McBirney and Johnson White Lead Company, 118
McClurg, A. C., 312
McCormick, Cyrus Hall, Sr., 124, 171, 172, 227
McCormick, Cyrus, Jr., 171, 172
McCormick, Edith Rockefeller, 12, 36, 124, 125, 128, 145
McCormick, Harold and Edith Rockefeller, house, 12, 123–130, 145
McCormick, Harold Fowler, 12, 36, 124–125, 128, 145, 171
McCormick, Mrs. Cyrus (Nettie) Fowler, 28, 124, 172
McCormick, Robert, 109
McCormick, Ruby, 227
McCormick and Company, 172
McCormick Institute of Infectious Diseases, 124
McCormick Reaper Works, 18, 30, 89, 124
McCormick Reaper Works Men's Club, 124

Index

McCormick Theological Seminary, 124, 172
McCormickville, 17
McGann, Grace Farwell, 30, 199, 201
McGann, Robert Farwell, 30
McGann, Robert Farwell, estate, 30, 199–202, 310
McIlvaine, William B., Jr., house, 304
McKim, Charles Follen, 61
McKim, Mead, and White, 61, 97, 231, 275, 309, 310, 314, 317
McKinley, William, 57
McKinley Music Company, 58
McKinnon, Robert W., house, 303
McPherson, Arthur G., house, 302
Mead, William R., 317
Meade, Frank B., 311
Meaning in Architecture (Gilbert), 318
Mears, E. Ashley, 29
Meeker, Arthur, 17
Mellody Farm (Armour, J. Ogden, estate), 12, 110–116, 254, 312
Melody, Patrick, 113
Michigan Drive, 195
Midway Gardens, 139
Miehle Printing Press and Manufacturing Company, 163
Mies van der Rohe, Ludwig, 11, 153, 313, 314
Milford, Pennsylvania, 53
Millard, Sylvester, house, 297
Miller, Art, 254
Miller, Arthur, Jr., 72
Milliken, Henry Outhort, 179
Mill Road Farm (Lasker, Albert D., estate), 244–251
Milman, Ralph, house, 304, 319
Mines, John, 158
Miralago (Everhardt, George, house), 299
Moholy-Nagy, Laszlo, 314
Monroe, Harriet, 72
Montecito Country Club, 103
Morris, William, 40, 70
Morris, William, wallpaper, 71
Morse, Charles Hosmer, 26
Morse, Robert Hosmer, house, 304, 322
motif rhythm theory, 13, 40, 82, 84, 93, 151
Muirfield Links (Scotland), 89
Municipal Tuberculosis Sanitorium, 309
Murphy, William Patton, 163
Museum of Modern Art (New York City), 222, 258, 311, 316
  Department of Architecture and Design, 283
Muthesius, Hermann, 136

N
National Housing Agency, 311
National Lead Company, 118
Navy Pier, 311
Newark, NJ, 313
Newark Museum, 313
New Haven, Connecticut, 310
New Orleans, 316
Newport, Rhode Island, 254
New Post Office Building, 310
New Republic, 317
New Trier Township, 22–23
New York Athletic Club, 310
New York City, 62
New York Metropolitan Museum, 231
New York Produce Exchange, 257

New York Stock Exchange, 133, 257
Nichols, Rose Standish, 118, 143, 3030
Nimmons and Fellows, 320
North Chicago, 34
North Shore, 11, 13, 15–34, 36–37, 38, 42, 43, 44–45, 143, 184, 188, 199, 200, 254, 264, 305, 307, 308, 309, 313, 316, 319, 322
North Shore Congregation Israel, 27
North Shore Country Day School, 309
North Shore Golf Club, 42
North Shore Improvement Association, 18–19
North Shore Line, 138
Northwestern Gas Light and Coke Company, 57
Northwestern University, 20–21, 29, 33, 52, 63, 85, 163, 165, 238, 294, 311
  Deering Library, 22, 318
  Fayerweather Hall, 312
  Fisk Hall, 22
  Harris Hall, 22
  Law School, 294
  Sorority Quadrangle, 318
  University Hall, 22
Notre Dame University, 308
Nutt, John, 24

O
Oak Bluffs, 32
Oak Park, 35, 39, 40–41, 44, 67, 155, 314, 320, 321, 322
O'Conner, James W., 231
octagonal house, 313. *See also* House of Tomorrow
Oklahoma A. & M. College, 320
Old Chicago (Tallmadge), 321
Old Elm Country Club, 79, 165
Olmsted, Frederick Law, 28, 30, 242, 256, 297, 309, 313, 317
Omaha, NE, 311
Onandaga Salt Company, 63
Orchard (house), 70
The Origin of the Skyscraper (Tallmadge), 321
Otis, William, 309
Otis and Clark, 309
Ouilmette Reservation, 23

P
Pabst Breweries, 306
The Packers, the Private Car Lines, and the People (Sinclair), 114
Paepcke, Elizabeth "Pussy" Hilken Nitze, 12, 98, 101
Paepcke, Hermann, 11–12, 95, 98, 101, 313
Paepcke, Hermann, estate, 11–12, 97–101
Paepcke, Paula Wagner, 98
Paepcke, Walter, 11–12, 98, 101
Page, Ruth, 260
Page, Ruth, house, 304, 310
Palladian villas, 200, 254, 283
Palladian windows, 11, 51
Palladio's house, 42
Palmer, Potter, 309, 320
Parrish, Stephen, 317
Parsons, William E., 307
Paterno Imports, 275
Patten, James, 314–315
Patten, James, house, 43, 80–85, 93, 314, 319

Patterson, Cissy, 109
Patterson, Erastus, 17
Patterson, Joseph Medill, 109
Pavillon de la Lanterne (Versailles), 179
Peabody, Francis Stuyvesant, 195, 316
Peabody and Stearns, 309, 311
Peacock's Dairy Bar, 24
Peck, Charles F., 25
Pembroke Hall (Jones, David B., house), 297
Pennoyer, Peter, 201
People's Gas, Light and Coke Company, 165
Perkins, Dwight H., 13, 38–39, 40, 41, 43, 102, 113–114, 148, 171, 174, 312, 316–317, 320, 322
Perkins, Fellows, and Hamilton, 171, 302
Perkins, Frederick Wainwright, 133, 317
Perkins, Lawrence, 260
Perkins, Wheeler, and Will, 25
Piatagorsky, Gregor, 29
Piazza San Marco, 20
Picture window, 312
Pierre Hotel (New York City)
  Cotillion Room, 316
Pinewold (Bernard Eckhart), 30
Pirie, John T., 195
Pittsburgh Plate Glass, 260
Platt, Charles Adams, 12, 123, 124, 125, 128, 130, 145, 317
Platt, William, 317
Poetry Magazine, 72
Pond, Allen Bartlit, 13, 29, 39, 40, 42, 113–114, 298, 299, 312, 317–318
Pond, Irving Kane, 13, 29, 39, 40, 41, 42, 113–114, 298, 299, 312, 317–318, 320
Port of Call, 223
Post, George B., 307
Potter and Robinson, 310
Powers, Horace Swett, 312, 320
Powers, Richard, 239, 318
Prairie School, 11, 20, 25, 28, 30, 33, 35, 38, 42, 43, 74, 78, 80, 91, 93–94, 102–103, 114, 117, 118, 125, 138, 139, 148, 151, 153, 205, 256–257, 313, 316, 320, 321
The Prairie School (Brooks), 40, 102, 320, 321
Prairie Tudor architecture, 42, 174
Prall, F. S., house, 297
Prallmere (Prall, F. S., house), 297
prefabricated houses, 260, 310–311
Price, Matlock, 227
Princeton University, 165, 318
Procter and Gamble factory, 306
Progressive architecture, 35
Prospect Park, 28
Prussing, E. E., house, 298
Pulaski Field House, 322
Pullman (town), 43, 306, 307, 318, 319
Pullman, George, 18, 226–227, 306, 307
Pullman, George, house, 306
Pullman Car Company, 260, 316
Pullman Strike (1894), 18
Purcell, William Gray, 41, 148
Purdue University, 318

Q
Queen Anne architecture, 11, 24, 41, 51, 78–79, 97–98, 101

R
Racine, WI, 321

[333]

Index

Ragdale (Shaw, Howard Van Doren, house), 13, 41, 67–72, 319
Ragdale Ring, 72
Rajkovich, Thomas, 275
Randall, Gordon, 22
Rathmore (Ambrose Cramer), 30
Ravenswood, 318
Ravine Bluffs Development, 28, 137–140, 322
Ravine Lodge (Millard, Sylvester, house), 297
Ravinia, 27, 43
Ravinia Park, 28–29
Reckitt, Ernest, 208
Reed, Helen Shedd, 277, 282
Reed, Kersey Coates, 277
Reed, Mrs. Kersey Coates, house, 276–283
Reed, Peter, 283
Renwick, James, 319
Research Council for Economic Security, 294
Revival architecture. *See* Classical Revival architecture; Colonial Revival architecture; Georgian Revival architecture; Spanish Revival architecture; Tudor Revival architecture
Richardson, H. H., 22, 24, 38, 84, 309, 310, 311, 316, 320
River Forest, 13, 39
  Coonley, Avery, house, 322
Riverside, 30
Robie, Frederick, house, 322
Roche, Martin, 41, 45, 312
Rockefeller, Edith, 12
Rockefeller, John D., 309, 318
Rogers, Anne Day, 124, 318
Rogers, James Gamble, 12, 22, 40, 41, 43, 89, 124, 318
Rogers Park, 20
Roman Catholic Archdiocese of Chicago, 257
Romanesque style, 20, 38, 51
Roosevelt, Theodore, 249
Root, E. T., and Sons, 58
Root, Frank, 58
Root, John, 13, 40
Root-Badger house, 58–62
Rosemor Lodge (Glaser, Edward L., house), 156–157
Rosenwald, Julius, 95–96
Rosenwald, Julius, estate, 28
Rosewood Park, 28
Rothschild, Maurice L., 268
Rubens, Harry, 28, 95, 101, 313
Rubens, Harry, estate, 91–93, 314
Rubenstein, Artur, 29
Rudolph, Emil, house, 93
Ruskin, John, 70
Ryerson, Edward L., 13, 28, 30, 36, 142–143, 145, 319
Ryerson, Joseph T., 143, 305
Ryerson, Joseph T., and Son steel company, 143, 165

S

Saarinen, Eero, 25
Saarinen, Eliel, 25
St. Gaudens, Augustus, 196, 317
St. Johns, 17
St. Louis, 316
St. Paul, Minnesota, 311
St. Petersburg, Florida, 313
Sandberg, Carl, 72
San Francisco plan, 307
Sara Lee Corporation, 268
Sarasota, FL, 305
Saxe, Albert Moore, 322
Schager, Edward, 205
Schager, Edward J. and Dorothy, house, 203–207
Schlitz, Joseph, Brewing Company, 101
Schmidt, Garden, and Martin, 313
Schultz, Henry W., house, 300
Schurz, Carl, 95
Schweppe, Laura Shedd, 317
Scott, Mackay Baillie, 70
Scott, Sir Walter, 24
Scully, Vincent, 74
Sears, Dorothy, 48, 51
Sears, Joseph, 24, 48, 51, 308
Sears, Joseph, house, 48–51
Sears, Roebuck, 28, 96, 310
Selling, Harold N., house, 303
Semper, Gottfried, 13, 40
Seng, Wendelin and Agnes, 203, 205
Servite Order of the Catholic Church, 163
Seyfarth, Robert, 43, 44, 301, 302, 318–319
Seyfarth, Robert, house, 319
Shadow Pond (Jackson, Arthur Stanley, estate), 252–257
Shaw, Frances Wells, 69, 71–72, 118, 319
Shaw, Howard Van Doren, 13, 26–27, 29, 30, 31, 36, 37, 40, 41, 43, 44, 67, 69, 71–72, 79, 102, 106, 109, 117, 118, 131, 133, 136, 142–143, 146, 157, 160–162, 199, 300, 301, 303, 305, 306, 319, 320
Shaw, Howard Van Doren, house, 13, 41, 67–72, 319
Shaw, Richard Norman, 38
Shaw, Theodore, 69
Shedd, John G., 277, 317
Shedd Aquarium, 277
Shell Union, 115
Shepley, Rutan, and Coolidge, 22, 311, 320
Sheppard, Robert Dickenson, 52–53
Sheridan, Philip, 19
Sheridan Road, 12, 19, 20, 24, 25, 27, 34, 43, 45, 152, 153, 197, 208, 211, 213, 227, 233, 267, 314, 319
Sheridan Shore Yacht Club, 195–196
Shingle Style, 24, 40–41, 51, 78–79, 308, 309, 320
Shipman, Ellen Biddle, 231
Shipman, S. V., 322
Shore Acres Country Club, 34
Sigma Chi Fraternity, 243
Silsbee, Joseph Lyman, 40–41, 78, 314, 320, 322
Simmons, Charles, 51
Simonds, Ossian Cole, 20, 256, 312
Sinclair, Upton, 114
Skillin, C. Percy, 155
Skillin, C. Percy, house, 153–157
Skokie School, 25
Skyscrapers, 19–20, 306
Smith, A. O., Company, 260
Smith, Carl, 18
Smith College, 310
Soane, Sir John, 146
Society of the Cincinnati, 36
Solti, Sir Georg, 29
Solway, Susan, 138
South Shore Country Club, 195, 315
Space, Time, and Architecture (Giedion), 314
Spanish Court, 24
Spanish Revival architecture, 196
Spencer, Robert Closson, Jr., 12, 13, 39, 40, 42, 102–103, 148, 174, 312, 320
Sprague, Albert A., 181
Sprague, Warner and Company, 181
Springfield, 151
  Supreme Court Building, 322
Spring Green, Wisconsin, 322
Stamford, CT, 310
Standard Oil Company, 318
Standard Oil of California, 115
Starett, Paul, 62
statistical mapping program, 311
Steinway Hall, 13, 38–39, 40, 102, 114, 148, 174, 312, 316, 320, 321, 322
Steinway Piano Company, 39
Stevens, Gary, 41
Stewart, Alexander H., house, 301
Stokowski, Leopold, 197
Stone, Edward Durrell, 221–222, 311
Stonebridge (Kelley, William V., house), 33, 42, 158–164
Stonegate Priory, 163
Stonehill, Charles A., 27
Stone Trust Association, 310
The Story of Architecture in America (Tallmadge), 321
The Story of England's Architecture (Tallmadge), 321
Strauss, Jesse, house, 302
Stravinsky, Igor, 29
Studebaker Building, 306
Studio, 40, 89
Suarez, Diego, 305
Sullivan, Louis, 11, 13, 38, 40, 41, 78, 84, 320, 322
Swedenborgian Church, 51
Swift, Louis F., 109
Swift, Louis F., estate, 299
SYMAP, 311

T

Taft, William Howard, 260, 310
Tague, Robert Bruce, 285, 287
Taliesion, 139, 322
Tallmadge, Thomas Eddy, 41, 43, 117, 300, 320–321
Tanglewood, 28
Tangley Oaks, 34, 271–275
Taylor, Anson, 17
Taylorsport, 17
Teatro del Lago, 24
Texas Panhandle, 201
Thatcher, Solomon, Jr., 32–33
Ticknor, James, 303, 306
Tiffany Studios, 29
Tigbourne Court, 136
Tomlinson, Henry, 312
Town and Country, 36
Townsend, H. M., 316
Traders Insurance Company, 63
Truman, Harry, 310

[334]

Tudor architecture, 20, 33, 35, 36, 176, 208, 211, 285, 307, 311, 318. *See also* English Tudor architecture; Prairie Tudor architecture
Tudor Gothic architecture, 34, 275
Tudor Revival architecture, 156, 316
Tunney, Gene, 249
Tuscan style, 143
Two Chicago Architects and Their Clients (Eaton), 37, 143

U
Uihlein, Edward G., 95, 101
Union Club, 309, 310
Union League Club, 238
Union Stock Yards, 18
United Educators, Inc., 275
United Jewish Charities of Chicago, 29
U.S. Treasury, 308
Unity Temple, 42, 321
Universal Oil Products, 115
University Club, 118
University of Chicago, 124, 249, 307, 309, 318
    Quadrangle Club, 319
University of Florida, 320
University of Illinois at Chicago, 312, 322
University of Indiana, 312
University of Michigan, 318
Upjohn, Richard, 254, 306
Urban Disorder and the Shape of Belief (Smith), 18
Utilities Power and Light Corporation, 238

V
Van Bergen, John Shellette, 43, 153, 155–156, 254, 301, 321, 322
Vanderbilt, George, estate, 37, 53
Vanderbilt family, 309
Van Osdel, John Mills, 296
Vaux, Calvert, 30
Veterans Bureau, 57
Vicenza, 42
Villa d'Este, 130
Villa Medici (Poggio a Caiano), 136
Villa Mondragone (Frascati), 128
Villa Pisani-Placco (Padua), 145
Villa Turicum (McCormick, Harold and Edith Rockefeller, house), 12, 123–130, 145, 172
Vista del Lago, 24
Vitale, Ferruccio, 254, 277, 3030
Voysey, Charles F. A., 40, 41, 69, 70, 102

W
Walcott, Chester, 309
Walden (McCormick, Cyrus H., Jr., house), 298
Walker, Anne, 201
War, U.S. Department of, 19
Warren, Edward Kirk, 322
Warren, Edward Kirk, house, 300
Washburne, Carleton, 25
Washington, Booker T., 25
Washington, D.C., 310, 317
Wasmuth, Ernst, 322
Watkins, J. R., Medical Company, 315

Watson, Vernon Spencer, 320–321
Waukegan, 15, 34
Waukegan Road, 115
Wavery (Sears, Joseph, house), 48–51
Wayside, 25
Webb house, Orient, Long Island, 227
Weber, Peter, 28
Webster, Edward Hutchins, house, 296
Welcome to Chicago (Granger), 271
Westchester County, 199
Western Architect, 31, 44, 148
Westleigh Farms (Swift, Louis F., estate), 299
Westmoreland (Dick, A. B., house), 86–89
West Point Military Academy, 307
Westwood Farm, 109
Wharton, Edith, 113
Wheelock and Clay, 316
Wheelwright and Haven, 320
White, Catherine M., 40
White, Catherine M., house, 40, 117, 299
White, Hugh A., 299
White, Marian, 95
White, Robert, 307
White, Stanford, 196, 305
White City, 61. *See also* World's Columbian Exposition
Whitehead, Russell, 314
White House, 310
Whitehouse, Francis, 312
Whitney, Ely, 172
Whitney family, 309
Wieboldts' Department Store, 237
Wight, Peter B., 31, 113
Will, Philip, Jr., 260
Willard, Frances E., 21, 33
Williams, Nathan Wilbur, 152
Williams, Nathan Wilbur, house, 12, 42, 148–152
Willits, Ward W., 79
Willits, Ward W., house, 13, 28, 35, 40, 42, 74–79, 153, 155, 322
Wilmette, 20, 21, 22, 23–24, 27, 43, 44–45, 197, 313, 315
    Baker, Frank J., house, 300
    Bersbach, Alfred, house, 301
    Bichl, Gerald and Helen, house, 203–207
    Bruning, Herbert, house, 284–289
    Indian Hill subdivision, 285
    Lake Avenue in, 23
    Marshall, Benjamin, house and studio, 192–198
    Miralago Ballroom, 24, 285, 313
    Plaza del Lago, 24, 309
    Schager, Edward J. and Dorothy, house, 203–207
    Skillin, C. Percy, house, 153–157
Wilmette Harbor, 23
Wilmette Historical Society, 23
Wilson, Walter O., house, 303
Winnetka, 17, 18, 21, 25, 27, 43, 44–45, 307, 309
    Beman, Spencer S., house, 302
    Chandler, Buckingham, house, 302
    Chestnut Street, 25

    Edgecliff (Epstein, Max, estate), 264–270
    Elm Street, 25
    Fisher, Walter T., house, 258–262
    Fisher Lane, 262
    Ickes, Harold L., house, 302
    Lowy, Felix, house, 208–213
    Magnus, Augustus, estate, 102–105, 151
    Maple Street, 25
    Municipal Building in, 309
    Oak Street, 25
    Page, Ruth, house, 304
    Schultz, Henry W., house, 300
    Wilson, Walter O., house, 303
Winnetka Village Hall, 24, 309
Winona, Minnesota, 315
Winona Savings Bank, 315
Winslow, William H., 13, 39
Woodlawn Cemetery, 310
Woodleigh (Granger, Alfred, house), 299
Work, Robert G., 69, 305, 319
World's Columbian Exposition, 17, 18, 38, 51, 61, 208, 306, 307, 309, 316
    Court of Honor at, 61, 62
    Ho-o-den Pavilion at, 78
    Transportation Building, 78
    Vermont State Building at, 64, 313
World War I, 57, 222
World War II, 311
Wren, Sir Christopher, 307
Wright, Frank Lloyd, 11, 12–13, 28, 33, 35, 37, 38, 39–41, 42, 44, 51, 67, 74–79, 80, 82, 102, 113–114, 117, 118, 124–125, 137–139, 148, 151, 153, 155, 256, 261, 300, 314, 316, 320, 321–322
Wyldwood (Carr, Clyde, house), 165–170

X
XIT Ranch, 201

Y
Yale University, 124, 310
    Hall of Graduate Studies, 318
    Harkness Memorial Quadrangle, 318
    Harkness Tower, 318
    Sheffield Scientific School, 143
    Sterling Law buildings, 318
    Sterling Memorial Library, 318
Yamasaki, Minoru, 27
Young Turks, 312

Z
Zimmerman, Saxe and Zimmerman, 304, 322
Zimmerman, William Carbys, 299, 300, 322
Zuber et Cie, 186, 235

Photography Credits

American Architect and Building News: 92-94 (1907) 96 (1907) 156-157 (1918)

Architectural Record: 26 (Oct.,1911), 31 (Oct.,1933), 81 bottom (April, 1904), 83 bottom (April, 1904), 95 (April, 1904), 116 (February, 1916), 122 top (Jan. 1924), 122 bottom (April, 1913), 128 (Jan.,1924) , 135 (April, 1913), 147 bottom (April,1913), 171-175 (March, 1918), 187-188 (Nov., 1923),192, 193 bottom-196, 198 (March, 1927), 202 bottom (Nov., 1927), 203, 204, 207 (Nov, 1925), 258-262 (March, 1930), 300 top left (Fuerman, Feb. 1906), 302 top left (March, 1918)

Architectural Forum: 232 (Jan., 1929), 304 top right (August, 1931)

The Architectural Review: 72 (Jan., 1904)

Architecture: 238, 240, 243 (Sept., 1929)

Architecture and Design. Ralph Milman and A. S. Morphett, 1937: 304 center left

Art Institute of Chicago: Historic Architecture and Landscape Image Collection, Ryerson and Burnham Archives: 23, 32, 75 top, 76, 77, 104 top right, 110-115, 137 (Gilbert Lane), 139 (Lane) 176-181, 244 (Chicago Aerial Survey Co.), 265, 269, 300 center right (Chi. Architectural Photographing Co.), 301 top left, 301 top right, 301 bottom right, 304 top left; Shaw Collection, Ryerson and Burnham Archives: 68-71, 117, 118, 120 top, 131, 142-146, 158-164, 301 center left, 301 center right, 303 top left; Architecture Department: 182, 183, 190 bottom, 234 top, 277

Ausgefuhrte Bauten und Entwurfe von Frank Lloyd Wright, 1910: 78 top

Susan Benjamin Postcard Collection: 21; photo: 216 top, 302 top right

Paul Bergmann, Stanley D. Anderson Archives 303 bottom left, 304 bottom left

Book of the North Shore: 300 top right, 300 center left

Stuart Cohen photo: 299 top left. 301 bottom left, 302 center left

Chicago Historical Society: 167-169, 185 (Trowbridge), 193 top, 224 bottom, 225, 227-231 (Raymond Trowbridge); 234 bottom-237 (Frederick O. Bemm); 246-248, 250-251 (Hedrich Blessing); 284-289 (Hedrich Blessing); 290-294 (Hedrich Blessing), 300 bottom right (Hedrich Blessing)

S. Creuer, A. Wirth (Arthur Jackson family) 252-257

David Adler Cultural Center: 184-187 top, Susan Beman Dahlmeyer and Ford Dahlmeyer, Spencer S. Beman archives: 302 bottom left

Domestic Architecture of H.T. Lindeberg: 170, 271-274, 303 center left,

Arthur D. Dubin Collection: Frontispiece

Classic Evanston courtesy of the Evanston Historical Society: 296 bottom left

Evanston Historical Society: 54, 55 top, 55 bottom, 56, 57, 63, 64, 65 top, 65 bottom, 66, 239, 241-243, 296 top left, 296 top right, 296 bottom right photo Barbara Bookbinder- Green, 300 bottom right

Glencoe Historical Society: 16, 97, 98, 99,100 top, 100 bottom, 101, 138, 140

Highland Park, 1896. 15, 297 top right, 297 bottom left, 298 top left

Highland Park Historical Society: 27,

House Beautiful: 190 (May, 1924)

Inland Architect: 39 (Feb., 1897), 52-53 (1896-97), 67 (July, 1899)80-81 top 82-85 top (August, 1903), 297 top left (Nov.1892), 297 center left (Oct.1895), 298 top left (May 1895), 298 center left (Nov. 1896), 298 center right (July 1899), 298 bottom left (April 1898),298 bottom right (July 1899), 299 top right (Jan. 1899), 52-52 (May, 1926)

Kenilworth Historical Society: 48, 50, 58, 59, 60 top, 60, 61, 299 bottom right,

Lake Forest-Lake Bluff Historical Society: 33, 86, 87 top 87 bottom, 88 top, 88 bottom, 123, 129, 132 top, 132 bottom, 133, 134 top, 134 bottom, 199-202 top, 297 bottom right, 299 center right

Lake Forest Preservation Foundation: 214-215, 216 bottom, 218-219

Betsy Mardin: 147 top

Terry McKay: 264, 266-268, 270

Luis Medina © Peter S. Reed: 276, 278-282

Shirley M. Paddock: 297 center right

David R. Phillips Collection: 74, 75 bottom, 91,165-166

The Prairie School. Photo H. Allen Brooks: 299 center left

The Architecture of Charles Platt: 125, 126 bottom, 127 top, 127 bottom, 130,

Martin and Maribeth Rahe: 215 upper right, 217, 220-222

Portfolio of the Work of Mayo and Mayo, courtesy of the Evanston Historical Society, 208-212, 303 top right, 303 center right

Lyn Redfield: 119, 120 bottom, 121

First Book of the North Shore: 300 top right (Fowler), 300 center left (Fowler)

Second Book of the North Shore: 19, 126 top, 299 bottom left

Ezra Stoller © ESTO: 189, 226, 233, 245, 302 center right

Elmer Vliet Historical Center, Lake Bluff: 223-224 top

"The Work of Frank Lloyd Wright." *Wendigen*: 124

Western Architect: 102, 103, 104 left top, 104 bottom, 105 (1914), 106-108 (1910), 148-152 (1920), 153-155 (1915), 302 bottom right (Dec. 1923)

Wilmette Historical Museum: 205-206

Winnetka Historical Society: 22, 303 bottom right